OLDER
ADULT EDUCATION

OLDER ADULT EDUCATION

A Guide to Research, Programs, and Policies

Ronald J. Manheimer
Denise D. Snodgrass
Diane Moskow-McKenzie

Published in Association with the
North Carolina Center for Creative Retirement,
University of North Carolina at Asheville

GREENWOOD PRESS
Westport, Connecticut • London

Library of Congress Cataloging-in-Publication Data

Manheimer, Ronald J.
    Older adult education : a guide to research, programs, and
policies / Ronald J. Manheimer, Denise D. Snodgrass, Diane Moskow-McKenzie.
        p.   cm.
    "Published in association with the North Carolina Center for Creative Retirement,
University of North Carolina at Asheville."
    Includes bibliographical references and index.
    ISBN 0–313–28878–X (alk. paper)
    1. Adult education—United States.   2. Continuing education—
United States.   3. Education and state—United States.
    I. Snodgrass, Denise D.   II. Moskow-McKenzie, Diane.   III. Title.
LC5251.M287   1995
374'.973—dc20   95–10277

British Library Cataloguing in Publication Data is available.

Library of Congress Catalog Card Number: 95–10277
ISBN: 0–313–28878–X

First published in 1995

Greenwood Press, 88 Post Road West, Westport, CT 06881
An imprint of Greenwood Publishing Group, Inc.

Printed in the United States of America

The paper used in this book complies with the
Permanent Paper Standard issued by the National
Information Standards Organization (Z39.48–1984).

10   9   8   7   6   5   4   3   2   1

Contents

Tables and Figures   ix

Acknowledgments   xi

Introduction   xiii

1 Lifelong Learning in an Aging Society   1
An Emerging Generation of Retirees: A Case Study   2
The Purposes of Education in an Aging Society   5
Attitudinal and Institutional Changes   12
Motivation for Education in Later Life   20
The Problem of Institutional Rationales   24
The New Paradigm: Lifelong Learning, Leadership, and
     Community Service   29
Conclusion: The Politics and Promise of Older Adult Education   32
References   33

2 Older Learners and Programs in Historical Perspective   37
The Concept of the Third Age   38
Emergence of Older Adult Education in the United States   40
Intellectual Functioning of Older Adults   42
Adult versus Older Adult Education   45
National Policies and Older Adult Education   46
An Institutional History of Older Learner Programs   48
Support of Older Learners   75
Note   77
References   77

3 *The Transformation of Older Learner Programs*   **83**
The Changing Picture   83
Five Models of Older Adult Education   84
A National Research Project on Older Adult Education   86
Research Findings   89
Determinants of Success   108
Prospects for the Future   109
References   110

**4 *The Impact of Institutional Policies on Older
Adult Education***   **113**
Public Policy and the Greying of the United States   114
Motivations of Major Stakeholders in
  Older Adult Education Policy   122
Governmental Policies before 1965   130
Public Policy Responds to Older Americans   131
Effects of the Older Americans Act:
  National Policies after 1965   135
State Initiatives   141
Policies of Institutions   146
Policies of National Aging and Education Organizations   150
Implications and Trends in Older Adult Education Policy   153
References   154

5 *Older Adult Learning in the Technological Age*   **159**
Education in the Computer Age   160
Seniors and Technology   160
Computers and the Older Learner   163
Computer-Assisted Instruction   167
Informal Learning and Communication   168
Distant Learning   169
Prognosis for the Future   170
References   170

6 *Generations Learning Together*   **173**
Intergenerational Learning   174
Rationales for Intergenerational Educational Programs   175
Transforming Effects of Intergenerational Education   179
Intergenerational versus Age-Segregated Programs   181
The Intergenerational Impulse and Imperative   182
References   184

Appendixes   **187**

A *Leadership Council of Aging Organizations*   **189**

B *Additional Organizations Interested in Older Adult Education*   **199**

C *Older Adult Education Resources* 201

D *The Older Americans Act of 1965 (as Amended in 1992)* 205

E *Survey of Age-Based Tuition-Waiver Policies* 207

F *Guidelines for Library Service to Older Adults* 213

G *Life-Enrichment Opportunities* 219

H *The Aging Network* 235

I *U.S. Department of Education Organizational Chart* 237

  Index 239

Tables and Figures

TABLES

1.1 Life Expectancy at Birth and Age 65 by
    Race and Sex, 1900–1987   6
1.2 Mean Age of Persons Initially Awarded
    Social Security Retirement Benefits by Sex, 1950–1989   7
1.3 Selected Characteristics of Participants in
    Adult Education: United States, 1984   16
1.4 Educational Attainment Age 25 Years Old and Older
    and 65 Years Old and Older, 1950–1989   17
1.5 Years of School Completed by Age, 1991   18
1.6 Educational Attainment by Age Group, Sex, Race, and
    Hispanic Origin, March 1989   19
2.1 Total Enrollment in Institutions of Higher Education by
    Level, Sex, Age, and Attendance Status of Student, Fall 1987 50
2.2 Civilian Labor Force and Participation Rates by Race,
    Hispanic Origin, Sex, and Age, 1970–1989,
    and Projections, 2000   74
2.3 Labor Force Participation Rates of Persons 85 Years
    and Over by Race and Sex, 1950–1980   76
3.1 Critical Pathways Taxonomy   90
3.2 Breakdown on Survey Response   92
4.1 Growth of the Older Population, 1900–1990   115
4.2 Older Adult Education: Key Legislation and Events   132
4.3 Selected Measures of Educational Attainment for
    People 25+ and 65+, 1950–1989   138

E.1 State Tuition-Waiver Policies   210

FIGURES

1.1 Life-Span Distribution of Education, Work, and Leisure   9
3.1 First-Year Planning Group Composition   94
3.2 Use Ongoing Planning Group   95
3.3 Actual First-Year Expenses   98
3.4 First-Year Funding Sources   99
3.5 Major Decision Makers Regarding Program   101
3.6 Significant Participant Involvement in
     Various Aspects of Program   102
3.7 Comparative Workload Distribution between
     Paid Staff and Volunteers   103
4.1 Median Age of the Population, 1950–2050   116
4.2 Population by Sex and Age, 1975   117
4.3 Population by Sex and Age, 2010   118
4.4 Population by Sex and Age, 2030   119
5.1 Familiarity with Information Superhighway by Subgroup   162
5.2 Penetration of High-Tech Products among Older Adults   164

Acknowledgments

We are grateful to several people who were instrumental in helping see this book to completion. Of the North Carolina Center for Creative Retirement staff, Carolyn Williams provided editorial guidance and management of the various manuscript drafts, while Susan Maas provided backup support for final corrections. Jim Verschueren, director of the Elderhostel Institute Network, read and commented on a draft of the manuscript and made useful suggestions. Sandra Timmermann, formerly director of education for the American Society on Aging and currently a private consultant on education and aging, generated a detailed critique and set of recommendations for improving the text. We are also grateful to the American Association of Retired Persons Andrus Foundation for funding the research that forms the main contents of Chapter 3. None of these individuals are responsible for any limitations or mistakes contained in the text, for which we assume full responsibility.

ABOUT THE NORTH CAROLINA CENTER FOR CREATIVE RETIREMENT

Established in 1988, the North Carolina Center for Creative Retirement (NCCCR) is an institute for examining and promoting meaningful and satisfying roles for older adults through lifelong learning, leadership, and community service programs. The NCCCR is part of the University of North Carolina at Asheville. The Center conducts a peer-learning and teaching program, the College for Seniors, a campus and community-oriented volunteer program, the Senior Academy for Intergenerational Learning, a public school volunteer program, Senior in the Schools, a research institute, a Leadership Asheville Seniors program, and a retirement planning program. The NCCCR operates in the greater Asheville area and collaborates with organizations throughout North Carolina and in other states on replicating Center programs or experimenting with new ventures. The Center has generated a variety of publications on older adult education and was instrumental in producing the *Older Americans Almanac* (1994), a reference work on aging in the United States.

Introduction

The role and importance of education in the lives of older Americans cannot be separated from the broader picture of changing lifestyles and choices, demographic dynamics, public policy on matters such as health care and income support, the new longevity of today's seniors, and unprecedented transformations in how people view (and what they expect of) the new stage of life we call retirement. That broader picture is made up of contrasting facts that reflect the diversity of the aging population and a spectrum of attitudes about later life.

EDUCATION AND THE COLLAGE OF AGING

Approximately one-third of the people traveling along golf course cart paths in the United States are individuals over sixty-five (Vierck 1993), while the percentage of older Americans who participate in credit-bearing and informal (noncredit) organized educational programs is an estimated 5 to 7 percent.

Consider that more than 30 percent of the vacation travelers and 60 percent of cruise passengers are people over sixty-five, who comprise less than 13 percent of the United States population. On the other side, almost 12 percent of the U.S. elderly have household incomes below the poverty level. Now add several additional facts to this list. Had you been born at the beginning of the century, you could have expected to live to age forty-seven and probably could not have counted on a retirement period lasting more than a handful of years. By 1990, the at-birth life expectancy had soared to seventy-five, and the average number of years one was freed, or forced, from the work force was seventeen.

The average age of retirement in 1990 was sixty-three, leaving most people a couple of decades to figure out the meaning and purpose of the so-called "bonus" years—a new, socially constructed part of the life course. Images of later life reflect both "boon" and "burden" attitudes toward the elderly. According to media reports, retirees have become big business. The over-fifty set is considered a phenomenally lucrative market segment. Meanwhile, Medicare, Medicaid, and Social Security are viewed as enormous national budget concerns. Some consider the older generation to be in an age–class struggle with younger generations over scarce resources (Longman 1987).

Given this collage of facts and attitudes, what profile might emerge about the role of education in the lives of older adults today and the huge population bulge of baby boomers soon to follow? Clearly, this profile must be seen against the backdrop of the broader national picture.

THE GUIDE: PURPOSE AND SCOPE

This book, *Older Adult Education: A Guide to Research, Programs, and Policies*, is an attempt to answer this question by capturing the profile of people engaged in various forms of organized learning who identify themselves with, or can be linked to, the later stages of life—whether that starts at fifty, fifty-five, sixty, or later. Emphasis is placed on the history of older adult education, related research, and policy development. Discussion of particular types of programs examine their organization's mission, goals, policies, curricula, relations to host institutions, forms of governance, costs (if any), and so on. Attitudes and motives, as well as intellectual abilities, of older learners are also explored but with a view to examining connections with the goals and policies of the institutional setting.

In this sense, the guide is not a close study of individual older learners, theories of adult cognition, or learning styles. Nor is it a how-to manual for setting up programs. Rather, the guide is an attempt to highlight certain institutional, research, and policy trends in how educational opportunities for older adults have been evolving—especially during the past fifteen to twenty years. As such, it should be useful to researchers studying older adult education, administrators of post-secondary educational institutions and aging programs, and others seeking to better understand the benefits and implications of such programs. The guide should also help those directly involved in education for seniors programs and people concerned about the history, current status, and possible future directions of these programs.

While the topic of older adult education is relatively distinct, the interrelationships of education for seniors to other aspects of our rapidly aging society make the context of the subject highly complex. The curricula and organizational forms through which older learners participate in types of organized educational settings are inseparable from political, economic, health, and cultural aspects of society, just as they would be for school children, traditional-age college students, or 30- and 40-year-olds upgrading their occupational skills. A major challenge is that, as our pastiche of statistics indicates, mature adults exhibit the greatest diversity of socioeconomic conditions and life experiences of any generation. Moreover, unlike individuals in earlier stages of life, older people have, on average, less time remaining to live; and most are not seeking educational opportunities related to the workplace. Hence, older adult education often requires a different rationale and set of justifications from that of education at other times of life.

EXCELLENCE AND LEISURE

Stretching your imagination a bit, today's retirement-aged generation could be compared to the leisure class of ancient Athens. Free, mostly male, adult citizens had the time and interest to learn, lead, and play in an amazingly rich cultural milieu. Today, in the United States and other countries, many seniors have joined a class of mature citizens with unprecedented leisure time for pursuing recreation, entertainment, travel, knowledge of the arts and humanities, fellowship, civic duty, and physical fitness. Flip open a copy of *Modern Maturity* (reaching 33 million people over fifty) or *New Choices for Retirement Living* (read by a couple million) and see what it means to near or arrive at the golden years. The images of today's elderly are without precedence.

The Athenian gentlemen would probably not have been as occupied with their grandchildren as today's over-fifty set. In fact, most would not have survived long enough to have gotten to know their grandchildren. But the Athenians would have been deeply interested in what fosters human excellence (the Greek term, *arete*) and in corresponding ideals of civic participation, leadership, and statesmanship. Similarly, our present-day leisure class of retirees might be looking around for models of excellence in dealing with adult children and their kids, managing their estates (whether big or small), volunteering for good causes, exercising leadership (such as serving in one of the numerous state senior legislatures), keeping fit, and wondering what makes for a good death. In other words, they may have discovered that what contributes to personal happiness in retirement and what goes into the ingredients that help form a good society are interrelated.

The quest for excellence in later life is probably not a self-conscious pursuit. Nevertheless, it is there. One has only to make an informal inquiry by going to the movies. Think of the 1987 film *Cocoon* and those Florida retirees discovering the fountain of youth in a swimming pool. They grapple with their quality of life, obligations to other generations, conditions of mortality, and prospects for spiritual transcendence. Take the mentoring role of Idgie (played by Jessica Tandy) in the 1992 film *Fried Green Tomatoes*, or that of the wizened, almost biblical role of the Jedi Knight, Yoda, in *Star Wars*. Popular culture is filled with images of older characters struggling heroically with finitude, the meaning of life and death, their own wisdom and folly, the legacy they would like to leave the young, and the burden they wish they could lift from the shoulders of youth. These are just a few of the many films that reflect our society's preoccupation with aging and the elderly: a mix of fear, fantasy, hope, and uncertainty.

Indeed, a society looks in the mirror of later life to wonder about the meaning and purpose of earlier stages. Put another way, the pyramid of life stages hangs from its apex rather than resting on its base (Gilligan 1982).

The achievements and productivity of later life are balanced by the decrements and vulnerabilities of aging. For many, there is protracted chronic illness, dwindling resources, multiple losses, despair, disappointment, isolation, and a life filled with meaningless distractions. It would be naive to argue that education could solve all the problems of old age or guarantee a pathway to self-transcendence.

While not presupposing that education in the later years is a panacea for virtue and happiness, the authors of this book hope to show that new forms of organized learning are meeting the demands of an unprecedented generation of mature adults, demands that are likely to increase dramatically with the size and make-up of the senior adult population in the United States. Though still greatly outnumbered by older golfers, seniors pursuing opportunities for continued learning (and many do both) are a growing segment and market of the emerging generation of retirees. Their motives for learning are diverse: Some seek to gain new skills that have practical application to everything from home repair to computerized financial management; others want to learn to paint, play the piano, swim, ski, acquire a foreign language, or delve into philosophy.

Many older people are independent learners. They use their public library for personal research, attend public lectures, visit museums, or raise orchids. They prefer to do these things on their own rather than in groups. Others enjoy the camaraderie of fellow seekers. They sign up for classes at senior centers, take educational trips together, attend Elderhostel courses, enroll in exercise classes, or participate in local senior athletic events such as Senior Games.

OBJECTIVES AND AUDIENCE

The objectives of this book are to capture some trends in organized educational programs for older adults and to describe the current state of research on how these educational programs have evolved, what needs and wants they aim to satisfy, how they are organized, the role that senior participants themselves play in determining the content and form of these programs, what policies guide them or are influenced by them, what institutions and organizations support and nurture them, and how technologies such as computers, telecommunications, and the information highway have already begun to affect their future.

We also explore how some programs link generations in learning with and from one another and how the volunteer spirit plays a role. An effort has been made to focus on the body of research literature, model programs, and policy development of the last fifteen to twenty years. Some earlier references are cited, often because they are seminal contributions with current relevance, or because they projected forward beyond their time.

A book of this type cannot do justice to all forms of education for older adults. While the scope of this book covers both those types of learning that help people solve problems and gain practical skills (so-called instrumental learning), as well as knowledge and information that is acquired for its own sake (so-called expressive learning), the educational contexts are primarily institutional settings of senior centers, colleges and universities, community colleges, department stores, churches, and synagogues. There is comparatively brief discussion of literacy programs, vocational education, remedial learning, job retraining, and health or consumer education. Nor are all organizations involved in some type of educational offerings to seniors covered equally. For example, agricultural extension programs and community school programs are only briefly mentioned.

What the reader will find is a synthesis of information on what we have determined to be the most dynamic, emerging forms of older adult education, ones in which seniors play active, even leadership, roles as they explore new norms and possibilities for this new stage of the life course.

We ask the reader's forgiveness for what may seem excessive emphasis on the North Carolina Center for Creative Retirement (NCCCR), our base of operation. We have used the NCCCR numerous times to exemplify a point or illustrate a trend because it is the program with which we are most familiar. We have, however, included examples from and citations to a vast spectrum of programs, mainly those found in the United States.

ORGANIZATION AND CONTENTS

The guide is organized into six chapters, with ancillary materials forming the Appendixes.

Chapter 1, "Lifelong Learning in an Aging Society," is a kind of musical overture to many of the themes, plots, and characters discussed in greater detail in subsequent chapters. This first chapter attempts to provide an overview of how older adult education looks today within the context of aging issues and programs. We explore purposes, goals, rationales, institutional relations, motivations, and emerging concepts of older adult education, and end with speculation on a new threefold paradigm linking lifelong learning, leadership, and community service.

Chapter 2, "Older Learners and Programs in Historical Perspective," moves from the notion of the third age as both an individual and societal concept to a review of how older adult education grew out of research on intellectual functioning of the elderly, the tradition of adult education, and forces operating within the relatively new field of gerontology. A review of numerous institutions hosting educational programs brings this historical review up to date.

Chapter 3, "The Transformation of Older Learner Programs," is a description of fifteen stages or phases of development in older learner programs as derived from a nationwide study conducted by the NCCCR of five institutional program types.

Chapter 4, "The Impact of Institutional Policies on Older Adult Education," aims at a comprehensive review of not only federal, state, and local public (meaning governmental) policies but policies of nongovernmental organizations both inside and outside the aging field.

Chapter 5, "Older Adult Learning in the Technological Age," examines the influence on older adult education of computer technology and forms of distance learning, such as telecommunications. We review the emerging literature on model programs and research regarding computer literacy among seniors, their motives for seeking knowledge of computers, and some preliminary findings of the benefits. How seniors may participate in the information highway is also discussed.

Finally, Chapter 6, "Generations Learning Together," considers recent emphasis on intergenerational programming and focuses on those programs inviting members of different generations to learn from one another and to take advantage of multigenerational perspectives in joint or colearning ventures.

The Appendixes to this guide contain documents that have been cited in the main text, resource lists, state tuition-waiver policies, and other items deemed useful to the reader. We have also included the background paper on "Life Enrichment" that was prepared for North Carolina's pre–White House Conference on Aging. North Carolina was one of the few states that made older adult education (as part of the broader term, Life Enrichment) one of its six major focus areas for recommendations to the 1995 White House Conference on Aging. The essay is included because it offers the reader a panoramic picture of the many forms of education (including recreational, political, spiritual, etc.) that may occur in a single state. The essay describes the tremendous differences between counties and regions of North Carolina in terms of available opportunities and resources. We believe that North Carolina is a microcosm of many other states and that this synoptic view will be useful in thinking about the status of older adult education in small towns, major urban areas, rural counties, and across diverse ethnic populations.

REFERENCES

Gilligan, C. 1982. *In a Different Voice*. Cambridge, Mass.: Harvard University Press.
Longman, P. 1987. *Born to Pay: The New Politics of Aging in America*. Boston: Houghton-Mifflin.
Vierck, E. 1990. *Factbook on Aging*. Santa Barbara, Calif: ABC-CLIO.

OLDER
ADULT EDUCATION

1

Lifelong Learning in an Aging Society

More than a dozen years have passed since David Peterson published his then-comprehensive treatment of older adult education, *Facilitating Education for Older Learners* (Peterson 1983). After carefully assessing national trends, he applauded those progressive institutions offering innovative educational programs to seniors, recognizing them as "beacons for society" that went beyond merely reflecting "current expectations." Given the rapid expansion of older learner programs through the 1970s, Peterson could justifiably proclaim: "The future, then, is bright."

If the future of older adult education looked promising then, it is positively brilliant now. Since the early 1980s, hundreds of new educational programs for retirement-age people have been launched and a whole new generation of retirees has turned up at registration day for educational programs offered by colleges, universities, churches, synagogues, hospitals, libraries, senior centers, and even department stores. So rapid has this growth been that several of these new educational organizations were not even mentioned by Peterson because they were still in fledgling stages. And some locations where he predicted little growth of older learner programs—for example, colleges and universities—have blossomed. As of 1994, over 200 institutions of higher education have become hosts to peer learning and teaching programs, generically described as Learning in Retirement Institutes (LRIs). The majority of these LRIs were started after 1985.

In 1983, Peterson could offer only a generic treatment of the stages of organizational development for older learner programs, highlighted by a few examples. Now these stages can be supported by survey statistics, numerous specific examples, and a multitude of variations.

What has happened to cause this expansion? Where is development of such programs headed? Who are the new retirees that want to continue or renew the learning process? Answers to these questions will help to update Peterson's study, integrate recent scholarship and research on the subject, and forecast developments likely to take us into the next century.

The aim of this chapter is to examine recent trends in education for seniors by (1) describing an emerging generation of retirees through examples of several older learners; (2) placing this generation in the context of the United States as an aging society; (3) examining attitudinal and institutional changes that illustrate new organizational forms and corresponding policy responses to older learners; (4) reviewing and critiquing the literature on what motivates people to seek lifelong learning; (5) comparing older learners' motives and goals with rationales articulated by host institution leaders (e.g., college and university administrators); (6) relating education for older adults to the concept of productive aging—a currently popular phrase that tries to capture the characteristics and activities of a new generation of retirement-age individuals; and, finally, (7) to crystallize some of the critical, social, and philosophical issues that surround older adult education. As such, this chapter will serve as an overview to this guide as a whole.

AN EMERGING GENERATION OF RETIREES:
A CASE STUDY

We begin with examples of three older persons whose continued participation in learning and the programs in which they learn reflect emerging trends that were identified through a national study of older adult education (Moskow-McKenzie and Manheimer 1993), which will be discussed at length in Chapter 3. Here, these anecdotes provide a microcosm of historical change.

The Hitchcocks and the North Carolina Center
for Creative Retirement

Earl and Marabeth Hitchcock decided that after twenty years of living, working, and raising a family in Bergen County, New Jersey, it was time to move. Earl, vice president of marketing for a manufacturing company, and Marabeth, a homemaker and community civic leader, were in their early sixties and thinking about retirement. Their three grown sons were married, and each lived in a different region of the eastern seaboard. Many of the Hitchcocks' friends had moved from New Jersey over the years, some because of corporate transfers, others to seek a friendlier climate. There were few compelling reasons to stay.

They wanted to live somewhere with four mild seasons, moderate housing costs, and a low crime rate. The location should be equidistant from their three sons. It should be a smaller town, possibly with a college or university which would ensure cultural activities such as plays, concerts, and lectures. Their taste for culture had developed over the years.

Earl had spent his childhood in France and Germany, depending on his father's European assignments as an engineer with International Harvester. Stories and firsthand experience of the Great Depression convinced Earl of the merits of an engineering degree. Though World War II broke out during his junior year in college, Earl was able to complete his degree under the "V7 Plan" that led him directly into the navy, following graduation. After the war, the degree helped Earl land engineering jobs; but he found them less satisfying than he had expected. Along the way to increasingly administrative roles, Earl discovered his bent for advertising and marketing. This did not surprise him, since writing had been one of his strong points in college. His career involved several geographic moves for the family until settling in Bergen County.

In 1985, Earl Hitchcock retired. He and Marabeth moved to a small city in the mountains of western North Carolina. They joined one of the migratory streams that carry approximately 5 percent of those over sixty-five to other states in retirement. Once established in the city of Asheville, they looked around for satisfying activities. They bought seasons tickets to the symphony. Marabeth served as a volunteer at a rehabilitation hospital. They joined the Episcopal church and got involved in visiting the homebound. Two years later, the Hitchcocks heard about a program for retirees started by the University of North Carolina at Asheville.

A College for Seniors had been established as part of the University's new North Carolina Center for Creative Retirement (NCCCR). The College for Seniors, modeled after other LRIs, offered a wide variety of peer-taught courses, primarily in the liberal arts. The Hitchcocks joined and began attending classes. After a while, Earl decided he might like to teach a course on how advertising influences social attitudes and opinions in the United States. The course was accepted by the curriculum committee, made up of retirees like Earl, and he began teaching. He was surprised and delighted by his unexpected good fortune in finding these unique retirement opportunities.

The Hitchcocks then discovered that the NCCCR offered yet another program, Leadership Asheville Seniors (LAS), designed to familiarize both newcomers and long-time residents with community issues, civic and governmental organizations, and some of the challenges into which retirees might like to channel their energies as volunteers or entrepreneurs. They decided to sign up. In one of the day-long LAS sessions devoted to issues of public education, Earl listened with rapt attention as Asheville High School principal, Larry Liggett, shared his vision of what the high school could be. Earl decided that a project involving retirees as volunteers with the schools was just the right type of activity. Marabeth agreed. And though they did not have any grandchildren in the area, the couple felt a general sense of responsibility for the education of children. It was, said Earl, "a kind of grandparenting instinct."

Earl arranged to meet with school principal Liggett and explained what he wanted to do. Liggett liked the idea and offered to help arrange a first organizational meeting in the school's media center. One evening, a few weeks later, sixty-eight people showed up; and a Seniors in the Schools project became a new arm of the NCCCR. Earl, aided by Marabeth, became its director. Within two years, over 100 senior volunteers were working with students in six schools, both in remedial and enrichment roles. Earl and Marabeth were amazed at their accomplishments. They had not dreamed of doing the things in retirement that evolved after their move to the area.

The Hitchcocks' retirement was nothing like either of their parents', the only model of retirement they had. Their fathers had worked pretty much until the onset of chronic ailments. The actual retirement period was only five and seven years for the fathers before they died, while the Hitchcocks' mothers lived on for another five and eleven years, mostly staying at home, traveling a little, visiting grandchildren, and socializing with a dwindling group of friends.

The Hitchcocks represent a newly emerging though still small cohort of retirees. Demographer Charles Longino calls them the "World War II foot soldier generation" (Fagan and Longino 1993). They share memories of the Great Depression, of World War II that made college possible for so many veterans, wartime and postwar corporate relocation, and participation in the booming U.S. economy. Reaching retirement, they are moderately affluent, in good health, well educated, and with entirely different kinds of expectations about the retirement years than their parents.

Moving away from a more or less permanent home was not new to them. They had done it four times over the years. Opportunities for broadening career and lifestyles horizons had come with the post–World War II period of educational opportunity and the benefits of participating in the economic boom of the 1950s and 1960s. Their penchant for community service derived from a strong sense of patriotism, from a belief that education could heal many of the wounds of poverty and prejudice, and from wanting to return something to others for what they had gained from society.

Elizabeth Houston and Senior Neighbors of Chattanooga

In many ways, the life of Elizabeth Houston could not be more different from the Hitchcocks. Born seventy-four years ago in Bristol, Tennessee, she grew up to become an elementary school teacher and, later, high school counselor. Teaching was not her favorite occupational path; but for an African-American woman in the South, it was one of the few professional opportunities available. After attending a historical black college, Houston became one of the first African-American graduate students to attend Eastern Tennessee State University shortly after desegregation. Her first marriage took her to Rochester, New York, for a period of years. Another marriage, which also dissolved, brought her back to Chattanooga, Tennessee, where she eventually retired after thirty-seven years in schools. But her life of learning did not end there.

At the age of sixty-five, Houston enrolled at the Young Women's Christian Association (YWCA) to learn how to swim. "I wasn't going to leave this world without knowing how to swim," she said. Her choice was not strictly recreational; it was also political. As a youth, Houston had few opportunities to swim, since public pools in the South were generally off-limits to African-Americans. Succeeding at swimming, she began to try out other educational activities.

Houston began to attend the Boynton Senior Center adjacent to the apartment building in which she lived, supported by Housing and Urban Development (HUD). There and at the main branch of Senior Neighbors of Chattanooga, a five-minute drive away, she studied Spanish, fine art (she prefers to paint in the abstract style), drama, and creative writing. When several of her paintings were exhibited, her grandchildren were enormously impressed by a talent they had never seen before. To these activities she added volunteering through the senior center in a program with youth called Kids on the Block, singing in her church choir, and other community activities. "There are a lot more opportunities now than when I was coming up. Anyway, I couldn't see myself staying home and doing nothing," she commented.

The Hitchcocks' and Houston's encounters with new educational programs serving older adults came at exactly the right time. They joined thousands of other older Americans in finding new opportunities to learn and new roles to play in their retirement years. The interplay between their personal motives and choices and the policies of a university and senior center that invited them to learn, teach, volunteer, and engage in community service reflects emerging trends in lifelong learning and changing attitudes toward aging that are, in part, a by-product of our nation's becoming an aging society. Their stories reflect individual motives, social changes, and the evolution of organizations adapting to a new portion of the life course—the retirement age.

Changes in access to education for seniors and the types of programs now available are part of a larger picture that can best be understood in the context of demographic change.

THE PURPOSES OF EDUCATION IN AN AGING SOCIETY

Understanding the societal potential for and public policy implications of education for older adults requires placing this development in context of recent history and an unprecedented trend: the overall aging of the U.S. population. Without grasping this connection, the significance of older adult education for the society as a whole will be lost.

The Changing Demographic Picture

The United States, like western Europe and Japan, is classified as an aging society because the population exceeds the demographer's average-age threshold of thirty, reaching thirty-three in 1990 and climbing toward forty by the year 2020. Victory over diseases of infancy and childhood in the earlier part of the twentieth century led to dramatic increases in the number and percentage of adults who survived to maturity. Advances in medical technology in the second half of the century have extended life expectancy in the middle and later parts of the life course. The postwar baby boom and a subsequent decline in fertility rates have also contributed to the aging of the population.

Since 1900, almost thirty years have been added to the average at-birth life expectancy of the U.S. population (see Table 1.1) and even more years to that of residents in countries like Japan and Sweden. The statistical aging of the population is socially accentuated given the remarkable contrast between the youth-oriented culture of the post–World War II period and today, when in the United States, teenagers represent a shrinking percentage of the population.

Middle-aged America, Europe, and Japan are on a course that will intensify issues of societal aging as these countries look ahead to 65-plus populations of between 20 and 25 percent by the middle part of the next century. Germany and Sweden already have 65-plus populations of 17 and 18 percent. For the next fifty years, apart from unforeseen diseases and natural or human-caused catastrophes, many countries will be drafting economic and social

Table 1.1
Life Expectancy at Birth and Age 65 by Race and Sex, 1900–1987 (values are in years)

Year	All races			White			Black		
	Both sexes	Men	Women	Both sexes	Men	Women	Both sexes	Men	Women
At birth									
1900[1,2]	47.3	46.3	48.3	47.6	46.6	48.7	33.0[3]	32.5[3]	33.5[3]
1950[2]	68.2	65.6	71.1	69.1	66.5	72.2	60.7	58.9	62.7
1960[2]	69.7	66.6	73.1	70.6	67.4	74.1	63.2	60.7	65.9
1970	70.9	67.1	74.8	71.7	68.0	75.6	64.1	60.0	68.3
1980	73.7	70.0	77.4	74.4	70.7	78.1	68.1	63.8	72.5
1987	75.0	71.5	78.4	75.6	72.2	78.9	69.4	65.2	73.6
At age 65									
1900-02[1,2]	11.9	11.5	12.2	-	11.5	12.2	-	10.4[3]	11.4[3]
1950[2]	13.9	12.8	15.0	-	12.8	15.1	13.9	12.9	14.9
1960[2]	14.3	12.8	15.8	14.4	12.9	15.9	13.9	12.7	15.1
1970	15.2	13.1	17.0	15.2	13.1	17.1	14.2	12.5	15.7
1980	16.4	14.1	18.3	16.5	14.2	18.4	15.1	13.0	16.8
1987	16.9	14.8	18.7	17.0	14.9	18.8	15.4	13.5	17.1

Source: Aging America, Trends and Projections, prepared by the U.S. Senate Special Committee on Aging, the American Association of Retired Persons, the Federal Council on the Aging, and the U.S. Administration on Aging, 1991, Washington, D.C., p. 20. Primary source: 1900 to 1980 data: National Center for Health Statistics. *Health United States, 1988*, DHHS Pub. No. (PHS)89-1232, Department of Health and Human Services,Washington, D.C., March 1989. 1987, data: National Center for Health Statistics. "Life Tables," *Vital Statistics of the United States, 1987*, Vol. 2, Section 6, February 1990.
[1]Ten states and the District of Columbia.
[2]Includes deaths of nonresidents of the United States.
[3]Figure is for the nonwhite population.

policies to accommodate an aging population. Meanwhile, the experience of aging and what it means to be old will continue to undergo a transformation.

Implication of the Longer Life Course for Education

It is difficult to predict how life after age fifty, sixty-five, or eighty will be experienced by future generations of individuals and regarded by social institutions, businesses, governments, and religious denominations. Indeed, today's 60-year-olds often look and act younger and are healthier than yesterday's 40-year-olds. Many people in their late seventies and eighties have already outlived their parents by fifteen and twenty years. In some ways, a longer lifetime means not only more years of later life, which is artificially demarcated anyway, but of mid-life as well. The whole life course is being stretched out in a rubber band fashion.

Extension of the life course changes the timing of life events and the socially determined segments of age-linked activities. Women are having first children when in their late thirties and into their forties. The age at which people retire has dropped from a mean age of 68.1 (for men) and 68.0 (for women) in 1950 to 63.7 (for men) and 63.4 (for women) in 1989 (Table 1.2).

Table 1.2
Mean Age of Persons Initially Awarded Social Security Retirement Benefits by Sex, 1950–1989

Year	Age	
	Men	Women
1950	68.7	68.0
1955	68.4	67.8
1960	66.8	65.2
1965	65.8	66.2
1970	64.4	63.9
1975	64.0	63.7
1980	63.9	63.5
1985	63.7	63.4
1989	63.7	63.4

Source: "Age at Retirement," *Family Economics Review* 5 (4;1992): 28–30. Primary source: Social Security Bulletin, *Annual Statistical Supplement, 1990*. Social Security Administration, 1990, p. 236, table 6B5.

Note: This table shows the decline in the median age of retirement. The source suggests that this decline, combined with an increase in longevity, "raise[s] the economic dependency burden the elderly place on younger cohorts still in the work force. This tends to make increases in per capita income harder to achieve, even as the cost of income transfers to the elderly rise."

On the education front, it is not uncommon for people in their thirties and forties to return to colleges and universities for additional degrees, upgrading of skills, and redirection in career paths or to expand their horizons. In 1988, according to the College Board, over 40 percent of the nation's undergraduate and graduate students were already nontraditional, that is, over twenty-five; and 40 percent attended on a part-time basis. The so-called older students may constitute a majority of college enrollments by the turn of the century. Corporate training and retraining has become a norm rather than an exception, and it is far from uncommon for people to have several different career specialties in a lifetime. Hence, being a student is not limited to one segment of life but becomes an episodic event.

As Crystal and Bolles (1974) point out, the changing life course involves an intermingling of activities rather than sequential boxes of life—periods of childhood, education, work, retirement. Periods of study and retooling, similar to college professor sabbaticals, may become commonplace in tomorrow's average life course experience. The distribution of education, work, and leisure activity may now look something like the life plans for the year 2000 in Figure 1.1.

Already there is discussion that the longer life span has created a "second middle age" (Bronte 1993) in the sixty to seventy-five age period. In the second middle age, individuals continue their life activities in modified form. They may work part-time in so-called bridge jobs that provide a gradual transition from full-time career to retirement. Meanwhile they are doing volunteer work, maintaining a busy social life, and participating in recreational and cultural events.

Reconceptualizing Later Life

This new flexibility in the timing of life events and the extended life course raises provocative questions about how coming generations will regard their own chronological age and the retirement period. Will second middle-agers identify with terms like "senior citizen," "older adult," and "senior"? Will they be comfortable joining organizations labeled as for "retired persons," go to "senior centers," or subscribe to magazines designed for "modern maturity"? We already see rapid changes reflected, for example, in the renaming of senior centers as "enrichment centers" and the reimaging of *Fifty Plus* magazine as it became *New Choices*. Are these harbingers of things to come?

Some gerontologists view the increase in longevity and loosening norms for prescribed age-linked behaviors as part of an emerging "age irrelevant" society (Neugarten and Neugarten 1986) or "age liberated" one (Gruman 1978). They reject the view that there are intrinsic age norms for later life, arguing that such norms are socially, economically, and culturally constructed and, hence, can be reconstructed. Groups like the Gray Panthers and the Older Women's League have set about to do just that.

Doing away with age norms can have political implications. Separating age norms from chronological aging may imply that entitlements like Social Security

Figure1.1
Life-Span Distribution of Education, Work, and Leisure

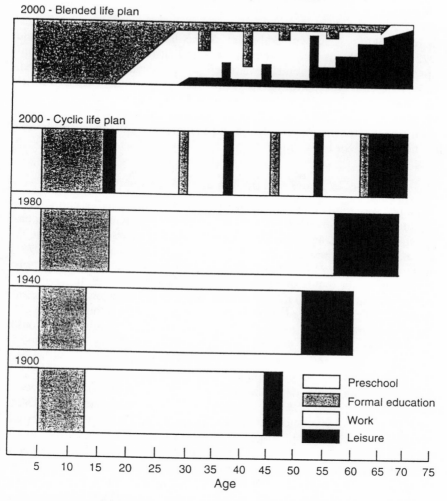

Source: Work in America Institute, *The Future of Older Workers in America* (Scarsdale, N.Y.: Work in America Institute, 1980). From Ronald J. Manheimer, ed., *Older Americans Almanac: A Reference Work on Seniors in the United States*, North Carolina Center for Creative Retirement, University of North Carolina at Asheville. Copyright © 1994 by Gale Research, Inc. Reprinted with permission of the publisher.

and Medicare should not be tied to a specific birthdate but to individuals' needs and economic situation. Such a position challenges senior interest groups and lobbies that have worked hard to improve the quality of life for older people in general. The United States and many other countries will have to ask whether their societies are able and willing to support a decent quality of life for all older persons based on an implied social contract between the generations.

Other scholars of aging agree that age stereotypes must be overcome and replaced by views that balance the strengths that come with age with the inevitable weaknesses and vulnerabilities. Some, like Moody (1988) and Cole (1992), believe that a more holistic view, one that recognizes interrelationships between generations and between segments of the life course, is needed. The holistic view would avoid perpetuating new generalities, such as the stereotype of the perpetually healthy and youthful senior. Instead, it would be grounded in traditional virtues emphasizing the dignity of later life; the potential for intellectual, emotional, and spiritual growth; and the nurturing role the old can play for the young.

Consciousness of Aging and the Women's Movement

Another way to understand changes in attitudes toward aging and old age is by drawing parallels to the history of the women's movement. A new consciousness about the aging process and later life can be traced to Simone de Beauvoir's 1970 literature-based study of old age, *The Coming of Age* (1973), and, more recently, to Betty Friedan's *The Fountain of Age* (1993). It is more than a coincidence that both authors first published epoch-making books that gave a powerful impetus to the women's movement (de Beauvoir's *The Second Sex*, in 1950; Friedan's *The Feminine Mystique*, in 1963) and then each, as she grew older, turned the same type of analysis to the subject of aging. One could argue that liberation from gender stereotypes set the pattern for consciousness raising about age stereotypes. Authors such as de Beauvoir and Friedan are not the only agents of social change.

The increasing power of senior organizations like the American Association of Retired Persons (AARP), the National Council on the Aging (NCOA), and the National Association of Senior Citizens (NASC) point to concerted efforts to bring older people together to push for better health care, protection from poverty, and age discrimination in the workplace. Television and film media now offer a greater number of older actors depicting positive roles of the elderly. And, again, like the women's movement that led thousands of women to return to the college campus for that all-important credential to a decent job, older adults are beginning to return to colleges and other educational institutions to achieve a wide variety of goals, including finishing a degree, getting trained for a second or third career, and enhancing personal discovery and enrichment, to name a few.

Education and the Reconstructed Life Course

Education, then, is not a one-time segment of the life course, but a repeated, indeed, lifelong series of reencounters. But the purposes of education, like the purposes of life at different times in the life course, may vary in objectives, structure, and format.

What education is like for children and adolescents is certainly different from that of undergraduate and graduate students. Similarly, corporate-based training programs, postgraduate seminars, and specialized certification programs have their unique qualities. When education is no longer designed for career enhancement, character building, or appropriation of basic life skills (reading, writing, and arithmetic), it takes on yet another meaning or set of meanings. But the purpose of education in later life, even including occupational retraining for remaining in the labor force or preparing for a volunteer position, raises a whole set of issues about the meaning of later life. And it invites questions like these: "Who decides what programs are offered?" and "Who should pay for them?" These are especially sensitive questions when public funds or resources (space, staff time, etc.) are involved. But even when programs are fully supported by older participants' fees (as with Elderhostel and many continuing education types of programs), identification with the sponsoring institution may raise questions of public image, fairness toward other special interest groups, and even discomfort about the presence of older people.

The largest percentage of people over fifty-five involved in education is found in noncredit, continuing education. Studies discussed in this chapter show variations in preference for practical, skills-oriented courses as distinguished from enrichment courses (the latter more popular with women and individuals from white-collar backgrounds). Unlike education geared for jobs and career advancement, learning for life enrichment has always met with objections from more utilitarian-minded educational leaders and policymakers who regard learning for its own sake—what is sometimes called the humanistic philosophy of education—as, at best, individually valuable for personal growth, important as an agent for building character and citizenship, or useful as an enhancement of critical thinking skills. At worst, they see education for its own sake as a questionable and possibly elitist luxury. Whatever ideology of education one holds, when older adults enter the picture, new complications and ambiguities are introduced, particularly when public dollars go into supporting these institutionalized opportunities.

For most educational administrators and policymakers, it is not too much of a stretch to justify work retraining or life-skills enhancement. But when an older person learns Spanish, fine arts, or about literature and history, how does society benefit?

If later life is viewed as a period of declining economic productivity and obsolescence of knowledge, a time during which, at best, people should keep mentally and physically busy in order to prevent premature physical and cognitive decline, then establishing a rationale for the existence of older adult education programs will be difficult. Indeed, as we shall find, institutional justifications and the motives of actual older people may have only tangential relevance to one another. How then has the changing consciousness about aging influenced social attitudes and institutional policies about education?

ATTITUDINAL AND INSTITUTIONAL CHANGES

The Four-Legged Stool

Retirement planning specialists and economists talk about the three primary economic supports in later life: the so-called three-legged stool of Social Security benefits, Medicare health care coverage, and the financial resource of private pensions. Announcing a variation on this theme, some people jokingly refer to Elderhostel as part of the four-legged stool of retirement. While still a tiny minority of the nation's elderly, the over 330,000 *hostelers* in 1994 make up a growing group of people who looked forward to turning sixty in anticipation of qualifying for Elderhostel, the residential college-level program that invites seniors to travel to college campuses, conference centers, national parks, and even social action centers, here and abroad, to continue learning while making new friends and seeing new places.

Elderhostel, which started in 1975 with a few hundred people, symbolizes changing personal and societal attitudes toward aging and retirement and reflects one aspect of the growth of educational opportunities for seniors during the past twenty years—learning as valued for its own sake. Certainly, seniors centers and community colleges should also be credited for their roles in reaching thousands of seniors since the 1971 White House Conference on Aging and 1973 amendments to the Older Americans Act promoted both the practical and developmental value of education for seniors. But community college and senior center programs had a tendency to emphasize recreational and practical aspects of education (e.g., crafts, exercise, sports, finances, and consumer safety) rather than expressive or intellectually reflective subjects. Even when arts and humanities courses were offered in these locations, they were often justified as having positive socialization and mental health benefits.

Elderhostel marked a sharp departure from this mind-set. For one, the curricular emphasis was on the liberal arts. Second, it was not a public institution but a private one. Third, people were expected to pay their own way—only a handful of scholarships were offered each year. Perhaps Elderhostel just appealed to a different socioeconomic stratum. But it showed by contrast that there are different concepts of the aims of education for seniors and different attitudes of seniors toward learning. Clearly, the purposes of learning in later life are based on fundamentally different assumptions.

Presuppositions of Learning in Later Life

The spectrum and development of educational programs and purposes can be put in perspective by examining their "philosophical presuppositions"

(Moody 1976, 1988). As Moody points out, the goals of providing education to seniors have ranged from (1) no goal at all ("older people don't need or deserve any more education"); (2) to the goal of ameliorating the negative factors of aging, for example, social isolation, depression, boredom, and intellectual decline; (3) to keeping seniors socially involved or "mainstreaming" them by encouraging traditional educational institutions to attract seniors to their regular offerings and to treat them the same as any other adults; and (4) to viewing later life as a special time for unique learning needs and desires that will help older individuals become "self-actualized." The move from regarding education for seniors as a form of distraction, amusement, therapy, or entertainment—while presuming the essential dependency of older people—to regarding education in later life as releasing hidden potential and creativity has parallel counterparts in institutional transformations.

From the 1950s to the 1970s, many educational programs for older adults were based on social service models (corresponding to goal 2 in the preceding paragraph) and tended to rely on foundation grants or local, state, and federal funding to make such programs freely available to presumably needy or dependent seniors. This reliance on private foundations and public funds led to discontinuities of educational programs: They appeared and disappeared within the time frame of grant start-ups and terminations or changes in funding priorities. Participants were rarely asked to pay even token registration fees.

While senior participants' appetites for education may have been whetted, the intermittent availability of programs often left them starving for more. Moreover, too often there was no institutional infrastructure to support continuity of programs. By not charging fees, the cost barrier was eliminated. But having no reliable source of funding and no revenue flow made it difficult to conduct long-range planning, develop an institutional infrastructure, maintain staff continuity, and identify long-term goals. The accumulated experience of running programs and gains in expertise on the part of personnel were often lost when projects terminated and staff members had to move on. Often they left no written record of achievements and lessons learned. Insights gained from programs and evaluation results were rarely turned into journal articles that could be accessed by future planners.

If the social work approach predominated in the 1950s through the 1970s, the mainstreaming approach overlapped and was characteristic of the 1970s. An effort was made to downplay the differences between old and young. Seniors were normalized by encouraging them to fit into existing educational institutions such as community schools, public colleges (on the basis of tuition-free, space-available programs), and community centers. "They're just like everyone else, just older," was the refrain. But most older adults were not the same; they had different learning goals and learning strengths and weaknesses, different schedules and access to transportation, and different contributions to make. Mainstreaming produced mixed results. The states with tuition-waiver policies saw relatively few older persons enrolling as credit or noncredit students in regular courses, while those states that offered community college courses at little or no cost (on-site or through senior centers) saw a large surge of enrollment.

The social service and mainstreaming approaches might be appropriate in certain settings with certain groups, but they were limited in scope, structure, and what they expected and drew from older adults. Self-actualization, a theory that endured from the humanistic psychology movement of the 1960s, suggested something more. There was still potential in those aging bodies and minds; untapped creativity waiting to be released; a passion for knowledge triggered by new-found leisure; a desire to make their resourcefulness available to their communities; and the ability to serve as role models for younger persons (McClusky 1990). But to make an institution out of self-actualization required new organizational forms that could embody this perspective.

New Organizational Structures of Older Adult Education

During the past twenty years, programs like Elderhostel and campus-based LRIs have emerged that charge fees, are completely or partially independent of public sector beneficence, and seek to establish their own infrastructure, sometimes as separate institutions (such as Elderhostel) and more commonly within the framework of a host institution. For example, the approximately 200 LRIs associated with colleges and universities across the United States are one form the new institutional structuring has taken. Similarly, community colleges and senior centers have increasingly adopted a low-fee format that may include state or community subsidies. And church- and synagogue-based Shepherd's Centers reflect another version of this permanent infrastructure approach, emphasizing a nonmonetized staffing pattern heavily reliant on volunteers. Even private businesses, such as the May Company department stores, have entered the picture by partially underwriting the cost and providing space for educational centers in department stores.

But infrastructure is not the only change. Older adult education has moved toward not only self-actualization but also empowerment as seniors are themselves taking over some of the leadership and curriculum decision making for their own learning opportunities. Community-based, consumer- or learner-oriented, participant-directed programs represent the innovative edge of older adult education today. This trend fits well with emerging ideologies of later life typified by phrases like *successful aging*, *productive aging*, and *creative retirement*.

New Roles for Seniors in Their Own Education

Older adult education represents a further evolution of adult and continuing education. While theorists of adult education such as Malcolm Knowles (1975) emphasized the importance of adult learner-centered pedagogy or "androgogy," new developments represent another step. Some programs and organizations have sought to encourage older adult learners to exercise greater authority over their educations, placing them in teaching, governance, and administrative positions. A national survey conducted during the years 1992–1993 by the NCCCR found that among 260 responding educational programs for seniors, an overall average of 27 percent used volunteers for 76 to 100 percent of the work, a percentage that is much higher for the more recently established LRIs (35 percent) and Shepherd's Centers (57.5 percent) than community colleges or senior centers. A fuller report on this research and corresponding trends is found in Chapter 3.

It is premature to predict whether consumer-driven or senior-led programs will come to predominate among older adult education organizations. Their appropriateness may vary according to situation and educational purpose. But the movement in this direction transcends earlier, rather sentimental ideas about roles older people can play, characterized in the 1970s and early 1980s by projects on the creative uses of reminiscence and oral history. Efforts to redeem the value of older adults by viewing them as cultural artifacts (i.e., turning them into storehouses of mythic knowledge, modern-day urban village mentors, wisdom keepers, bearers of folk knowledge and traditional folkways, and so on) were noble, to be sure. But few seniors actually seek these roles or hold these aspirations. They represent new stereotypes based on younger persons' needs to find something good about growing old or trendy concepts possibly useful for securing a grant or selling a program. Certainly, the Foxfire publications kindled some wonderful student projects and recognition that many ordinary older people have special talents and knowledge that are being ignored. But few older people are mountain weavers or folk healers wise in the ways of herbal medicine.

Dickerson (1990), following some ideas of Moody (1986), saw one role of older adults as providing the "high-touch" counterbalance to society's increasing high-tech orientation. Their wealth of life experience and tendency to be contemplative, argued Dickerson, "can be harnessed to provide society with high-touch contributions." There reflection on the meaning of life and their capacity as storytellers, oral historians, and the like enable older people to help younger generations in the transition to a self-help future lifestyle. Again, these qualities may fit some older people and not others. To generalize in this way is to create new stereotypes. More appropriately, this line of thinking does suggest that many older people have unique strengths that are enhanced by their longer years. They can, and often want, to play contributive roles. How can institutions respond to these needs?

Participation Rates

While the recent evolution of older adult education is dramatic when compared to what was available just twenty years ago, the actual number and percentage of participants is still rather modest. The most recent comprehensive data are those drawn from a 1984 survey of adult education participation rates conducted by the National Center for Education Statistics (NCES) (see Table 1.3). That study indicated that 4 percent (900,000) of the sixty-five and over population participated as full-time or part-time students in high school or college degree programs, a percentage that increases to 5.7 percent (2.7 million) when the fifty-five and over group is considered.

One has to put these figures in perspective. For example, participation in adult education by all age groups increased from 10 percent in 1969 to 14 percent at the time of the 1984 survey. Analysis of subgroups is also of great interest. Women adult education participants (14.1 percent) outnumbered men (12.8) as women increasingly sought out educational opportunities to secure entry or reentry to the work force while they continued to take courses for personal enrichment. Others estimate that for the 65-plus population, a figure of 6 to 7 percent may obtain for the 1990s. These figures do not include many hard to survey informal educational programs such as those conducted at senior centers, LRIs, and public humanities programs funded by the National Endowment for the Humanities (NEH) or state humanities councils, both of which tend to draw strong participation of older adults; and they do not

Table 1.3
Selected Characteristics of Participants in Adult Education: United States, 1984 (numbers in thousands)

Characteristics of Participants	Number of adults Population	Students in High School or College Degree Programs					
		Full-Time		Part-Time		Total Enrolled	
		Number	%	Number	%	Number	%
Total: All Age Groups	172,583	1,118	0.6	22,184	12.9	23,303	13.5
Age Breakdown							
17–34	71,891	948	1.3	10,756	15.0	11,704	16.3
35–54	52,303	152	0.3	8,712	16.7	8,864	16.9
55+	48,388	18	0.0	2,717	5.6	2,735	5.7
Sex							
Men	81,700	485	0.6	9,961	12.2	10,446	12.8
Women	90,883	643	0.7	12,224	13.5	12,857	14.1

Source: U.S. Department of Education, Center for Education Statistics, "Current Population Survey, May 1984, Survey of Adult Education," conducted by the Bureau of the Census, unpublished tabulations (prepared in 1986).

Note: Data are based upon a sample survey of the civilian noninstitutional population. Because of rounding, details may not add to totals.

include activities of independent learners whose classroom may be the local public library or a self-help group.

The number and percentage of older adults who participate in education is likely to grow. As Cross (1981) and others have found, the primary predictor of participation in education is prior participation. The more formal education people have received, the more they are inclined toward further learning opportunities. As shown in Table 1.4, the median years of schooling has risen from just over eighth-grade level for those 65-plus in 1950, to over twelve years of formal education for the same age group in 1989 (U.S. Bureau of the Census 1989). In 1989, 11 percent of those age 65-plus had completed four or more years of college, a figure that will rise to over 20 percent by the year 2010. Tables 1.5 and 1.6 show percentages of age segments with four or more years of college. Table 1.5 shows that while 10.5 percent of those over seventy-five completed four years of college as of 1991, almost 17 percent of

Table 1.4

Educational Attainment Age 25 Years Old and Older and 65 Years Old and Older, 1950–1989

Year and Age Group	High School Education	Four or More Years of College	Median Years of School
1989			
25+ years	76.9	21.1	12.7
65+ years	54.9	11.1	12.1
1980			
25+ years	66.5	16.2	12.5
65+ years	38.8	8.2	10.0
1970			
25+ years	52.3	10.7	12.1
65+ years	27.1	5.5	8.7
1960			
25+ years	41.1	7.7	10.5
65+ years	19.1	3.7	8.3
1950			
25+ years	33.4	6.0	9.3
65+ years	17.0	3.4	8.3

Sources: U.S. Bureau of the Census, Unpublished data from the March 1989 Current Population Survey; idem, "Detailed Population Characteristics," 1980 Census of Population, PC80-1-D1, United States Summary (February 1973); idem, "Characteristics of the Population," 1960 Census of Population, Vol. 1, Part 1, United States Summary, Chapter D (1964).

people fifty-five to sixty-four had. Thus, the cohorts nearing retirement age contain markedly higher percentages of likely participants for continuing education types of programs. If prior education holds up as the primary predictor of educational participation in the later years, then we can expect a strong increase, especially after the turn of the century.

Predictors of education in later life also suggest that programs will be largely populated by white students. Lower levels of educational attainment among African-Americans (in 1989, 24.6 percent for African-Americans compared to 54.9 percent for whites completing high school) and other minorities implies smaller increases in educational participation among minority populations even while these groups will form an increasing percentage of the older population. However, other cohort and socioeconomic factors (e.g., concepts of leisure, family obligations, and roles) may have equal or greater influence on minority groups and their choice of learning options in the later years.

As mentioned, prior education is indicative of the desire for further education, and to this must be added income level as another key predictor. Based on analysis of the 1984 data, some researchers (e.g., Arbeiter 1989) predict that by 2010, the generation that will be forty-five to sixty-five (approximately 80 million people) will include a high percentage of well-educated, relatively well-off older adults. This is based on data which show that while 10.6 percent of adults who have completed high school participate in adult education, almost 20 percent do of those with one to three years of college.

Table 1.5
Years of School Completed by Age, 1991 (for persons 25 years old and older, as of March)

Age	Population (1,000)	Percent of population with:		
		4 years of high school or more	1 or more years of college	4 or more years of college
Total persons	158,694	78.4	39.8	21.4
25 to 34 years old	42,905	86.1	45.3	23.7
35 to 44 years old	38,665	87.7	50.2	27.5
45 to 54 years old	25,686	81.2	41.1	23.2
55 to 64 years old	21,346	71.9	31.4	16.9
65 to 74 years old	18,237	63.5	25.3	13.2
75 years old or over	11,855	49.0	20.8	10.5

Source: U.S. Bureau of the Census, *Statistical Abstract of the United States: 1992*, 112th ed. (Washington, D.C., 1992), p. 144. Primary source: U.S. Bureau of the Census, *Current Population Reports*, series P-20, No. 462.

Table 1.6

EducationalAttainment by Age Group, Sex, Race, and Hispanic Origin, March 1989

Measure of educational attainment and age	Sex			Race and Hispanic origin								
	Total	Men	Women	White			Black			Hispanic origin		
				Total	Men	Women	Total	Men	Women	Total	Men	Women
Median years of school completed												
25+	12.7	12.8	12.6	12.7	12.8	12.7	12.4	12.4	12.4	12.0	12.0	12.0
60 to 64	12.4	12.5	12.4	12.5	12.5	12.4	10.7	10.6	10.7	9.3	9.6	8.9
65+	12.1	12.1	12.2	12.2	12.2	12.2	8.5	8.1	8.7	8.0	8.1	8.0
65 to 69	12.3	12.3	12.3	12.4	12.4	12.4	9.5	9.1	9.8	8.4	8.5	8.3
70 to 74	12.2	12.2	12.2	12.3	12.3	12.3	8.4	8.2	8.6	8.0	8.1	7.9
75+	10.9	10.5	11.3	11.6	11.1	11.9	7.8	7.0	8.2	7.1	7.0	7.1
Percent with a high school education												
25+	77	77	77	78	79	78	65	64	65	51	51	51
60 to 64	66	65	67	69	68	71	39	43	37	34	37	31
65+	55	54	56	58	57	59	25	22	26	28	26	29
65 to 69	63	61	65	67	65	68	31	28	33	33	31	35
70 to 74	57	56	58	60	59	62	21	20	22	25	21	29
75+	46	44	48	49	47	50	21	18	23	23	21	24
Percent with four or more years of college												
25+	21	25	18	22	25	19	12	12	12	10	11	9
60 to 64	14	19	10	15	21	10	5	7	4	6	5	7
65+	11	14	9	12	15	10	5	4	5	6	7	5
65 to 69	13	16	10	13	17	10	5	3	6	9	9	9
70 to 74	11	13	9	11	13	10	3	3	3	9	9	9
75+	10	12	9	11	13	9	6	4	6	4	7	3

Source: Aging America, Trends and Projections, prepared by the U.S. Senate Special Committee on Aging, the American Association of Retired Persons, the Federal Council on the Aging, and U.S. Administration on Aging, 1991, Washington, D.C., p. 192. Primary source: U.S. Bureau of the Census. Unpublished data from the March 1989, *Current Population Survey*.

Note: Data exclude people in institutions.

[1]People of Hispanic origin may be of any race.

Arbeiter also predicts that the trend of increasing educational attainment will be reversed in the twenty-first century because of the aging of the poverty population and the powerful trend in students dropping out before high school graduation. Hence, baby boomers will be strong consumers of adult education while there will be a decline in overall adult education participation tied to declines in prior educational attainment.

The demographic picture of present and future educational participation of older adults in relation to the larger population is both speculative and problematic. Many factors will alter predictions. Nevertheless, it is clear that many groups, such as new immigrants, aging high school dropouts, underclass minorities, and others will have great need of remedial and adult education, and other groups in the work force will need periodic retraining to accommodate changes in technology. How will the educational needs and interests of older adults compare in terms of availability and importance? To what extent might older persons provide guidance, tutoring, and mentoring to these especially needy groups and how much will these roles form part of what it means to be an older learner? We will return to these questions in Chapters 2 and 6.

MOTIVATION FOR EDUCATION IN LATER LIFE

The curriculum of educational programs for older adults would suggest a broad range of participant learning goals. For example, among participants in LRIs where the curriculum is heavily weighted toward the liberal arts, one might expect education to be regarded by participants as an end in itself, having its own intrinsic value. On the other hand, a community college series of courses on life skills for seniors (e.g., managing finances in retirement, maintaining physical well being, and coping with stress) suggests a learning process geared toward an outcome that lies beyond the educational activity itself. Correspondingly, learner motives vary in relation to involvement in different types of curricula. Is there a systematic basis on which to classify the educational motivations of older adults?

What Motivates Older Learners?

A considerable amount of research, based on the work of Havighurst (1976) and then of Londoner (1971, 1978) who made direct application to older adults, centered around the dichotomous pair of terms *expressive* and *instrumental* to characterize learner motives. Learning for its own sake has been classified as expressive, while learning directed toward some further outcome or external objective is said to be instrumentally oriented. Whether expressive and instrumental orientations are viewed as opposites (dichotomous) or as forming a continuum, the distinction poses many conceptual problems.

Expressive and instrumental motives for learning blur one into the other. For example, learning French might be desirable in and of itself for the person who enjoys learning languages or wants to read Moliere in the original. But for the person who hopes to command some mastery of the language for the two-month visit to Provence, the motivation is instrumental. Similarly, the popularity of computer courses among seniors may stem, on the one hand, from the pleasure of gaining facility with a new technology or keeping up with the grandchildren, or, on the other hand, from a desire to acquire skill with Lotus 1-2-3 in order to computerize household bookkeeping or to land a part-time job. Londoner has himself noted that the same educational activities can be viewed as simultaneously expressive and instrumental, depending upon the learner's goals (Londoner 1978).

Other difficulties in classifying the motives of older learners stem from this dual perspective: the intrinsic character of the educational activity and the learner's goals. For example, numerous studies (Boshier and Riddell 1978; Bova 1981; Kingston and Drotter 1983; Bynum and Seaman 1993) have shown that "intellectual stimulation," a seemingly expressive orientation, is the most important value of education for those enrolled in LRIs, Elderhostel programs, Shepherd's Centers, and similar programs (NCCCR 1993). But the term intellectual stimulation can conceal a variety of submotives. For some it may mean the chance to increase appreciation of literature, philosophy, or history, while for others it suggests a desire to glean information that will help the individual keep up to date with current social and cultural issues.

Some are motivated by a fear of cognitive decline. For them, intellectual stimulation, like the jogger's workout, is intended to offset or prevent decline arising from disuse of mental functioning. For others, intellectual stimulation is a way of belonging to one's chosen social group, has entertainment value, or stimulates curiosity.

Other motivations more likely to be found in community college settings have to do with clearly instrumental goals. These would be reflected in such courses as how to take care of a frail spouse, manage one's budget, learn word processing in order to obtain a part time job, or prepare for passing the realtor's exam. Instrumentally motivated education is also often connected with hobbies such as woodworking, basket weaving, or gardening.

Studies of older persons' motives for enrolling in formal and informal educational programs have yielded a wide disparity of results. Some surveys have concluded that people are more likely to be instrumentally oriented (Londoner 1971, 1978) and others have found expressive motives to be predominant (Lowy and O'Connor 1986). This, in part, may be a function of when the studies were conducted, what population was studied, and which categories or taxonomy were assumed. For example, studies conducted at senior centers in the early 1970s are likely to yield instrumental orientations since the types of programs offered tended to deal with coping issues and hobbies. By contrast, studies of participation in Elderhostel, which did not really attract a sizeable enrollment until the late 1970s, tend to yield the opposite results as most people elect these courses for intellectual and personal enhancement. The survey instruments themselves, as Wirtz and Charner (1989) point out, may presuppose a jargon and taxonomy (e.g., the hypothesized expressive–instrumental continuum) which forces participants into artificial categories. Hence, inconsistent findings may be the result of utilizing scales that lack psychometric validity.

Wirtz and Charner (1989) did, in fact, attempt to study the validity of the expressive–instrumental continuum by surveying a nationwide random sample of 490 retired union members. Their subjects had the following characteristics: 61 percent were between sixty-five and seventy-four; 21 percent were younger than sixty-five; 18 percent were seventy-five or older; 76 percent had finished high school; 77 percent were married; 69 percent were men; 88 percent were white; and 56 percent had annual retirement incomes of at least $15,000. The researchers found that the largest percentage of their subjects reported both instrumental and expressive learning motivations. Some 66 percent endorsed the motive of gaining general knowledge and 55 percent acknowledged becoming more well-rounded as important. Wirtz and Charner found no support for the existence of an expressive–instrumental continuum. They found instead that nearly two of every three members of the sample (64 percent) endorsed at least one expressive item and at least one instrumental item on a list of choices.

Wirtz and Charner's subjects, diverse as they may seem in terms of educational background and geographic distribution, hardly represent the typical member of an LRI who tends to be well educated (typically, at least one third have masters degree level educational attainment) and affluent (annual household incomes well over $30,000). If prior education is a key to understanding an older person's inclination to participate in educational programs, then this highly educated, usually professional group is going to be quite different from Wirtz and Charner's unionists.

The problem of categorizing motivation to participate in educational programs is that a broad survey is likely to yield aggregate results too general to be characteristic of any particular group, while studies of more homogeneous groups (e.g., Elderhostelers and LRI members) is likely to yield characteristics of only that group. Why, then, bother to study older learner motivation? Two central purposes of studying motives of older learners are the following: (1) to anticipate and plan for the curricular needs of senior clientele, and (2) to develop a justification and rationale to support institutional and government policy regarding the availability of and access to education for seniors. The key is in knowing which audience planners are hoping to reach and being wary of overgeneralizing.

The problem with most motivation theories is that they are already biased toward the ideological commitment of a sponsoring organization or toward the predispositions of certain socioeconomic senior groups. There is no national study of the motives of older learners that spans a wide variety (e.g., age, class, ethnicity, and location, including urban, rural, and suburban) of participant types. Moreover, earlier studies have been limited by the existing range of programs available to any given senior population. For example, in 1975, when the NCOA initiated its NEH-funded humanities reading and discussion group series, the Senior Center Humanities Program (later called Discovery through the Humanities), many people, including educators and senior center directors, predicted failure. They thought that because the senior population frequenting senior centers averaged less than eight years of formal education, it was unlikely that a program inviting people to read short stories, poems, essays, and other forms of literature based on programmatic themes would attract or hold the interest of local clientele. But they were wrong. By organizing the textual materials around lively and popular topics (e.g., local history, work experience, family history, contemporary ethical dilemmas), and by offering the reading and discussion programs to people in a familiar place (at first, senior centers), the NCOA humanities program managed to overcome many barriers and to attract, initially, a few hundred, and later, thousands of seniors. In this instance, motive was triggered by opportunity. Hence, NCOA's leadership helped to create a clientele whose preliminary experience generated further interest in and growth of the programs.

Lowy and O'Connor (1986) probably had the most useful idea for reviewing motivation among seniors. They constructed a matrix that combined expressive and instrumental orientations with categories of educational needs (e.g., coping, contributive, influencing) developed by McClusky (1974) to produce a holistic overview that would accommodate a wide range and mix of learner goals and orientations.

A major problem of studying seniors' motivations for educational programs, as pointed out by Jeffrey Leptak (1987) in his literature review, is that most of the research is quantitative. While methodologically correct from a social science perspective, the use of preference rankings falls short of providing deeper insight into how older participants think about their own motives. Cognitive interest and intellectual stimulation are abstractions distant from the older person's actual fascination with a particular subject matter.

Lessons from Reviewing Categories of Motivation

The lesson in the review of seniors' educational motives is to recognize that, like adult learners in general, seniors exhibit a wide diversity of needs, interests, and wants that may be conditioned by socioeconomic and educational backgrounds, institutional setting where programs are offered, and existence or availability of opportunities. Theories of the motives of older learners are useful as hypotheses for planners, but they should not become constraints on imagination or openness to exploring the possibilities of what seniors in a given area may want or need to learn, how they prefer to learn it, and from whom they prefer to learn—including one another.

Another lesson in this review is that motives of older learners may be the product of educational institutions' own motivations. For example, LRIs located within colleges and universities are likely to favor intellectually challenging liberal arts types of curricula. This best fits the institutional identity, setting, and faculty resources available. Programs of this type will attract seniors with certain types of motivation and not others. Nor should one discount the image that LRIs and host colleges may prefer to project. Similarly, technical and community colleges are more likely to offer and promote handicraft, life skills, and support groups and to recognize corresponding senior learner motivations.

Adaptational and Transformational Frameworks

Another way of thinking about motives of older learners is offered by Manheimer (1992), who proposed that theories about developmental change in later life tended to emphasize either an adaptational or transformational standpoint. An adaptational approach would tend to focus on the skills, knowledge, and information that people need as they age in order to cope with the challenges and obstacles of health, finances, housing, and other life necessities. A transformational approach would focus on the unique opportunities of later life as a special part of the life course, whether this referred to self-actualization, spiritual growth, or a renewal of the learning process.

Learner motivation is clearly a function of many factors. One might presume that institutions offering educational programs have conducted studies to determine needs, wants, and feasibility. They in turn will account for and justify their programs in terms of the fit between older learners' motives and their institutions' capability to respond. But this is not quite the case, as we shall see.

THE PROBLEM OF INSTITUTIONAL RATIONALES

David Peterson, in *Facilitating Education for Older Learners* (1983), points out that theorists and educators often tend themselves to predetermine the needs of older learners. They want to be able to show how these are "consistent with the idealized values of education and social service organizations," and are defensible when seniors' consumption of resources is called into question. However, while these needs imply institutional rationales that are "attractive to society at large," such needs may in fact not correspond to the actual educational wants of older people. Lack of correspondence between educational needs and the wants of older adults may lead to curricular offerings that are unattractive to a given senior population; or, if older learners are given a free hand in drafting curricula, it may lead to course offerings that seem peripheral to or inconsistent with the main mission of the host institution.

Example of Rationales of an Institution of Higher Education

A review of the mission statement or rationale for sponsoring older learner programs as articulated by the higher education host institution and by the programs for older adults which these institutions host may reveal both congruities and incongruities. For example, at a 1993 University College seminar on "The Implications of the Extended Life Course for Continuing Education" sponsored by the University of Wisconsin's Extension Division, key elements of the University's rationale were articulated by a variety of deans. Their justifications for institutional support of older adults' access to higher education include the following purposes: (1) to assure an informed citizenry, (2) to provide equal access, (3) to make use of available, possibly underutilized resources, and (4) to cultivate future givers.

The first two positions are ideological in nature. In the first instance the chain of reasoning goes like this. One of the roles of a public university is to provide community service (the other roles being research and teaching). The strength of a democratic society depends on how well informed its citizens are. Older adults represent an important part of a democratic society and the highest percentage of voters by age group. Therefore, as part of its public service mission, the university is obliged to help ensure that older citizens be kept well informed so that they can continue to participate actively and intelligently in societal decision making.

The equal access argument involves a set of similar assumptions. A public college or university is expected to provide equal access to adult citizens of diverse ages and backgrounds. As taxpayers, older adults deserve opportunities for continued learning. Therefore, as part of its mission and in support of diversity, the institution is committed to opening its doors to older adults.

This second argument is consistent with the public policy momentum of the 1970s which sought to mainstream older adults into existing educational programs by creating tuition-free, space-available access to college courses in twenty-eight states. Interestingly, the equal access/mainstreaming approach paralleled the normalization policy that ushered in community-based mental health services and emptied mental hospitals across the United States. Seniors, it was argued, are no different than other adults and should not be treated as either second class citizens or as social work cases. They should be encouraged to participate on an equal and similar basis to other students.

Although the tuition-free/space-available policies were passed by many state legislatures, they were less likely to be promoted by colleges and universities who feared, perhaps unrealistically, that they would be inundated by older students. Unlike the politicians, college administrators saw little to gain financially or otherwise from older students (Danner, Danner, and Kuder 1993). Community colleges, on the other hand, in many states received extra state funding for each older person enrolled. In some states this became a thriving business for community colleges. But for four-year institutions, it turned out that traditional college courses held little appeal to most older adults who were not attracted to lengthy course commitments nor to large lecture halls where traditional college-aged students listened passively.

The third, pragmatic rationale was frequently adopted by housing directors and continuing education leaders who, especially during the late 1970s and early 1980s, saw empty dorm rooms in the summer or declining daytime enrollments. As a way to beef up enrollments, they had the idea that older adults might be induced to rent dorm space as part of an Elderhostel-type program or even as a semester-long apartment on campus. Huron College in Huron, South Dakota even sold one of its unused dormitory buildings to a local senior group who used federal grants and loans to convert the building into apartments and turned the ground floor into a senior center. This brought a whole new audience of seniors to the college campus. Western Washington University in Bellingham created its Bridge Project at Fairhaven College to provide apartment living for thirty older persons and developed a series of intergenerational educational and cultural programs. These examples suggest something more substantive than economic opportunism since they combine ideals of bringing generations together around educational endeavors. But there are other examples where no special educational objectives were involved; mostly economic considerations and marketing decisions prevailed.

Finally, in the back of the minds of campus development officers was the lingering notion that involving older adults in campus programs would create the potential for eventual financial contributions to the institution. Indeed, this has occurred in many instances, and beyond annual contribution, more substantial gift giving has occurred, especially where a campus lacked adequate space for senior programs and where fundraising for a building involved mutually beneficial use of space. For example, the University of Delaware's Academy for Lifelong Learning raised over three million dollars (matched by the university) to help finance a new continuing education building which the seniors' program shares with continuing education. A similar project was carried out at California State University, Fullerton.

Institutional Rationales and Participant Motives

Rationales for lifelong learning programs and the motives expressed by older learners may coincide with host institutions' rationales. Informed citizenry and equal access rationales are not uncommon as part of learning in retirement institutes' mission statements. But as we examine older learner motivation and less overt, more indirect articulations, we find something rather different emphasized. Where do intellectual stimulation and fellowship, the top senior motives found in numerous surveys, fit with host institution rationales of informed citizenry and equal access? Being an informed citizen should be intellectually stimulating, but such stimulation usually holds a much broader meaning. For example, world affairs and current events courses, highly popular at most LRIs, would contribute to an older person's functioning as a well-informed citizen. But equally popular are literature courses, fine arts, computer training, and so on. These could have an application to fostering an informed citizenry, but are not reducible to that purpose. Many seniors are clearly interested in learning as an end in itself and in the community of fellow students who help make that process exciting and meaningful.

Intellectual stimulation takes on a completely different meaning in the example of one very large LRI at Florida Atlantic University (FAU). In the program's newsletter, which includes information on fundraising for a new building, a reprint of an article is featured on research showing that there are fewer incidences of Alzheimer's Disease among better educated people and among those who continue to learn. What is hinted at in the article is made overt in another column of the newsletter which comes right out and says that by taking courses at FAU's LRI, the older person stands a better chance of avoiding cognitive decline and dementia, one of most seniors' worst fears.

Intellectual stimulation would seem to be much broader than what is suggested by the purpose of helping promote an informed citizenry. Fellowship seems to have little to do with access and more to do with a sense of community. Participating in educational activities to sustain cognitive functioning and to feel productive introduces additional purposes and motives that go beyond the deans' ideas. These reasons and purposes are not necessarily in conflict, but they seem tangential to one another. The administrative voice and that of students has probably always been different; for one thing, there are generational differences. But in the case of older learners and their host school, the differences are more problematic.

An institution's argument that it has an obligation to serve older adults (either on the informed citizenry or access basis) can encounter opposing arguments of the same order. What about the educational needs of other special groups such as minorities, veterans, the poor, or immigrants? Are they adequately served? Is there competition for scarce resources such as space, parking, faculty, and administrator time? In the eyes of many people, older adults are already receiving enough in the way of entitlements and do not deserve more. Still others believe that education is wasted on the elderly. This view is reflected, perhaps unintentionally, in a proverb inscribed on a special wall of a new education building for the state of North Carolina in Raleigh, which reads, "Learning in old age is writing on sand, but learning in youth is engraving on stone." The Arabian proverb could be interpreted to mean that older people are more flexible. More likely, the point being made is that education in one's youth is more primary and enduring. Unintentionally, the choice of this saying amounts to an insult to all adult learners. Ageism has an interesting way of creeping in to both private and public arenas.

The rationales justifying support of older adult education—informed citizenry and equal access—when placed in the wider context of competing demands for access, resources, and priority of needs, seem weakly persuasive and more disputable. Moreover, they avoid dealing with the deeper needs and wants of today's senior adults which have more to do with entering a unique and unprecedented time of life, the retirement or *third age* (Laslett 1991) in which one has reached a pinnacle of life from which certain perspectives are now possible. But this idea of the third age—both a matter of individual life stage and a social phenomenon—is so new and the underlying concept of a new stage of life development so fragile, that most educational institutions simply have not caught up with the change.

The new zeitgeist of third-age learners is partially captured in the currently popular phrase *productive aging*, which attempts to expound the contributory role that older people can continue to play in society. Education for older adults may fit well with this new norm of older adulthood. But how does the concept of productive aging fit with the social responsibilities of educational institutions. A close look at one of the first institutions to offer tuition-free courses for older adults is illustrative of the possibilities and challenges.

Rationale and Social Responsibility

In 1989 the University of Kentucky celebrated the twenty-fifth year of its Donovan Scholars Program (DSP), an institutional arrangement, apparently the first in the country, by which people sixty-five and over could take regular university courses on a space-available, tuition-free basis or could choose from a small number of special courses offered specifically to seniors. Research conducted in review of the DSP's history noted that it took twenty-five years to attain an annual enrollment of 250 participants. This was attributed to findings that most people learned about the program through word-of-mouth, primarily from friends, and because of limited publicizing on the part of the university (Danner, Danner, and Kuder 1993).

Authors of the research assumed the informed citizenry/equal access rationale for the DSP, stating that institutions of higher education have a "social responsibility" to "enrich the lives of the nation's older citizens." The study showed that the clientele for the DSP were predominately female (64 percent), white (98.3 percent), well-educated individuals who were motivated to take advantage of the program first because of cognitive interests ("to seek knowledge for its own sake"), second for the opportunity for socialization ("to participate in group activity"), and third because of a "desire to become more effective citizens." Participants' self-esteem, the study noted, was enhanced when they discovered that although their speed of learning and retention had slowed with age, experience and perspective enhanced their abilities as learners.

The question remains: Has the University of Kentucky fulfilled its social responsibility to older adults by annually enrolling a relatively privileged handful of people over sixty-five? Moreover, does the research bear on or clarify what it means to "enrich" the lives of older adults? Institutional assumptions and older learners' perceived value of these programs may, at best, be parallel, but may also be on divergent paths. The DSP is simply one example reflecting hundreds of other similar situations: Institutional distribution of educational opportunities to a small number of relatively privileged older adults is a reasonable and benevolent act on the part of the university, while its rationale assumes a condition of scarce resources and narrow purpose not necessarily consistent with, though not in opposition to, the motives of older learners. Institutional rationale and older learner motive are like two points not quite connected by a straight line. What is lacking is the third point that would complete the connection.

THE NEW PARADIGM: LIFELONG LEARNING, LEADERSHIP, AND COMMUNITY SERVICE

The stories of Earl and Marabeth Hitchcock and Elizabeth Houston at the beginning of this chapter are worth revisiting to help explore ways to close the gap between host institution (especially nonsenior-service organizations like colleges and universities) rationales and the rationales of educational programs for seniors these institutions have chosen to host. Institutional motives and older learner motives intersect at a point outside themselves in the example of the Hitchcocks and Houston. The third point that makes the triangle is the Hitchcocks' and Houston's volunteer community service.

For the university, the Hitchcocks' initiative leads from relatively passive lifelong learning into active community service—one of the three purposes of a public university. For the Hitchcocks, community service furthers their desire to continue to learn and to contribute to society, especially to the lives of the young. Working in schools with young people furthered the Hitchcock's learning experience, as would other forms of actively helping other people to learn or accomplish some goal. In this triad, a model of intergenerational justice is suggested and an incomplete picture completed: nothing less than a concept of the social good. The relationship of old to young need not be one-way either. There are many examples (some of which are described in Chapter 6) of younger people helping seniors and of mutual helping or equal partnerships that are part of a broader educational context.

Likewise, Houston's involvement in volunteer community programs, some of which included working with youth, complemented her lifelong learning objectives.

By serving others and seeking to benefit society, the Hitchcocks and Houston demonstrate reciprocity and integrity. They are not trapped in a narrow conception of self-actualization, viewed atomistically as the fulfillment of private wishes and desires, nor are they empowered only, though importantly, to benefit others of their own age group (special interest group entitlements). The Hitchcocks demonstrate a voluntary desire to engage their community and members of the younger generation for the purpose of a larger common cause—the general welfare. The university, in this context, serves as an enabling force to transform the energies of one generation into an educational aim that benefits other generations (for surely the parents of these children indirectly participate in the Hitchcocks' contribution to their children).

What brought Earl Hitchcock to Seniors in the Schools was a leadership program that encouraged civic involvement on the part of seniors. And what brought Houston to community volunteerism was the broader vision projected by Senior Neighbors of Chattanooga. Lifelong learning, leadership, and community service form the triad of purposes that create the model of education in later life and close the gap between institutional objectives and the personal motives of older adults. This holistic model transcends the territorial mentality of special group interests in conflict over scare resources as it shows the shortcomings (and incompleteness) of fragmentary rationales. But can one argue that there is an ethical imperative for older adults to model their lives upon the notion that the good life in retirement consists of both personal enrichment and serving others? Especially in a society that lacks coherent models of intergenerational justice, of clear rights and obligations between different stages of the life course, and in which aging, old age, and death are feared, it is hard to imagine universal agreement and clear guidelines for social policy.

Arguments and normative exhortations have been advanced for what might be termed an *elder imperative*, which says that older adults act in such a way that they provide to other generations an image of dignity and composure even under duress and in the face of close proximity to death (Callahan 1987). However, fostering a disposition is one thing and imposing a social obligation is another. Building the opportunity for community service into lifelong learning programs for seniors simply opens a pathway, it does not force passage.

A Lesson from *Star Trek*

The aims of older adult education raise the basic question of the purposes and meanings of later life. A longer and healthier life course is both a benefit and a burden to the older individual and society. What is to be done with this added time? And for whose good? Uncertainties, anxieties, and confusion about these issues can be found in many forms of social expression. For example, one finds many recent movies such as *Cocoon* and *Cocoon II*, *The Whales of August*, *Fried Green Tomatoes*, *Batteries Not Included*, *Tough Guys*, and numerous others in which older actors take the roles of older people caught in dilemmas around the issues of longevity, disability, productivity, isolation, social worth, and social responsibility.

Television also has its share of such plot structures. An example, which may at first may seem remote but will eventually bring us back to the main point, is found in the popular TV series *Star Trek: The Next Generation*. In one episode, three cryogenically frozen bodies are discovered floating in a space capsule by the Starship Enterprise's android, Lieutenant Data. Data is programmed to preserve or save life. But his introduction of the capsule into the Enterprise poses a conflict for its commander, Jean Luc Picard. It seems that the threesome has been floating in space for over 300 years. The frozen ones were terminally ill former residents of earth (the United States, to be more precise). The primitive technology of cryogenics was applied to them in hopes that a cure for their illnesses would eventually be found and then they could be brought back to life and healed. But for Picard to save them now is to interfere with both the natural order of things and with history—something members of the enlightened Federation are prohibited from doing. Nevertheless, the threesome are already aboard the Enterprise, so to place them back in space means both withholding medical intervention and condemning them to permanent death. Given the options, Picard is obligated, in the words of Deuteronomy, "to choose life."

The dilemma of this futuristic space adventure is none other than the dilemma of prolongevity on late-twentieth-century earth. Should people's lives be extended at any cost, despite decline in their quality of life? Should one withhold advanced medical technology when prolonging a life is a questionable act? In the *Star Trek* episode, the frozen ones are healed with the use of a hand-held electronic device that, aptly or ironically, looks like a television channel changer. Then they are thawed out and revived. Of course they are surprised by their surroundings. Rather comically and tragically, they are totally baffled by their new lives in the culture of space travel. Their era and age cohort have long vanished, but here they are: the still youthful Texan who calls for a whiskey and a guitar; the young woman, a cancer victim, who wants to see her sons; and the middle-aged entrepreneur who wants to check on his stocks and find out how things are going back at the office. In the context of future space travel, their lives are both irrelevant and poignant. They have traveled beyond their natural life span.

The drama focuses at one point on the entrepreneur's persistent demands for access to his financial resources. Finally, in exasperation, Captain Picard explains to the irrepressible capitalist that his avarice is pointless since material scarcity and physical vulnerability are no longer the basic conditions of life. In the Federation's advanced society, material well being is available to everyone as is extremely advanced health maintenance that, while not preserving life forever, basically guarantees radical compression of morbidity, a long and full life course free from illness until the very last moment in advanced old age. The entrepreneur is shocked that society no longer operates within the assumed framework of scarcity, competition, and differentiation of mortality. What remains then as the purpose of life? What is there to live for? Picard answers: "Self-improvement and service to others."

The *Star Trek* episode dramatizes the paradox of extending life quantitatively but not qualitatively: To what end would people live longer? It also offers television viewers a teleological explanation of human purpose in a hypothetical world free of the limitations of poverty and disease. Though the idea of a universal order of this type is hard to imagine, so would be the remarkable improvements in twentieth-century health if foretold to someone in the year 1900. More central to the present discussion, this futuristic life bears an interesting resemblance to the world in which the Hitchcocks and Houston already live. While they are not impervious to chronic ailments—Earl has spinal problems and late onset diabetes, and Marabeth suffers from arthritis and high blood pressure—compared to earlier generations they are representatives of a lengthened life course, relatively free of serious disabilities, financially secure, inclined toward continued self-improvement, and willing to be of service to others. They are not space voyagers, *Star Trek*'s "the last frontier," but time travelers whose retirement age has brought them to the frontier of the human condition. They have not outlived their time, nor are they purposeless. Rather, their involvement in education combines self-improvement and service to others. The Hitchcocks' and Houston's lives articulate a clear answer to the profound and doleful question asked in the title of Robert Butler's 1975 Pulitzer Prize–winning critique of old age, *Why Survive?*

Education and Abundance

The examples of the Hitchcocks and Houston underscore the productive aging theme that has been gaining popularity since it was coined in 1986 by geriatric physician, Robert Butler. It is not simply that the Hitchcocks, to take one example, are keeping usefully busy. Rather, they and the institutions in which they are active (the university, school system, etc.), are generating *abundance*, to use Harry R. Moody's term (1988), by demonstrating a way to move beyond an assumed conflict of older adults competing for entitlements against the needs of other generations. Rather than redistributing a fixed pool of scarce resources, their example reflects a way of moving toward a politics of generativity. In other words, the Hitchcocks and Houston are enriching others as they are themselves enriched. This single, small example can be multiplied by the thousands as reports come in from across the nation about intergenerational projects involving older adults being of service to young people at risk of dropping out of school, pregnant and unwed teens, deprived children, and so on.

CONCLUSION: THE POLITICS AND PROMISE OF OLDER ADULT EDUCATION

Older adult education, in the context of the United States as an aging society, cannot be separated from the sociopolitical reality that surrounds such programs. By ignoring the larger context or avoiding the implications of discordant public and private motives, leaders in the field will find themselves on shifting sands as attitudes about the value of educating older learners fluctuate with economic ups and downs.

One has only to think of the dramatic reversal in many of California's community colleges. Where state and school policies had encouraged participation of tens of thousands of seniors through the 1970s and 1980s, the economic crises in California in the early 1990s brought new criticism that older persons' use of space and time on community college campuses was indefensible in light of other pressing needs. Hence, tuition-free policies were eliminated on many campuses and the number of seniors enrolled plummeted. The organization of Community College Educators of Older Adults (CCEOA) had failed to anticipate this reversal, believing that education for older adults had arrived permanently. One finds the same phenomenon in North Carolina where a 1988 drop in community block grant funds for community colleges led to a sharp decrease in tuition-free courses and participation rates among seniors (see background essay on "Life Enrichment Opportunities" in North Carolina, Appendix G).

Education that involves older adults remains peripheral in most schools. Seniors themselves would not like to think that they are competing with other generations for scarce resources. In times of limited resources, educational administrators show their true colors by voting for their priorities of which programs (and students) will stay and which will go. Since they and we as a society lack a comprehensive picture of the life course and the interrelationship of its stages or ages, it is difficult to promote a philosophy of older adult education that brings wide acknowledgment and support.

It is probable that the sheer size of the population increase among retirement-age people, especially in the next decade, will bring an expansion of learning opportunities. For now, we are faced with the task of thinking through the purposes of older adult education in an aging society and, by implication, the meaning and purpose of later life.

The meaning of aging and the role of education for older learners are inextricably bound together in the history of adult education and lifelong learning in the United States. To appreciate the dramatic advances and institutional innovations of the last thirty years it is useful to examine the emergence of new organizational forms and the modifications of others in the context of earlier and more recent historical events and trends. Accordingly, our next chapter traces the roots of older adult education, examines the dynamics of demographic and social change captured in the term *third age*, and profiles some of the new educational programs for third-age learners.

REFERENCES

Arbeiter, S. 1989. "Higher Education and Older Adults in the 21st Century (1990–2010): Who Will Be Learning? Who Should Be Learning?" In *Higher Education and an Aging Society*. Washington, D.C.: Gerontological Society of America.

Boshier, R., and G. Riddell. 1978. "Education Participation Scale Factor Structure for Older Adults." *Adult Education* 28: 165–175.

Bova, B. M. 1981. Motivational Orientations of Senior Citizens Participating in the Elderhostel Program. Paper read at the National University Continuing Education Association Regional Meeting. ERIC Document Reproduction Service No. ED 206 927.

Bronte, L. 1993. *The Longevity Factor*. New York: HarperCollins.

Butler, R. N. 1975. *Why Survive? Being Old in America*. New York: Harper & Row.

Bynum, L., and M. A. Seaman. 1993. "Motivation of Third-Age Students in Learning-In-Retirement Institutes." *Continuing Higher Education Review* 57(1&2): 12–22.

Callahan, D. 1987. *Setting Limits: Medical Goals in an Aging Society.* New York: Simon & Schuster.

Cole, T. 1992. *The Journey of Life: A Cultural History of Aging in America.* Port Chester, N.Y.: Cambridge University Press.

Cross, K. P. 1981. *Adults as Learners.* San Francisco: Jossey-Bass.

Crystal, J., and R. Bolles. 1974. *Where Do I Go from Here with My Life?* Berkeley, Calif.: Ten Speed Press.

Danner, D. D., F. W. Danner, and L. C. Kuder. 1993. "Late-Life Learners at the University: The Donovan Scholars Program at Age Twenty-Five." *Educational Gerontology* 19(3): 217–239.

de Beauvoir, S. 1953. *The Second Sex.* New York: Knopf.

———. 1973. *The Coming of Age.* New York: Warner.

Dickerson, B. E. 1990. "A 21st Century Challenge to Higher Education: Integrating the Older Person into Academia." In *Introduction to Educational Gerontology.* 3d ed. Edited by R. H. Sherron and D. B. Lumsden. New York: Hemisphere.

Fagan, M., and C. F. Longino, Jr. 1993. "Migrating Retirees: A Source for Economic Development." *Economic Development Quarterly* 7(1): 989–1006.

Friedan, B. 1963. *The Feminine Mystique.* New York: W. W. Norton.

———. 1993. *The Fountain of Age.* New York: Simon & Schuster.

Gruman, G. J. 1978. "Cultural Origins of Present-Day Ageism: The Modernization of the Life Cycle." In *Aging and the Elderly: Humanistic Perspectives in Gerontology.* Edited by S. F. Spicker, K. M. Woodward, and D. Van Tassell. Atlantic Highlands, N.J.: Humanities Press.

Havighurst, R. 1976. "Education through the Adult Life Span." *Educational Gerontology* 1: 41–51.

Kingston, A. J., and M. W. Drotter. 1983. "A Comparison of Elderly College Students in Two Different Geographic Areas." *Educational Gerontology* 9: 399–403.

Knowles, M. S. 1975. *Self-Directed Learning: A Guide for Learners and Teachers.* New York: Association Press.

Laslett, P. 1991. *A Fresh Map of Life, The Emergence of the Third Age.* Cambridge, Mass.: Harvard University Press.

Leptak, J. 1987. Older Adults in Higher Education: A Review of the Literature. Ohio State University, Department of Education: Policy and Leadership. ERIC Document Reproduction Service No. ED 283 021.

Londoner, C. A. 1971. "Survival Needs of the Aged: Implications for Program Planning." *International Journal of Aging and Human Development* 2: 113–117.

———. 1978. "Instrumental and Expressive Education: A Basis for Needs Assessment and Planning." In *Introduction to Educational Gerontology.* 2d ed. Edited by R. H. Sherron and D. B. Lumsden. Washington, D.C.: Hemisphere.

Longino, C. F., Jr., B. J. Soldo, and K. G. Mauton. 1990. "Demography of Aging in the United States." In *Gerontology Perspectives and Issues.* Edited by K. F. Ferraro. New York: Springer.

Lowy, L., and D. O'Connor. 1986. *Why Education in the Later Years?* Lexington, Mass.: Lexington Books.

Manheimer, R. J. 1992. "The Narrative Quest in Qualitative Gerontology." *Journal of Aging Studies* 3(3): 231–252.

McClusky, H. Y. 1974 "Education for Aging: The Scope of the Field and Perspectives for the Future." In *Learning for Aging.* Edited by S. M. Grabowski and W. D. Mason. Washington, D.C.: Adult Education Association.

————. 1990. "The Community of Generations: A Goal and a Context for the Education of Persons in the Later Years." In *Introduction to Educational Gerontology.* 3d ed. Edited by R. H. Sherron and D. B. Lumsden. New York: Hemisphere.

Moody, H. R. 1976. "Philosophical Presuppositions of Education for Older Adults." *Educational Gerontology* 1:1–16.

————. 1986. "Late Life Learning in the Information Society." In *Education and Aging.* Edited by D. A. Peterson, J. E. Thornton, and J. E. Birren. Englewood Cliffs, N.J.: Prentice-Hall.

————. 1988. *Abundance of Life: Human Development Policies for an Aging Society.* New York: Columbia University Press.

Moskow-McKenzie, D., and R. J. Manheimer. 1993. *Organizing Educational Programs for Older Adults: A Summary of Research.* Asheville, N.C.: North Carolina Center for Creative Retirement.

Neugarten, B. L., and D. A. Neugarten. 1983. "Age in the Aging Society." *Daedalus* 115(1): 31–49.

North Carolina Center for Creative Retirement (NCCCR). 1993. Identifying Critical Pathways in Organizing Educational Programs for Older Adults. Final report submitted to the AARP Andrus Foundation. Asheville, N.C.: University of North Carolina at Asheville.

O'Connor, D. 1991. "Free Tuition for Elders: Intentions and Effects of the Massachusetts Policy." *Journal of Aging and Social Policy* 3(1/2): 57–72.

Peterson, D. A. 1983. *Facilitating Education for Older Learners.* San Francisco: Jossey-Bass.

U.S. Bureau of the Census. 1989. *Current Population Reports, Special Studies.* Washington, D.C.: U.S. Government Printing Office.

————. 1992. *Statistical Abstract of the United States.* Washington, D.C.: U.S. Government Printing Office.

Wirtz, P., and I. Charner. 1989. "Motivations for Educational Participation by Retirees: The Expressive–Instrumental Continuum Revisited." *Educational Gerontology* 15(3): 275–284.

2

Older Learners and Programs in Historical Perspective

In 1983, Genevieve Dienstbach was walking through the Famous-Barr department store in the Northland Shopping Center near St. Louis on her way to pick up something for her mother. Recently retired after working some forty-five years in the accounting departments of two area manufacturers, Dienstbach spent her time taking care of her invalid mother who lived with her. She had never married and was, as she saw herself, "an unclaimed treasure." Dienstbach was somewhat at loose ends concerning how to spend her time. She had a few hobbies, read a little, looked after the house, and visited friends. Like many people, she had never thought much about what she would do in retirement.

But on this day something caught her eye that changed her life. It was a sign telling about the department store's special program for retirement age people, the Older Adult Service and Information System (OASIS), an in-store education center. Dienstbach had only a high school education, but she wanted to learn new things and meet new people. She decided to drop in at the OASIS center and find out about the classes that were being offered. Eventually she found her way into fine arts classes for which, she discovered, she had a flair.

"I could hardly draw a straight line," she explained in an interview, "but I learned that in today's art world, that wasn't such a bad thing." After several years of classes, the OASIS staff asked Dienstbach if she would help out by teaching a beginning art class at one of the area senior centers. She had never thought of herself as a teacher of art, but with encouragement and some training, she took the plunge. She discovered she had a talent for teaching art.

At one point during the years of her association with OASIS, Dienstbach needed a serious operation. While recovering at home, and still tending to her aged mother, she found it difficult to go shopping. But a married couple whom she had met through OASIS offered and continued to do her shopping for a full year's time.

On close examination, stories of people like Genevieve Dienstbach reveal that educational opportunities for older adults are a multidimensional experience. Discovering talents and abilities, learning new skills, gaining knowledge and awareness, developing self-esteem and confidence, finding that one has the capacity to be of service to others, and making close and important friendships are interrelated benefits for many who participate. These outcomes are a far cry from the idea of senior education as a form of pacifying entertainment.

Programs like OASIS, which started in 1975, did not originate in a vacuum. There were important historical precedents, some policy inducements from the federal government in the form of available grant money, demographic changes, and a growing awareness that education could play an important continuing role throughout a person's life.

This chapter examines some of the historical background of lifelong learning in the United States and follows the emergence during the last twenty-five to thirty years of new programs and institutions that have led to the flowering of older adult education in the last decade of the twentieth century. We try to show ways in which older adult education evolves from adult education in general, as well as from research and policies that have a gerontological foundation. National policies on adult and older adult education are discussed briefly as part of this historical perspective, but a fuller treatment is reserved until Chapter 4. We include a discussion of intellectual functioning of older adults because, as we hope to show, the changing focus and emphasis of research is both a cause of revised attitudes toward the capabilities of senior adults and itself the by-product of changing social attitudes and the advocacy of organizations representing the well elderly. Hence, we view research on intellectual functioning as part of historical change.

One way to introduce and conceptualize how the nexus of personal, social, and economic developments has influenced the historical shape of older adult education is to begin with the larger framework suggested by the term third age.

THE CONCEPT OF THE THIRD AGE

The term third age has both individual and societal meanings, often blurred together. In the United States it is often used to refer to a time and condition of life—the period of continued activity, social involvement, and productivity of retirement-age individuals. In this sense, third age suggests an attitude and an outlook on life. But third age, especially as described in the European setting where it originated, refers to a class of people and a socioeconomic event that happened sometime in the 1950s or 1960s, depending on the country. It refers to a threshold over which many were passing as they reached their mid-sixties. They were not going to become poor or sick or invisible. And there were going to be many of them. In this sense, Genvieve Dienstbach exemplifies the third ager's mentality and represents the emergence of a new social group.

The popularized version of the term third age connotes the active lifestyle of the well elderly in the United States, Europe, and other postindustrial societies. The catchy phrase goes back to the French L'Université du Troisième Age (University of the Third Age, or U3A) first proposed by its founder, Pierre Vellas, in 1973. Vellas recognized the combined vitality and longevity of many older persons in France and thought that French universities should promote a combination of instruction for seniors, research emphasizing the well elderly, and opportunities for personal development. Mental challenge, a judicious amount of physical exercise, and contact with younger students were the key elements of the U3A program which has subsequently spread through Europe, Britain, Australia, Canada, and, to some degree, the United States.

The idea of a third age is based on a traditional way of dividing life into quarters or four ages. The first age, youth, is a time of dependency when education helps prepare us for future work and family. With the second age comes independence and responsibility for earning a living and supporting a family. The third age is one of personal achievement and learning for self-development; the fourth age is the period of frailty and decline.

British sociologist Peter Laslett (1991), who helped to establish the U3A movement in England by starting a group in Cambridge (though independent from the university—the British model diverged from the French in making the participants their own authority for teaching and learning together), gave a more precise sociohistorical conceptualization of the third age.

He dated the arrival of the third age in Britain to the 1950s. Laslett observed that until quite recently in the twentieth century, most people never attained the third age. Before this, only a fortunate few, the wealthy and healthy, had a third age. For the rest, the fourth age came before they had a chance to enjoy the third.

But with the new characteristics associated with retirement that emerged in the 1950s—better health, economic security through pensions, and an improving societal- and self-image of the older person—the third age was born. Hence, the third age is a product of demographic expansion of retirement-age individuals, economic security through national public policy, improvement in health care and access to care, and changing attitudes of and toward older adults. The third age, says Laslett, "is an attribute of a population, indeed of a nation, as well as of particular men and women."

It is only when people can anticipate with a high degree of confidence that they will live long enough to experience the third age that they can begin to plan for it. Thus, the settled features of the third age only became widely recognizable in Britain in the 1980s and probably a decade earlier in the United States. Given the social and personal dimensions of the third age, Laslett was able to identify the critical question: How will society respond through its public policies and institutions to the presence of this new segment of the population?

Laslett thought that the new-found period of relative leisure must be met with opportunities for people of all classes to deepen their sense of culture and to participate in educational programs that would enable them to appreciate art, history, philosophy, music, and other subjects that were valuable to experience simply for the sake of learning. Without educational engagement the third age would, says Laslett, "turn out to be indolence indefinite." He recommended not only that third-age learners take classes and teach one another, but that they get involved in doing some type of research.

Given the conception of the third age as both a personal and societal achievement, a kind of populist aristocracy in which broad segments of the public can enjoy the fruits of leisure, what forms of education and lifelong learning might be possible? The arrival of the third age and of recent forms of older adult education in the United States have their own convoluted histories that reflect both social change and transformed individual expectations.

EMERGENCE OF OLDER ADULT EDUCATION IN THE UNITED STATES

Adult educational opportunities in the United States date back to the 1700s when coffee houses functioned as adult educational institutions, mainly for disseminating political propaganda. The potential for influencing the thinking of a large number of adults was sometimes enhanced by political parties, such as the Whigs, who oftentimes owned the coffee houses. Many of the coffee houses in New York City also provided writing and reading materials for their customers (Long 1981).

The earliest leaders of our country believed that democracy depended on the educability of the citizenry. Through widespread educational efforts, the public decision-making process could be improved. Benjamin Franklin, a great believer in this theory, established one of the first adult education activities in the colonial United States, called Junto. Established in 1727, Junto was a weekly study group of twelve people who met to discuss community and social issues and was responsible for the formation of the first local lending libraries. It lasted for thirty years. Almost 100 years later a lecture series, given the name Lyceum (in ancient tradition, an association providing public lectures, concerts, and entertainment) was established. The Lyceum series introduced adult citizens residing in small towns and rural areas to scholarly knowledge. These lectures were an attempt to raise the educational levels of participants who had not completed an elementary level education. The lecture series lasted well over 100 years, bringing intellectual stimulation to many of the rural areas of the country (Peterson 1983).

Approximately fifty years later, the Chautauqua movement began introducing adults to religious studies, liberal arts education, and the performing arts.

Established at Lake Chautauqua, New York, in 1874 by the Methodist Episcopal Church, it was basically nondenominational and drew audiences from all over to the summer assembly tent performances. Similar "tent Chautauquas" were held across the country. The New York Chautauqua village is still in existence today and attracts increasing numbers of older people. The program offerings have expanded to include vocational, personal, civic, and community education, as well as programming designed specifically for older adults (Chautauqua Institution 1992).

Until the early 1950s, a cultural bias toward youth appears to have had a detrimental effect upon the growth of educational programs for older adults. An emphasis on youth was prevalent in the majority of publications in the field of education. Yet, in 1949, a Committee on Education for Aging was established under the Department of Adult Education of the National Education Association (NEA). In 1951, this committee became a part of the Adult Education Association of the United States. For the first time in history, a descriptive book on educational programming for older adult learners, *Education for Later Maturity: A Handbook*, was developed by this committee.

The period of the 1960s and early 1970s saw the confluence of interest in older adult education flowing from two sides: adult education and the burgeoning field of gerontology. For example, as an outgrowth of the 1971 White House Conference on Aging, where some emphasis had been placed on the needs of older learners, the Administration on Aging awarded a two-year grant to the American Association of Community and Junior Colleges (AACJC). Funds went toward enabling the nation's community colleges to explore ways for them to highlight the needs of older persons and contribute to their quality of life. In addition, several community colleges tapped new funds made available through Title I of the Higher Education Act of 1965 and Title III of the Older Americans Act of 1965 to hire coordinators or part-time program directors to design and implement courses for seniors (Brahce and Hunter 1990).

Still, the prevailing thinking in this period was to focus on providing seniors with knowledge and skills to cope successfully with the problematic aspects of growing older. According to Peterson (1983), "Educational programs emphasized the crisis of adjustment to retirement and the need for outside assistance to overcome the trauma of role change." As discussed in Chapter 1, this approach is similar to what Moody (1976) characterized as the "social service" model of older adult education in which aging is regarded as a problem that education can help to ameliorate.

During the 1950s and 1960s, only a few educational administrators considered offering educational programs for older adults. The few programs in operation were experimental in nature with no research base.

In the early 1960s, gerontological researchers devoted considerable energy to examining links between aging, intelligence, and memory. The combined emphasis on the youth culture and research on age-related cognitive declines continued to have a negative impact upon attitudes toward older adult educational programs (Timmermann 1979). During this period, the trend that emerged for program planners was to segregate older learners because their integration in ongoing adult educational programs was deemed undesirable. Most practitioners pointed to the differences, not the similarities, between young and old (Timmermann 1979).

By the mid-1960s, small inroads were made in removing the educational bias toward the young, while attitudes toward older adults began to change. For example, social workers trained during the 1940s and 1950s had been instructed to discourage reminiscing among older people because it was viewed as a form of pathology—the person denying or having lost contact with the present. However, between the late 1950s and early 1970s, this view changed dramatically. The work of Butler (1963) and Erikson (1964), working from geriatric and developmental psychology perspectives, respectively, helped service providers and educators recognize a universal life review process and a quest for personal integration occurring normally among the elderly. It was deemed that this process could serve as the basis for therapy and educational programs by building on older persons' life experiences and histories.

Some researchers and educators went even further. They described elements of wisdom and creativity in the life review process (Kaminsky 1984). Not only were older adults still capable of learning and expressing themselves; because of their treasure house of past experience, they could be the best possible students a teacher might find. And they could make some of the best teachers. Hence, the concept of lifelong learning was stretched beyond the middle years of life.

Although the expression lifelong learning has been in use for many years it is only recently that the concept has been applied to the older adult learner. As gerontology became an established field of practice and research, it influenced the adult education movement, and educators began to consider older adults as potential students of lifelong education (Lowy and O'Connor 1986).

Parallel to the emergence of older adult education as meriting the attention of adult educators and gerontologists (and revisions in thinking about the needs and goals of older learners) were changes in appraisal of cognitive functioning among older persons. While a focus on the decline of older persons' intellectual powers characterized early research, more recent research and findings have pointed to stability in cognitive functioning over time. While recognizing decrements in some areas, researchers also emphasized older learners' relatively undiminished capacities and fascinating shifts in the type of intellectual abilities that may come with aging.

INTELLECTUAL FUNCTIONING OF OLDER ADULTS

Maintaining intellectual functioning and capacity is one purpose of education in later life. However, a popular stereotype still prevails that decline in intellectual functioning is usual with advancing age. This stereotype was supported by a body of literature generated in the 1960s and 1970s. K. Warner Schaie, director of the Gerontology Research Institute at the University of Pennsylvania stressed the importance of analyzing the limitations of the research upon which these conclusions were based (Casey 1984).

Schaie (1975) questioned the assumption that older people tend to function less well intellectually than younger people. If one draws the conclusion that the maximum intellectual peak is reached in the years of young adulthood, then it is not surprising that we assume there is a decline that accelerates during old age. In taking this point of view, one would need to explore whether the developmental change in intelligence is a uniform phenomenon. Measures of intelligence are derived from responses to items on tests. The intellectual behavior of an individual is based on an index number arrived at by examining various dimensions that are important for effective mental functioning. When examining the results of studies on intellectual functioning, one must take into consideration that people who differ by age frequently differ by other characteristics. Differences in age mean differences in life experiences. Schaie contended that it did not follow that all older adults exhibit intellectual decline. Individual differences must be taken into consideration.

Some longitudinal studies have shown that many remarkable individuals gained in level of performance from age seventy to age eighty-four. There may be two explanations for these individuals' differences. People who have had a significant and chronic physical illness may be disadvantaged. Also, people who grew up or lived in limited and static environments (substandard housing, lack of food and clothing, limited educational opportunities) will also likely show some decrement (Schaie 1975).

Riley and Riley (1987) undertook a series of studies on intellectual functioning that showed improvement with age under certain conditions. The researchers found continuity in intellectual functioning where life situations continued to be stimulating and challenging and people had an opportunity to use their skills. Also important was that the social environment provide incentives as well as opportunities for learning. Experiments involving people with a mean age of seventy have focused on intellectual skills such as spatial orientation and inductive reasoning in which older adults have been most likely to show declines in test performance. The results of these experiments have shown that intellectual performance does improve when the social environment has provided incentives and opportunities for learning. Test subjects in many studies have shown improvement following training (Riley and Riley 1987).

As Labouvie-Vief (1980) pointed out, the early phase of geropsychology was heavily influenced by the prevailing decrement model of aging. Research presumed that physical and mental processes manifested "primary, inherent, universal, and irreversible biological concomitants of aging." But as a developmental model began to influence the direction of research, geropsychologists began to more carefully differentiate gains and losses in cognitive functioning. Hence, psychologists applied the distinction between two forms of intelligence:

crystallized (derived from experience) and fluid (more biologically determined). While the latter may show marked signs of decline with aging, the former shows less decline and longer stability. Later, the distinction between competence and performance was used to indicate differences in intellectual functioning.

Labouvie-Vief's own research was influenced by her elderly subjects who told her that her "battery of tasks was altogether unrelated to what they felt should define intelligent behavior." Many of the test tasks struck them as demeaning and uninteresting. She recognized that this might be because the standardized test presupposed "regressive change." She began to wonder whether a better understanding of cognitive change with age might not be understood as a process in which knowledge is reorganized and represented. Accordingly, she developed a "trade-off view" of cognitive development as a process in which some forms of intellectual integration are dissolved while new forms of integration occur, particularly around adaptations in relation to "pragmatic necessities." We will return to this point of view in discussing Paul Baltes's more recent research.

Based on a number of recent studies, Swindell (1991) agreed that no significant loss of intellectual functioning need be associated with older adults if they are cognitively stimulated throughout their lifetime. A report from the Panel on Behavioral and Social Sciences Research, National Advisory Council on the Aging in the United States, explained that education may actually slow the onset of some consequences of old age. The standardized tests used to measure intellectual functioning were designed for the young, primarily for use in schools. The Rileys (1987) contend there may be other areas of intelligence that do not develop until middle age or later in life. These areas would include experience-based decision making, interpersonal competence, and the wisdom to evaluate, set priorities, and take appropriate action. For years, the strengths and potentials of older learners have been grossly underestimated. More and more researchers and educators are acknowledging the importance of providing productive and rewarding roles to older citizens.

An important theorist who has brought new insight to changes in cognitive functioning and intelligence in later life is Paul Baltes (1993). Baltes and his colleagues at the Max Planck Institute for Neurological Research in Berlin distinguished two types of mental activity. First, there is the architecture of mental functioning. Using the analogy of computer language, he called it the biologically shaped "hardware of the mind," which operates the speed and accuracy of memory, sensory input, our ability to make distinctions and comparisons, and our ability to put things into categories. By contrast, the "software of the mind" is more a product of culture, upbringing, and environment. It includes reading and writing skills, language comprehension, professional skills, knowledge about ourselves, and the skills that help us master or cope with life.

Baltes and his associates found that while older persons' memory capacity would increase if they participated in memory training techniques, they would still not reach the level of younger persons who received the same training. Hence, they concluded, the hardware of the mind does show a decline with age.

But when it came to real-life problem-solving tests that challenged people to think aloud about how they would deal with a threatened suicide, for example, or how they would advise a 15-year-old girl who wanted to get married, they found no major differences between those thirty to seventy years of age. In fact, those over sixty were as likely to be among the top 20 percent of "wisdom performers" as younger adults. Baltes also compared a group of nominated "wise" older persons with professional psychologists and other professionals in similar real-life tests and found that the wisdom nominees predominated at the top range of performers.

The implications of Baltes's work is similar to that of Peter Laslett's view discussed earlier, that the "world record in wisdom-related knowledge and skills may very well be held by someone in the last season of life" (Baltes 1993). Many older persons are ideally equipped to benefit from continued opportunities to learn and teach and may play critically important roles in societies preoccupied with short-term, often short-sighted, planning and values.

Paul Baltes's work asserts that there are qualitative differences in how some older people think; that is, with declines in some areas offset by advances in others. Most recent research findings suggest that chronological age is not the key determinant of cognitive ability and that attempts at formulating a general theory of older learners may be a misguided effort. While there clearly are declines in memory and intellectual functioning associated with aging, these declines vary widely with individuals, while certain capabilities seem enhanced with age. Future research may be conducted more profitably by examining the persistence of learning styles, strategies, and intellectual habits shaped by prior education and training.

ADULT VERSUS OLDER ADULT EDUCATION

Many educators have addressed the importance of past experiences in enhancing the older adult's learning experience. Education has been defined by John Dewey (1938) as the "continuous reconstruction of experience." Adult educator Malcolm Knowles (1980) further contends that life experience distinguishes child learning from adult learning. Accumulation of experience means the older learner knows what he or she wants to explore, has a foundation to build on, and has the perspective of years to evaluate the worth of continued, renewed, or newly initiated learning. Then is older adult education simply an extension or subspecies of the principles of adult education? For some, the answer is yes, for others, no.

Differing views of the relationship between adult and older adult education derive from the professional orientation of the theorist (i.e., whether he or she approaches the subject from the field of aging or of education) and the theorist's presuppositions of life course development. For example, if later life is regarded by an adult educator as a continuous extension of middle age, then approaches to adult education would be sufficient to cover later life—part of the continuum of adult education. However, if later life is regarded as a unique developmental stage with its own special tasks and opportunities, then education in the later years may be regarded as distinct from adult education. For example, Moody (1990) has argued that, unique to old age, some older learners are capable of understanding philosophical and spiritual matters that only a lifetime of experience could make possible. Just when does a person reach that threshold of unique insight? Again, it is probably not a matter of chronology but of maturity.

Peter Laslett (1991) suggests that older learners are capable of a greater capacity for drawing on subjective time perspectives because they have reached a state of "completion and arrival" in the life course. People entering the third age are better prepared by a lifetime of experience to understand the deeper meanings of love, work, family, history, suffering, and joy than younger persons.

Other researchers such as Clayton and Birren (1980) have focused on the search for wisdom in later life as a unique characteristic of older persons. Old age, being the last stage in the course of life, may be viewed as an attempt to explore the meaning of one's experiences and to integrate an understanding of these experiences acquired throughout a lifetime. Many gerontologists and adult educators believe that self-actualization should be the ultimate goal of every older adult educational program (Peterson 1990). However, Moody (1987) has pushed his own model of philosophical presuppositions of learning in later life beyond culmination in self-actualization. He postulated a fifth presupposition of education for seniors, that of *emancipation.*

In line with the European philosophical tradition of critical theory, and based on a unique blend of Marxism and phenomenology, Moody argued that beyond self-actualization (which is itself heavily ideologically laden since it places primary emphasis on the individual) education has as a social purpose the liberation of individuals from prejudice and stereotype through critical awareness, public debate, and social change. Accordingly, older adults may take charge of their lives and educations through voluntary associations in self-help groups, community activism on their behalf as well as on the behalf of those of other generations, and peer-learning and teaching programs in which seniors assume a high degree of control and responsibility.

NATIONAL POLICIES AND OLDER ADULT EDUCATION

While a fuller discussion of public policy as related to older adult education will be found in Chapter 4, it is appropriate in the context of this chapter to examine how the history of older adult education has been influenced by changes in government policies toward older adults and, more specifically, toward their educational possibilities.

The change in societal attitudes has had a significant impact on federal policies regarding the education of older adults. The first major development came with the creation of the Older Americans Act in 1965. This act established the Administration on Aging and provided needed funding for gerontological training and research at colleges and universities. The act opened the door for new educational opportunities for older adults and extended educational gerontology, workforce training, and multidisciplinary graduate programs, as well as research in addressing the needs of older adult learners.

As mentioned in Chapter 1, another departure from the prevailing attitudes occurred in 1971 when the White House Conference on Aging advanced recommendations which paved the road for educational programming for older adults. The national event had a significant impact on the attitudes of educators and gerontologists. Education received special attention at the conference, where recommendations called for increased funding and human resources to provide older adult educational programs in the private and public sector.

Congress enacted the Older Americans Comprehensive Services Amendments of 1973 to strengthen the Older Americans Act. Under this act, the Administration on Aging was reorganized under the U.S. Department of Health, Education, and Welfare (HEW) and the Federal Council on the Aging (FAC) was created, as well as the National Information and Resource Clearinghouse for the Aging (NIRCA). Grants were given to state governments for special library and education programs for older adults. Research in the field of aging and grants for training personnel to work with older adults were encouraged (Brahce and Hunter 1990).

In addition to federal policies concerning older adult education, many states began to establish guidelines within their statutes to allow or require a waiver or reduction of tuition fees for older adults who might enroll at state-supported institutions of higher education (U.S. Senate Special Committee on Aging 1991). A more detailed discussion of tuition-waiver policies can be found in Chapter 4.

The private sector also became involved in the educational pursuits of older adults during the 1970s. An initiative was taken to design projects that would enable older adults to become involved in new careers and further their knowledge so that they might continue to contribute to society. Private-sector programs established to meet the needs of the aging included those of the AARP, the National Retired Teachers Association (NRTA), the National Association of Retired Federal Employees (NARFE), the National Association for the Spanish Speaking Elderly (NASSE), the National Center on the Black Aged, Inc. (NCBA), the NCOA, the NCSC, the National Farmers Union (NFU), and the National Indian Council on Aging (NICA).

The Edna McConnell Clark Foundation funded many research projects to determine the best utilization of services for older adults. One of their projects included a grant to the AACJC to extend career opportunities to older adults by assisting them to prepare for further careers before and after retirement (Brahce and Hunter 1990).

Federal, state, and local policies have partially shaped funding streams and institutional missions in promoting older adult education. To some extent, these policies have served to motivate or catalyze a variety of institutional developments. But new initiatives have also occurred, independent of governmental policies or foundation support. The following section reviews this broader scope of organizations serving older learners and how these have changed during the last few decades.

AN INSTITUTIONAL HISTORY OF
OLDER LEARNER PROGRAMS

Four-Year Colleges and Universities

In the 1980s, institutions of higher education were confronted with difficult economic challenges. Since the 1970s there had been periodic declines in the proportion of full-time, traditional-age students (eighteen to twenty-two years of age). Along with this decline in the population of traditional-aged students, costs for providing education continued to rise (Romaniuk 1983). In the 1980s, educators predicted that the decline in enrollment of traditional-age students would also have an impact on the use of facilities, need for faculty, and the relevance of curriculum (Peterson 1981). Today, institutions of higher education are not having as serious an enrollment problem as had been expected. Nontraditional-age students twenty-five years and older are making up for part of the decline in enrollment of traditional-aged students. Enrollment is predicted to climb from 14.1 million in 1991 to 16 million in 2002 according to the U.S. Department of Education. The projected 13 percent increase is attributed to rising college enrollments of eighteen- to twenty-four-year olds beginning in 1996. A big part of this increase will be made up of minority and female students. Additionally, 23 percent of the enrollment in 2002 is predicted to be made up of students thirty-five and older (Evangelauf 1992).

Older adults are usually welcomed in the regular academic programs; but because older adults' goals, priorities, and schedules are less compatible with traditional college classroom teaching, the vast majority of nontraditional-age students tend to be in the 25- to 45-year-old bracket (Thorson and Waskell 1991). Fischer (1992) has found that until the past ten to fifteen years, older adult education was an issue of speculative discussion among administrators rather than practice. Since that time, higher education institutions have begun to recognize that the college campus is no longer just for the traditional-aged student and that realization has created a positive climate for older adult learners as well. Fischer contends that there is a new creative and innovative spirit at work in higher education which focuses on adults fifty-five and older as well as students in their twenties to forties. This view is confirmed by the large and growing number of LRIs that have sprung up around the country, primarily in associating with four-year institutions of higher education. Whether older adults enrolling in regular college courses are well received is not well documented.

Among institutions of higher education attracting older learners (55-plus), programs have developed that are both credit-bearing and noncredit. In a 1976 survey conducted by the Academy for Educational Development (AED) of a selected sample of 814 colleges and universities believed to be offering programs for older adults throughout the United States, researchers found that colleges and universities offered educational programs for older adults that fell into three categories: (1) those offering courses specifically designed for older adults; (2) those providing regular or continuing education courses at reduced tuition rates or free of charge, either for credit or on an auditing basis; and (3) those offering courses of special interest to older adults through a continuing education program (Scanlon 1978).

In 1981, a Louis Harris survey sponsored by the NCOA found that adults sixty-five and over were most often enrolled in older adult educational programs at colleges and universities as opposed to their place of business, high school, community or senior center, church, library, museum, or by correspondence. In another survey conducted by the National Center for Education Statistics (NCES) in 1981 concerning the location preferred by older adults, NCES reported that 32 percent of the courses taken by persons sixty-five and over were taken in educational settings: elementary or high schools, two- and four-year colleges, business, trade, or vocational schools, and particularly at community colleges (Ventura and Worthy 1982).

The NCES (1991) reported that, in the fall of 1987, 239,029 students fifty to sixty-four years of age and 94,875 students sixty-five and older were enrolled in undergraduate credit programs at higher-education institutions throughout the United States; 2,078 students fifty to sixty-four years of age and 272 students sixty-five and older were enrolled in first-professional programs at higher education institutions; and 51,591 students fifty to sixty-four years of age and 7,494 students sixty-five and older were enrolled in graduate programs at higher education institutions (Table 2.1).

Community Colleges

In 1989, the League for Innovation in the Community College (LICC) and the AARP conducted a national survey of League member institutions (community colleges). From the approximately 600 community colleges responding to the survey (Doucette and Ventura-Merkel 1991), the researchers

Table 2.1
Total Enrollment in Institutions of Higher Education by Level, Sex, Age, and Attendance Status of Student, Fall 1987

Attendance status and age of student	All levels			Undergraduate		
	Total	Men	Women	Total	Men	Women
1	2	3	4	5	6	7
All students	12,766,642	5,932,056	6,834,586	11,046,235	5,068,457	5,977,778
Under 18	207,085	87,168	119,917	206,271	86,732	119,539
18 and 19	2,696,652	1,253,984	1,442,568	2,695,892	1,253,615	1,442,277
20 and 21	2,392,038	1,168,820	1,223,218	2,375,398	1,160,289	1,215,109
22 to 24	2,025,725	1,078,235	947,490	1,724,576	915,014	809,562
25 to 29	1,839,916	926,756	913,160	1,327,828	639,577	688,251
30 to 34	1,242,344	558,441	683,903	921,165	386,317	534,848
35 to 39	882,763	337,774	544,989	647,596	231,380	416,216
40 to 49	872,120	288,231	583,889	654,007	209,118	444,889
50 to 64	291,698	98,263	193,435	239,029	80,086	157,943
65 and over	102,641	38,507	54,134	94,875	33,904	60,971
Age unkonwn	213,660	95,877	117,783	160,598	72,425	88,173
Full-time	7,231,085	3,610,888	3,620,197	6,462,549	3,163,676	3,298,873
Under 18	113,938	48,513	65,425	113,659	48,348	65,311
18 and 19	2,331,202	1,088,972	1,242,220	2,330,703	1,088,703	1,242,000
20 and 21	1,919,332	948,534	970,798	1,905,791	941,234	964,557
22 to 24	1,251,794	716,088	535,706	1,034,268	590,066	444,202
25 to 29	727,279	412,056	315,223	462,354	246,357	215,997
30 to 34	371,825	181,798	190,027	248,644	107,274	141,370
35 to 39	217,470	90,852	126,618	148,050	53,779	94,271
40 to 49	170,162	62,796	107,366	119,511	41,946	77,565
50 to 64	38,224	14,556	23,668	27,116	10,122	16,994
65 and over	9,330	5,463	3,867	6,565	3,209	3,356
Age unknown	30,529	41,250	39,269	65,888	32,638	33,250
Part-time	5,535,557	2,321,168	3,214,389	4,583,686	1,904,781	2,678,905
Under 18	93,147	38,655	54,492	92,512	38,384	54,228
18 and 19	365,450	165,012	200,438	365,189	164,912	200,277
20 and 21	472,706	220,286	252,420	469,607	219,055	250,552
22 to 24	773,931	362,147	411,784	690,308	324,948	365,360
25 to 29	1,112,637	514,700	597,937	865,474	393,220	472,254
30 to 34	870,519	376,643	493,876	672,521	279,043	393,478
35 to 39	665,293	246,922	418,371	499,546	177,601	321,945
40 to 49	701,958	225,435	476,523	534,496	167,172	367,324
50 to 64	253,474	83,707	169,767	210,913	69,964	140,949
65 and over	93,311	33,044	60,297	88,310	30,695	57,515
Age unknown	133,131	54,617	78,514	94,710	39,787	54,923

Source: U.S. Department of Education, National Center for Education Statistics. Integrated Postsecondary Education Data System. "Fall Enrollment, 1987" survey. (This table was prepared in March 1990.)

First-professional			Graduate		
Total	Men	Women	Total	Men	Women
8	9	10	11	12	13
258,332	170,129	98,203	1,452,075	693,470	758,605
47	33	14	767	403	364
194	106	88	566	263	303
7,269	4,102	3,167	9,371	4,429	4,942
99,604	53,181	36,463	201,505	100,040	101,465
95,381	63,701	31,680	416,707	223,478	193,229
33,065	20,691	12,374	288,114	151,433	136,681
16,159	9,368	5,791	219,008	97,026	121,982
9,898	4,959	4,939	208,215	74,154	134,061
2,078	1,114	964	51,591	17,063	34,522
272	156	116	7,494	4,447	3,047
4,325	2,718	1,607	48,737	20,734	28,003
241,807	153,668	88,139	526,729	293,544	233,185
45	31	44	234	134	100
190	103	87	309	166	143
7,170	4,037	3,133	6,371	3,263	3,108
96,885	61,446	35,439	120,641	64,576	56,065
86,390	57,807	28,583	178,535	107,892	70,643
26,779	16,682	10,097	96,402	57,842	38,560
12,130	6,968	5,162	57,290	30,105	27,185
6,737	3,296	3,441	43,914	17,554	26,360
1,261	683	578	9,847	3,751	6,096
197	113	84	2,568	2,141	427
4,023	2,502	1,521	10,618	6,120	4,498
26,525	16,461	10,064	925,346	399,926	525,420
2	2	0	533	269	264
4	3	1	257	97	180
99	65	34	3,000	1,166	1,334
2,759	1,735	1,024	80,864	35,464	45,400
8,991	5,894	3,097	238,172	115,586	122,586
6,286	4,009	2,377	191,712	93,591	98,121
4,029	2,400	1,629	161,718	66,921	94,797
3,161	1,663	1,498	164,301	56,600	107,701
817	431	386	41,744	13,312	28,432
75	43	32	4,926	2,306	2,520
302	216	86	38,119	14,614	22,505

51

found that (1) most older adult educational programs came under organizational units such as Community Services, Adult Education, or short courses; (2) the majority of the colleges conducted noncredit courses with fees ranging between twenty-five and fifty dollars per course; (3) some colleges allowed students sixty and older to audit credit courses with fees waived; (4) half of the League colleges had a special program and/or center for older adults at their college; (5) three-fourths of the colleges reported offering noncredit classes to older adults; and (6) full-term credit courses were often taught at off-campus sites (Charles and Bartunek 1989).

Catherine Ventura-Merkel, then Senior Education Specialist in the Special Projects Section of AARP, and Don Doucette, then Associate Director of the LICC, reported that the types of courses being offered in the community colleges were traditional classes in exercise and nutrition, avocational arts, crafts, and hobbies, as well as trips and financial management programs on retirement and estate planning.

The courses least likely to be offered were in fact the ones demographers and other analysts contended are most needed by the older adult population. These courses included skills training for second and third occupations, personal development courses, and health care programs. Ventura-Merkel and Doucette concluded that only a small number of community colleges were offering programs and services for older adults. The colleges offered programs that were mostly designed for groups of retired seniors.

Colleges reported that lack of funding was a major obstacle in offering more programs and services for older adults. Ventura-Merkel and Doucette proposed that the most logical explanation for the few programs offered for older adults by community colleges was that this particular population did not realize what community colleges could offer to them. Older adults were only likely to demand such programs as they began to realize their need for new skills that would assist them in adapting to a fast-changing world and to the personal changes of aging and retirement (Doucette and Ventura-Merkel 1991).

Charles and Bartunek (1989) have identified several community colleges that provided outstanding programs and services designed specifically for older adults. One example, Cuyahoga Community College in Warrensville Township, Ohio, provided a comprehensive range of educational services that included seminars, workshops, and special events; courses in the humanities and social, behavioral, and biological sciences; and courses on a variety of special interest topics related to health and well-being in the later years. The program was designed for adults fifty-five and older and offered in forty locations throughout the county where older adults live or meet. The offerings were held in cooperation with the Office on Aging, Title III nutrition sites, and community and senior centers and residences.

A special program, Elder's Campus, is a day-long, weekly program held on the eastern and western campuses of the college. The participants in that program assist in planning and implementation, serve as the Advisory Committee, and function as teaching faculty (Charles and Bartunek 1989).

Barriers to Participation in Colleges and Universities. There are many kinds of barriers, real or perceived, that may prevent older adults from participating in educational opportunities. These barriers may be categorized as situational, dispositional, and institutional. Situational barriers may include a lack of mobility or knowledge about the educational opportunities that are available or the cost of programs. These barriers pertain to one's situation at the time of the educational offering. The dispositional barriers include how the person views himself or herself as a learner. For example, many adults believe they are simply too old to learn.

Some older adults have limited educational backgrounds. As a result of this limitation, the older adult may have a lack of interest in further education, feelings of insecurity concerning the ability to learn, and lack of ability to see the need for education at this time in his or her life.

Institutional barriers are practices or procedures within an institution that may discourage participation. Inflexible schedules, expensive fees, inappropriate course offerings, complicated application and registration procedures, inaccessible buildings, and lack of communication concerning what educational opportunities are available are all examples of institutional barriers (Cross 1981).

Ruth Weinstock believes there are many barriers to education for older adults that can be overcome. Admissions procedures and registration of college credit courses is a difficult experience for all students and should be modified for the older adult learner. When an applicant has to request permission to audit a course from a professor, the professor's office location, telephone number, and office hours should be readily available. Weinstock suggests that modifications be made for the older adult learner such as campus orientation and publication of an older student handbook (Weinstock 1978).

John Scanlon cites Fordham University's College at Sixty as an example of a college reaching out to older adults to enroll them in credit classes. College at Sixty's enrollment is open to college and noncollege graduates alike who express an interest in reading and demonstrate the ability to undertake college-level work. Upon successful completion of four seminars offered by the College at Sixty program, a certificate is awarded to the student entitling him or her to enter Fordham's College of Liberal Arts without having to meet any of the other admission requirements (Scanlon 1978).

The research literature on educational programs for seniors in institutions of higher education reveals that there are many other strategies that may be used by educational programs for increasing older adult's participation, including reduced or waived tuition, courses designed specifically for older adults, support services (orientation workshops and counseling), and outreach strategies to include older adults.

As the need for educational programs for older adults continues to grow, educational institutions and community organizations are attempting to meet these demands by developing programs to serve this special population. At many institutions the barriers are simply not understood; therefore, efforts to overcome them are not universal (Peterson 1983).

Elderhostel

From their inception in 1975 to the mid-1980s, Elderhostel programs were exclusively conducted at college campuses. But in recent years, Elderhostel has gone beyond higher education sites. Because of its prominence and size, it belongs in a class by itself.

Elderhostel is an international educational network providing opportunities for adults over sixty (lowered to fifty-five in 1995) to participate in noncredit educational activities on college campuses and in other educational settings (Gelfand 1988). Founded in 1975 by Martin Knowlton as a short-term residential college program, Elderhostel originally operated under the auspices of the Center for Continuing Education at the University of New Hampshire in Durham. The first Elderhostel programs in 1975 were run by a small group of colleges and universities in New Hampshire with 220 older adults participating in course offerings. In 1977, Elderhostel became an independent, nonprofit organization with the full support of the University. A national office was established in Boston to coordinate all Elderhostel activities. In 1979, a computerized national mailing list system was installed, and the national office began registering participants by phone or mail for any Elderhostel program anywhere in the country (O'Donnell and Berkeley 1980).

Since 1986, Elderhostel has grown at a rate of 15 to 25 percent (U.S. Senate Special Committee on Aging 1991a). The program is operating in more than 1,800 sites in the United States and Canada and in forty-five countries worldwide. The enrollment averages over 300,000 annually. The sponsoring institutions are largely four-year colleges and universities, but environmental study centers, scientific research stations, and conference centers serve as program hosts. Variations in programming also allow the participants to bring their recreational vehicles to programs offered in state and national parks in the United States (Goggin 1991). In 1993 Elderhostel began offering a social action component for people who wished to travel to a site and become affiliated with a local community service project where they could both serve and learn.

Elderhostel's international activity provides opportunities for Elderhostelers to study abroad. The catalogue of courses for studying abroad is published three times a year. Catalogues of the courses in Canada and the United States are published four times annually (U.S. Senate Special Committee on Aging 1991b).

Participants are responsible for their room and board, transportation, and course fees. The cost of an average one-week stay (as of 1994) is $275 in the

United States, which includes a campus dorm room, cafeteria meals, three college-level courses, and extracurricular activities.

The AARP's Institute of Lifetime Learning grants 200 scholarship awards annually for attendance at Elderhostel programs in the United States. Applicants must be sixty years or older (their spouses need not meet the age criterion), a member of the AARP, and must have given a significant amount of volunteer time in their communities. Special consideration is given to those who could have difficulty paying the Elderhostel fee. Applications are available from the AARP Fulfillment, Elderhostel Application Form D 12309, P.O. Box 2400, Long Beach, California, 90801.

A perhaps surprising aspect of Elderhostel is that none of the courses offered take old age as the subject matter. This is based on the view that courses that deal with aging teach people to be old (Peterson 1983). The program mainly focuses on the expressive needs of students, using a liberal arts curriculum that is preselected by the institution's administration (Lowy and O'Connor 1986). The courses are generally designed for a one-week period. Generally three courses are offered in each of the one-week programs (Gelfand 1988). The courses do not require homework, involve grades, or require a prior knowledge of the subject matter. The noncredit course offerings afford students the opportunity to participate for the sheer enjoyment of learning (Goggin 1991).

Participation in Elderhostel ranges from exploring the Alaskan mountain range to studying the culture and society of China. At Denali National Park, location of Mount McKinley, Elderhostel class sessions include lectures, slide presentations and guided tours of the wildlife, natural history, history and management, and glaciers and glacial geology of Denali. Participants are housed in two-room cabins on the banks of the Nenana River.

The Elderhostel program in China is organized in cooperation with the Chinese American Educational Exchange (CAEE) based at the New York University. The Chinese Culture and Society program is designed so that participants may achieve a deeper understanding of the Chinese people, their lives, and their cultures as reflected in the differences dictated by the history and traditions of the various geographical areas in which they live. The programs are offered in the provinces of Hebei and Shandong. Each program is three weeks long and held in university settings. All programs offer the opportunity for observing both rural and city life and for studying a large, modern city and a smaller, ancient city, as well as the chance to view various aspects of country life through visits to agricultural villages.

An example of Elderhostel programming in the continental United States is "Colorado's Colorful History: Peaks, Poems, and Pokes," located at Colorado Mountain College/Springwood Valley Center in Glenwood Springs. Participants explore the history of Aspen, Redstone, Markie, and Glenwood Springs through art, cowboy poetry, old photographs, and field trips.

Learning in Retirement Institutes (LRIs)

An LRI is an organization of retirement-age learners dedicated to meeting the educational needs of its members. LRIs generally fall into one of two general program categories: institution-driven or member-driven. Francis A. Meyers of the Association of Learning in Retirement Organizations in the Western Region (ALIROW), a consortium of LRIs, defines the institution-driven model as an educational offering traditionally designed by professional staff and taught by the regular higher-education faculty. The member-driven model is developed, designed, and taught by the members with the cooperative sponsorship of a higher-education institution. The members also take an active role in governing the organization by electing directors and officers (Meyers 1987).

A set of common characteristics has been identified in LRIs: (1) LRIs are typically designed to meet the educational needs of older adults that live within commuting distance of the program; (2) the offerings are varied and cover a broad spectrum with the majority consisting of college-level material; (3) LRIs are sponsored by accredited colleges or universities, institutions, or organizations working in collaboration with an accredited higher-education institution or an organization or institution sponsoring a comparable college- or university-level program; (4) LRIs are nonprofit organizations which charge a modest tuition or membership fee; (5) a need-based scholarship program is available; (6) affirmative action goals are of utmost importance; (7) many times, members serve as volunteer teachers or course leaders; (8) social, cultural, and physical experience are a part of the offerings; and (9) participants are encouraged to be involved in planning, evaluating, teaching, and (when appropriate) administering the program (Fischer 1992).

There is some confusion over the acronym for learning in retirement institutes. Those institutes that qualify for membership in the umbrella organization, Elderhostel Institute Network (EIN), a subsidiary of Elderhostel, are termed by that organization Institutes for Learning in Retirement (ILRs). The acronym LRI (Learning in Retirement Institute) is simply a generic classification and does not denote a specific type. Generally, ILRs are characterized by membership roles of teaching and self-governance.

The New School for Social Research in New York City was the first to establish an Institute for Retired Professionals (IRP) in 1962. The IRP is often cited as the beginning of the LRI movement. In 1993, the New School's IRP ran into a conflict with the school's administration and after 30 years of on-site affiliation was asked to consider finding a new host institution. Further discussion on the relationship of LRIs to their host institutions will be taken up in Chapter 4.

During the 1960s and 1970s, colleges and universities began replicating or adapting the IRP model. Several national conferences were devoted to the

LRI concept; and the number of LRIs has increased dramatically (Elderhostel Institute Network 1991).

In 1989, Elderhostel established the EIN to advance and promote LRIs (Goggin 1991). This voluntary association of independent institutes is dedicated to extending the LRI concept to new people in new institutions and strengthening and supporting the effectiveness of established LRIs. In 1994, an estimated 200 LRIs had been established in the United States. Over 160 of these were members of EIN; and of these, 80 percent were started after 1989 (Elderhostel Institute Network 1991).

The LRI programs include core courses and classes in the humanities and liberal arts. Literature, history, public affairs, and music and art appreciation have proven to be the most popular among participants. Many times the core curriculum is supplemented by classes in computer science, foreign languages, painting, and writing. Recreational and physical fitness programs are also offered. Classes are not limited to the traditional classroom setting. Field trips including one-day or overnight travel to museums, historical sites, and cultural events are frequently part of the LRI's offerings (Lipman 1992).

During the past few years, the EIN began offering national study/travel opportunities. These programs include such opportunities as an exploration of the myriad aspects of Rome, a naturalist's study in a naturalist's paradise (Costa Rica), architectural studies in London and Dublin, the study of European unification focusing on the position of smaller countries like Belgium and Holland, and numerous other ventures.

There are many outstanding LRIs in the United States and Canada today. One example is the College for Seniors established in 1988 at the NCCCR, University of North Carolina at Asheville (UNCA). This member-driven institute provides life enrichment courses to anyone fifty-five and over who pays the required membership fee of eighty dollars per eight-week semester (scholarships are also available). The fee allows members to enroll in from one to five courses, depending on space available, and includes parking privileges and use of the university library. Most courses are taught on a volunteer basis by other retirees. Between 800 and 1,000 individuals take part each year.

There are no educational prerequisites and no exams or grades in College for Seniors. The program is founded on the desire of adults to pursue learning for pleasure and stimulation, and to do so in the company of others similarly motivated. Participants are involved in more than taking classes. From teaching to working on a newsletter, from registering participants to designing curriculum, there is much in which to become involved. The curriculum provides a variety of substantive courses in almost every field—music, literature, history, fitness and wellness, art, religion, environmental issues, psychology, philosophy, computer science, political science, foreign language, and current events of interest to the older adult population. The College for Seniors is an organization that creates a welcoming atmosphere by involving participants in the shaping and creating of its offerings. It is able to offer a full and varied program because of its members, people who give freely of their time and knowledge.

While the College for Seniors is similar to many of the over 200 LRIs established by 1994, the context in which it operates, the NCCCR, is comparatively unique. The NCCCR conducts programs in campus and community service, leadership, intergenerational collaboration, research, volunteerism, wellness, and retirement planning. The Senior Academy for Intergenerational Learning (SAIL) matches retired civic and professional leaders with undergraduate students and UNCA faculty to work together on learning projects. The SAIL volunteers share their time and expertise with students. For example, senior adults work with university athletes sharing career interests, and retired scientists serve as research partners in undergraduate research projects. The SAIL program provides an opportunity for retirees to continue to contribute to their professions and community (U.S. Senate Special Committee on Aging 1991b).

Another NCCCR program, Leadership Asheville Seniors (LAS), provides an intensive learning experience for its older adult participants. Local political leaders, agency directors, representatives of industry, and civic leaders present information about community issues through lectures and problem-solving sessions. The LAS participants take part in these activities in order to improve their leadership skills which will enable them to make more meaningful contributions to the community.

The Center also runs a humanities outreach program through reading and discussion groups led by trained volunteers at churches, community centers, and other various sites in the rural areas of western North Carolina. The Center, in cooperation with the NEH and the North Carolina and South Carolina Humanities Councils, provides other humanities programs in the multistate area that are led by paid, trained scholars. Public libraries in North Carolina, South Carolina, Tennessee, and Virginia are the cosponsors of a recent program entitled "The Carolina Special—Railroads through the Carolinas and Beyond as Reflected in Literature and History."

The Center also conducts wellness programs. For example, for several years it sponsored the Senior Wellness Program, a sixteen-hour course that prepares graduates as Wellness Ambassadors who assist with the Senior Wellness Day. This day-long annual event is cosponsored with a local hospital that offers a series of workshops and health screenings. The program has also coordinated two mall-walking programs in conjunction with a local hospital.

The Center's Retirement Planning program offers corporations and individuals retirement seminars. The Research Institute has studied the economic and social impact of retirees migrating into the region and conducted a national survey of older adult educational programs. The latter study (see Chapter 3) provides a national perspective on certain forms of educational programs for older adults in the United States by examining critical variables in the success of these programs and highlighting organizational features that might lend themselves to replication in other programs, whether already existing, in the planning process, or simply as ideas in the minds of senior leaders, college administrators, or administrators of community organizations.

The Center serves as a laboratory for North Carolina and the nation by designing, implementing, and evaluating innovative educational programs. It's long-range mission is to encourage development of an age-integrated society. In a future age-integrated society, retirement-aged persons will take advantage of educational opportunities to help them find new and satisfying roles and join with other generations in programs, projects, and entrepreneurial enterprises that add to the general quality of life while tapping seniors' unique talents, experiences, and abilities. While seniors will continue to identify, in part, with their age peers, they will also identify strongly with young people and with those who share a vision of the future (Manheimer 1992).

Duke University's Institute for Learning in Retirement (DILR), established in 1977, is another good example of programming for people fifty and older. Older adults participate in peer-taught academic classes in a year-round program. Numerous benefits are available to students enrolled in the program, including use of the library, swimming pool, language labs, and the faculty dining room. The class offerings range from drama to religion to literature to science. Approximately forty courses are offered each semester. These classes meet once a week for ninety minutes over a twelve-week period. The class offerings are determined by faculty availability, student interest, and variety. Membership in the program is $100 per semester, which entitles the students to enroll in as many as five classes. These students are involved in volunteer activities, including teaching some of the courses, leading study groups, acting as teaching assistants, and assisting with administrative tasks (Fischer 1991).

Another example is The Renaissance Society at the California State University, Sacramento. Established in 1986, the program provides a number of study discussion groups on life-enrichment topics where each member or a team of members is encouraged to investigate the past of a topic under study and participate in an informal discussion with a coordinator presiding. There is a writer's group that meets in the homes of members, a group studying the opportunities of aging in today's society, and field trips that enhance the learning taking place in the classroom. The various study groups are led by volunteers from the membership. Each semester opens with a free public forum featuring a speaker who addresses a timely topic. The forum also affords current and prospective students an opportunity to learn more about the purposes of the society, the curriculum for the next semester, and procedures for joining. No specific educational background is required for admission, and an annual membership fee covers the courses offered during the year, as well as a campus parking permit (The Renaissance Society 1992).

Each LRI may have similar characteristics, but each is as unique as the creativity of its participants.

Certification Programs

While LRI participants are pursuing educational courses for the sheer enjoyment of learning, some older adults require educational courses that prepare them for retraining and second and third careers. Certification programs
provide this type of training.

As noted in Chapter 1, the demographic profile of the United States is
changing. Fewer younger workers are projected to be available and many
employers may soon begin to increasingly hire or retain older workers to meet
their labor requirements (Gelfand 1988). Many of these positions require
employees to have specific skills and certification in order to meet the challenges of the job. The complex labor force picture is difficult to predict. Corporate downsizing, attributed to competition in the global economy, has
thrown many 45- to 55-year-olds into premature retirement. Some find ways
to return to work, others do not or choose to stop working or to launch more
independent self-employment ventures. If this trend continues, then older
workers, especially white collar managerial and technological workers, will
alter this picture of labor market shortages.

Many colleges and universities are establishing special programs and making the older learner's transition back into the educational environment more
appealing, as well as preparing them for new careers or new job challenges.
One such program is Kingsborough Community College's My Turn. This
special tuition-free college education program has waived all admission requirements with the exception that students must be residents of New York
state and sixty-five years of age by the first day of class. Many students are
working toward a General Equivalency Diploma (GED) while others are
working toward an associate degree (U.S. Senate Special Committee on Aging 1991b).

Another such program is at the University of Massachusetts, Boston campus, where qualified students over sixty prepare to serve as professionals in
the field of gerontology. During the past five years the Gerontology Program
has grown without excessive demands on faculty time or the need for major
outside funding. The educational backgrounds of the students vary. Not all
have high-school degrees and only one-third have college degrees. The University has sought diversity in the backgrounds of the students as well as age
and ethnicity. Classes are scheduled during the daytime hours and are held in
easily accessible buildings. Tutoring services and administrative assistance is
provided to students when needed. After completing two terms of intensive
study, an equivalent of thirty undergraduate hours, students receive a State
Certificate in Gerontology. Graduates of the program have found job opportunities in government agencies serving the aging, in nursing homes, working for political candidates, and administering programs for the aging (U.S.
Senate Special Committee on Aging 1991b). In order to compete successfully
in today's job market, older adults must acquire the skills and certification

(when appropriate) to meet the challenges of an ever changing world of technology. Certification programs provide one avenue.

The Role of Public Libraries

Many older adults find themselves with increased leisure time, reduced income, and declining health at a time when their information needs are increasing. As they become more socially isolated, older adults have fewer opportunities to seek answers from traditional sources such as daily communication with other people (Hales 1985). The public library is a community service that may fill this void.

Older adults are one of the many publics that the library serves on a regular basis. Public libraries were established to serve the community as a whole, from preschoolers to the oldest citizens. The purpose of the library is to facilitate informal self-education of all people in the community, enhance the subjects being undertaken in formal education, meet the informational needs of the total population, support education, civic, and cultural activities of groups, and encourage recreation and the constructive use of leisure time (Hendrickson 1973).

The concept of library services for older adults is not new. The movement to provide direct library services to older adults began in the 1950s with establishment of the Adult Education Department of the Cleveland Public Library and the beginning of the department's Live Long and Like It Library Club for adults over sixty. The club served as a study and discussion group that began with a mailing list of fifty and grew to sixteen hundred participants. As a result of the Cleveland program's success, similar programs were established across the United States. In 1956, Congress passed the first Library Services Act which recognized the need for libraries to expand their community service operations. Preparations for the 1961 White House Conference on Aging spurred an intense interest by libraries to serve older adults. Between 1957 and 1961 the American Library Association (ALA) established the Adult Services Division and appointed a permanent Committee on Library Services to the Aging (in the 1970s, renamed Library Service to an Aging Population). In 1957, the Office of Education funded the committee to conduct a survey of library services to older adults. The study revealed that many libraries were offering some special services to older adults, such as supplying books, publicizing materials for the older adult, providing services to the homebound, and working with other agencies serving older adults (Turock 1982).

In 1964, Congress approved amendments to the Library Services and Construction Act (LSCA), formerly called the Library Services Act, which provided funding for the construction of libraries. This legislation and funding enabled libraries to alter their physical structure to meet the needs of the physically disabled and older adults. Title I of the LSCA also became the primary funding source for the initiation of library programs for older adults.

The LSCA was also responsible for funding the large-print collections and services. In 1966, the thirty-year-old Pratt–Smoot Act was amended to provide a wider range of large-print materials and to make more persons eligible for participation, including older adults who were unable to use conventional books (Turock 1982).

Title III of the Older Americans Act increased library services to the homebound and institutionalized older adult. Even though library services for older adults were being developed and implemented across the United States, many librarians did not have the educational background and training to provide these services. In 1965, Title II-B of the Higher Education Act provided funding for workshops, institutes, and research programs that would provide the special training needed (Turock 1982).

In preparation for the 1971 White House Conference on Aging, the U.S. Office of Education and the Cleveland Public Library conducted an extensive study of library services, the National Survey of Library Services to the Aging, which revealed that library services for older adults had not increased at a pace consistent with the increase in the older adult population. The researchers concluded that development had been inhibited by a lack of recognition of services to older adults in federal, state, and local library plans. As a result of the survey findings, an amendment was added to the LSCA through Title IV, Older Readers Service, which was passed into law in 1973. This title proposed that the federal government provide a program of grants to states for older readers' services. The title has never been funded. There are several contributing factors to the failure of the program: The library community did not instigate the resolution for the title and did not push for appropriations (Turock 1982).

The 1981 White House Conference on Aging was nonproductive in terms of library service to the aging. Conference coordinators denied the ALA's request for an official delegate and would not permit the distribution of literature by the association. Even though the 1981 White House Conference was disappointing, some progress has been made in library services for older adults (Turock 1982).

For many years, special programs from public and state libraries have provided library services to the aging via bookmobiles, cable television, and books-by-mail. Many bookmobiles are provided with hydraulic lifts that raise patrons into the bookmobile, making accessibility easier. Books-by-mail connect the older learner with a free, prepaid mailing of selected readings, including large-print materials. Regular on-site library programs have been established in which older adults participate in discussions, films, videos, arts and crafts demonstrations, exhibits of older adults' hobbies, concerts, forums on consumer issues and health concerns, and life-enrichment programs (Manheimer 1984). Many of the library programs are brought directly to retirement and senior centers and in some cases transportation is provided to the library for special programs (Casey 1984).

One outstanding packaged educational program for older adults available to public libraries is the Discovery through the Humanities program (mentioned in Chapter 1) available from the NCOA (1991a, 1991b). For a complete description of the program, see the humanities program section of this chapter.

Librarians and volunteers make visits to the homebound, residents of nursing homes, and other institutional settings providing reading materials and many times reading the materials to their audience.

Talking books and closed-captioned video tapes are also provided by the public library. These materials are excellent resources for the visually and hearing impaired older adult (AARP 1991).

Public libraries also serve as an information and referral service for educational opportunities. Older adults may acquire information on where to learn a specific skill, who teaches desired courses, where to get a specific type of educational program, and what the eligibility requirements are for the program (Turock 1982).

There are many library programs available to older adults today. The Brooklyn Public Library's Service to the Aging (SAGE) program for older adults is a nationally-recognized example of what can be accomplished (Hales-Mabry 1990).

The SAGE project's older adult volunteer program sends older people into the community to establish library-based senior groups, to organize educational programs using films, lectures, and television, to oversee trips to cultural events, and to expand the homebound service. These volunteers recruit older adults to teach minicourses on crafts, art, music, and photography. They also organize intergenerational projects that bring older adults in touch with young children (Turock 1982).

The Monroe County Library System (MCLS) in Rochester, New York, provides a program of live entertainment for and by older adults. Older adult performers include magicians, pianists, and collectors. Another service of MCLS is helping older adults learn skills of advocacy on their own behalf. The older adult advocates have presented their views to local, state, and federal offices on various issues. MCLS also publishes a directory of services for older adults, nursing homes, and housing for seniors. Older adult patrons write a newsletter, *Sunburst*, that is sponsored and published by MCLS (Turock 1982).

As the older adult population grows, so does library service to older adults. There was a new emphasis in the 1970s and 1980s on educating librarians to provide library and information services for older adults, and attention was given to meeting the needs of the aging by meeting the needs of their service providers (Turock 1982). That emphasis appears to have declined in recent years.

In 1987, the Library Services to an Aging Population (LSAP) committee of the Reference and Adult Services Division (RASD) of the ALA prepared

Guidelines of a Library Service to Older Adults, which was adopted by the RASD Board of Directors (ALA 1987). The guidelines provided an important standard of ideal service to older adults that spanned information services concerning preretirement and later life career opportunities for utilizing older persons as resources for intergenerational programming. The policy implications of the Guidelines will be discussed further in Chapter 4.

Humanities and Arts Programs

Humanities programs are learning experiences based on the study of history, literature, philosophy, and history and criticism of the arts. An information paper, "Lifelong Learning for an Aging Society," prepared by the U.S. Senate Special Committee on Aging (1991b) cites David Shuldiner's definition of humanities programs as educational programs that explore and interpret the human experience. Shuldiner contends that good humanities programs involve participants in lively discussion, critical thinking, and life review, all of which add information and insight to the topics at hand.

A major development in this direction took place in 1976 with the establishment of the Senior Center Humanities Program by the NCOA with a grant from the NEH. The program was designed to provide life enrichment and self-discovery through the humanities (Lowy and O'Connor 1986). In 1984, the program expanded to other sites besides senior centers and was renamed Discovery Through the Humanities. The program is organized around informal discussion groups which are initiated in local communities.

NCOA lends Discovery materials on literature, history, philosophy, and the arts to any group or organization that serves older adults. Some fifteen different large-print anthologies are used as a basis for a discussion series inviting participants to explore the works of distinguished writers and artists, to relate what they read and hear to their own experiences, and to consider issues of profound meaning for every generation. At the local community level, older adults meet on a regular basis to reflect on the readings and to share their responses with the guidance of discussion leaders. Today, the NCOA humanities program is offered free of charge at libraries, community colleges, retirement communities, senior centers, nutrition sites, nursing homes, adult day-care centers, housing complexes, churches, and synagogues. For a small fee to organizations, the NCOA provides the program materials, discussion leader guides, publicity materials, and audiotapes for conducting the program (NCOA 1991a).

Organization of the program requires a volunteer discussion group leader, a meeting place for twenty people or less to meet, eight to twelve weekly meetings, and a promotional program to recruit participants. The Humanities program encourages new interest in cultural, educational, and social activities that translates into expanded participation in community events (NCOA 1991a).

The Discovery through the Humanities programs are based on different themes. The program is organized into the following units:

1. We Got There on the Train
2. A Family Album
3. Americans and the Land
4. The Remembered Past: 1914–1945
5. Work and Life
6. The Search for Meaning
7. In the Old Ways
8. The Heritage of the Future
9. Words and Music
10. Exploring Values
11. Portraits and Pathways
12. Art in Life
13. The Family, the Courts, and the Constitution
14. Roll on, River
15. Remembering World War II

Many other types of humanities programs are attractive to older adults. Esther Mackintosh, in conjunction with the Federation of State Humanities Councils (FSHC), has compiled a resource book, *Humanities Programming for Older Adults*, in which she reports that many state humanities councils purposely publicize to and recruit older adults into humanities programs. She contends that older adults are a ready and growing audience for these programs; they have the time to devote to humanities activities as participants and volunteers, and they are a responsive and interested audience because they seek out intellectual stimulation. The lifetime of experience that older adults bring to these programs will only serve to enrich and enliven the programs. No other age group can provide the oral history as older adults can. Older adults who are homebound or institutionalized may benefit from the intellectual and social qualities that humanities programs have to offer (Mackintosh 1988).

For the past twenty-three years, Hospital Audiences, Inc. (HAI) has brought arts and humanities programming to over seven million people in New York City, including the frail elderly. City, state, and federal agencies—as well as the private sector—support HAI. It has three components: (1) institution oriented, (2) community oriented, and (3) advocacy. The institutional component provides the In-Facility Program which brings live music, dance, and theater by professional artists into institutions. One of these programs, the Senior Composers Program, enables composers to share their talents and experiences as performers for the aged. The community-oriented Access Program provides an opportunity for thousands of homebound, frail elderly to attend cultural events throughout the year. These events include the New York Philharmonic and Metropolitan Opera concerts in the parks, the Delacorte Theater, and Macy's Fourth of July Fireworks and Thanksgiving Day Parade. Daytime appearances of renowned artists at auditoriums selected for accessibility are also available. In its advocacy role, HAI has formed the Arts Access Task Force, a consortium between HAI, the Arts and Business Council, Inc., and the New York Foundation for the Arts. The mission of the task force is to make the arts more accessible to people with disabilities. A guide to neighborhood restaurants, movies, and other leisure sites for and by consumers with disabilities, *Access NY*, is available from the HAI office (HAI 1992).

Another unique program is Museum One, which offers arts and humanities programming to thousands of older adults sixty years of age and older in the Washington, D.C. area at more than 100 facilities, including nursing homes, retirement communities, senior centers, adult day-care centers, and senior apartment complexes.

Programming includes course titles such as: Impressionism, American Heritage and Traditions, Renaissance Artists, Modern Art, Afro-American Art, Art and Aging, American Women Artists, and Latin American Art.

Special courses and workshops are designed for intense geriatric rehabilitation of mentally ill, hearing impaired, and blind and visually impaired older adults in hospitals, senior centers, and retirement communities.

In addition to local programming, Museum One has developed educational and training materials, called Enriching Life through the Humanities: Workshops for Practitioners in Aging. These materials—designed specifically for professionals working with older adults—focus on how staff can utilize the arts to better communicate with their groups and clients (Hart 1992).

Other programs with strong arts orientations range from Liz Lerman's intergenerational dance troupe, Dancers of the Third Age, to the Senior Neighbors of Chattanooga's drama ensemble, the Ripe and Ready Players. In general, senior theater has enjoyed rapid expansion of amateur performance groups and even a yearly conference. Some arts programs mix creative dramatics with a therapeutic orientation, such as the New York–based Elders Share the Arts (ESTA) organization which combines living history and performance or designs creative movement exercises that are both expressive and therapeutic (Fisher 1989). Considerable work using music therapeutically has been done with Alzheimer's patients and others suffering from dementia.

Senior Centers

A senior center is a physical facility, resulting from or part of a community planning process, which offers a wide variety of services and activities for older adults (Krout 1989). Senior centers are the outgrowth of senior clubs that can be traced back to 1870. These senior clubs served as associations of peers providing social support for their members (Gelfand 1988). In 1943, the first senior center, the William Hodson Community Center, was established specifically for low-income elderly in New York City by the Public Welfare Department under the direction of Harry Levine and Gertrude Landau. Social workers in the community have been credited with the idea of senior centers because they recognized the need for human contact and communication required by their older clientele. These social workers concluded that older adults could benefit from a setting that would enable them to socialize and participate in activities with other older adults. As a result of the Hodson Community Center, other centers began to develop in San Francisco (1947); Philadelphia (1948); and Bridgeport, Connecticut (1951) (Lowy and O'Connor 1986).

In 1959, the first state senior center association was organized in Ohio. During the late 1950s, there were approximately 200 senior centers throughout the United States. These centers were supported by local resources and sponsored by nonprofit organizations and/or local government agencies (departments of social service or recreation). At this time there was no federal or state legislation in place that funded the senior center concept (Krout 1989).

In 1962, the NCOA published "Centers for Older People: Guide for Programs and Facilities," an overview of the concept and operation of senior centers. This was the first national attempt to provide a comprehensive overview of senior centers. In 1963, the NCOA held its first annual conference of senior centers (Leanse 1978).

During the next decade, the multiservice senior center concept began to flourish. Activities and services available at these centers included hot meals and nutrition education, health education, employment services, transportation assistance, social work services, educational activities, creative arts programs, recreation, leadership, and volunteer opportunities (Lowy and O'Connor 1986).

In the 1970s, federal legislation began making funds available for the development of senior centers. Title V, Section 501 of the Older Americans Act was amended to include the new "Multipurpose Senior Centers" title. Title V provided funds for the renovation or construction of senior centers. Title III of the Act then made operational monies available for the development and delivery of specific services (Gelfand 1988).

In 1970, the NCOA sponsored the National Institute of Senior Centers (NISC), a network of 1,200 centers in all parts of the country. By the late 1980s the NCOA reported 9,000 senior centers being in existence in the United States (Krout 1989). In 1991, the NISC reported that approximately eight million older adults participate in senior centers nationwide (U.S. Senate Special Committee on Aging 1991b). The NISC classifies the senior center services into three categories: individual, group, and community. The individual services include counseling, employment, and health maintenance. Group services involve recreational, nutritional, and educational activities as well as group social work. Participants in senior centers provide services to the local community through volunteer work in community institutions or organizations (Krout 1989). Senior center services depend on the resources, facilities, and community support available. Many of these services can be provided by the center staff. When this is not feasible, appropriate agency staff are assigned to the center or the agencies rotate through the center (Gelfand 1984).

While some senior centers provide a wide range of offerings, many provide largely recreational and educational activities (Krout 1989). The recreation–education component of senior center programming varies with availability of community resources and interests of participants. Some of the more common activities include arts and crafts, nature studies, science and outdoor life, drama, physical activity, music, dance, table games, special social activities, literary activities, excursions, hobby or special interest groups, speakers, lectures, movies, forums, round tables, and community service projects (Gelfand 1988). As mentioned earlier, one popular educational program used by senior centers is the NCOA Humanities Program.

At one senior center in Brooklyn, New York, off-campus instruction in the liberal arts has been conducted under the auspices of the Institute of Study for Older Adults. Under the direction of the Institute, members of local senior centers help design courses and the local community colleges provide faculty to teach them on site. Liberal arts courses and self-help instruction are popular among the clientele that attend these centers (Moody 1988).

In Iowa City, Iowa, approximately 75,000 older adults were served in 1991 at the Iowa City/Johnson County Senior Center. Educational courses are offered in the applied arts, performing arts, art appreciation, crafts, exercise, and computers. Special workshops are also featured with topics varying from medication to chair caning. In Sioux City, Iowa, at the Siouxland Senior Center, a program called Talk Show was developed and implemented in the 1970s providing opportunities for older adults to meet newsmakers, discuss current events, or talk with a doctor or lawyer. The program has made many changes over the years. The program is held weekly from 10:30 A.M. to 12:00 P.M., where approximately sixty-five older adults meet to hear about a selected topic and discuss it (U.S. Senate Special Committee on Aging 1991b).

One key problem faced by many senior centers is an aging in place phenomenon. Senior center populations are, on the average, growing older, and centers are having an increasingly difficult time attracting younger retirees. Educational programs provide one avenue for attracting new participants.

Older Adult Service and Information System (OASIS)

OASIS is a consortium between business and not-for-profit organizations designed to challenge and enrich the lives of adults age fifty-five and older. Educational, cultural, health, and volunteer outreach programs are offered at the OASIS centers to provide participants an opportunity to remain independent and active in community affairs (OASIS 1991).

Marylen Mann, Executive Director of OASIS National, and Margie Wolcott May established OASIS in St. Louis in 1982. The May Department Stores Company. the major national sponsor, provides OASIS with dedicated meeting and activity space in many of its stores. Initial support for the program was provided by the Administration on Aging (OASIS 1991). The program is administered nationally from St. Louis. The national office establishes program quality requirements and overall management and operations guidelines. Management training, new programs and materials, and ongoing support to the local program directors is also provided by the national headquarters.

Currently there are centers operating in Portland, Los Angeles (two centers), Long Beach, San Diego, Escondido, Phoenix (two centers), Tucson, Denver (two centers), Houston, San Antonio, St. Louis (three centers), Chicago, Indianapolis, Akron, Cleveland (two centers), Rochester, Buffalo, Pittsburgh, Hyattsville, Boston, Enfield, and Waterbury, with over 129,000 members participating. Each center has permanent and specially designed space for offices, student lounges, and meeting rooms. In many cities, a local hospital and a not-for-profit community agency serve as sponsors, along with the May Company-owned department stores. People from all socioeconomic, cultural, and educational backgrounds are invited to participate. The OASIS membership is free, and programs have minimal or no charges. Courses are scheduled by calendar quarters or trimesters and are held during daytime hours, usually once a week from one to twelve weeks. Courses are offered in areas of visual arts, music, drama, creative writing, contemporary issues, history, science, exercise, and health. Many courses are held in collaboration with local cultural and educational institutions (OASIS 1991).

Volunteer outreach is an important component of the OASIS program. Many participants are trained in the Older Adult Peer Leadership (OAPL) program to teach classes in the community and to work in intergenerational programs helping young children. In 1990, more than 2,000 volunteers gave over 110,000 hours of their time to run the OASIS sites (OASIS 1991).

The OASIS Centers in St. Louis are housed in three Famous-Barr department stores and other area locations. The programs are sponsored by Famous-Barr and its parent company, the May Company, as well as the Jewish Hospital of St. Louis and Washington University School of Medicine. Volunteers are on duty from 10:00 A.M. to 3:00 P.M., Monday through Friday, to enroll students sixty years of age and older in the classes. All health-related classes are free of charge, and most other programs require a nominal fee of one dollar. A variety of courses are offered including wellness, liberal arts, and vocational training. OASIS/OAPL are provided to older adults throughout the St. Louis Metro area by the OAPL Outreach program. Volunteers are trained in subject matter and leadership skills and conduct these classes at libraries, churches, residential and senior centers, and other sites (OASIS 1991). In 1990, the St. Louis OASIS Centers established the OASIS Award to recognize outstanding volunteer contributions to the St. Louis community made by the area's older adults.

Special events and travel programs are also an integral part of the OASIS Centers in St. Louis. Events such as the Opera Theatre St. Louis, Picnic at the St. Louis Zoo, and an Evening at Queeny Pops provide OASIS participants an opportunity to experience local cultural activities free or at a nominal charge. Travel programs to the Winston Churchill Memorial, Inn of the Ozarks, McDonnell–Douglas aerospace center, or a cruise on the Belle of St. Louis (just to name a few) provide adventure and new learning experiences for the OASIS members (OASIS 1991).

The OASIS Center is the central gathering point for classes, seminars, and special events offered throughout the year. OASIS strives to empower adults fifty-five and older to live independently and continue to expand their knowledge and remain productive individuals (OASIS 1992).

Chautauqua

The Chautauqua Institution is a 750-acre complex on the shores of Chautauqua Lake in southwestern New York. Established over a century ago, the Institution provides educational, religious, recreational, and cultural opportunities for persons of all ages from all parts of the United States and abroad (Chautauqua Institution 1992).

Chautauqua Institution's 55 Plus Weekend, established twenty years ago, is an important component of the multifaceted Chautauqua experience. Each weekend a topic is presented through discussion, workshops, lectures, films, cassette tapes, or any other appropriate means. Cultural programs are scheduled for Saturday evenings. Weekend themes and discussions have included topics on political ideologies, the presidential campaigns, and election years. Housing and meals are available on site. The registration fee covers all programs and accommodations. In addition to the weekend programs, a special week-long program, The Chautauqua Experience, introduces older adults to lectures, music, recreation, drama, and group fellowship (Chautauqua Institution 1992).

Shepherd's Centers

A Shepherd's Center is a nonprofit community organization sponsored by a coalition of religious congregations committed to the delivery of services and programs for older adults. In 1972, the first Shepherd's Center was founded by Dr. Elbert C. Cole in Kansas City, Missouri. Twenty-three churches and synagogues joined in an interfaith effort to provide a ministry by, with, and for older adults. In 1972, the original Center began with only six volunteers. Today, eighty-seven Shepherd's Centers in twenty-five states comprise a network of 15,000 volunteers serving over 175,000 older adults. The services and programs of the Shepherd's Center are designed to empower older adults to lead creative, productive, meaningful, and interdependent lives. The Shepherd's Centers are controlled and operated by older adults (Shepherd's Centers of America 1991).

Dr. Cole reports that Shepherd's Centers are an expression of congregations in a defined area. By working together, the congregations may accomplish what can not be done alone. The Shepherd's Centers focus on neighborhoods or specifically defined territories. The participants develop an attitude of ownership which empowers them to take responsibility for their well being. Centers are governed by a self-perpetuating board of trustees, appropriately representative and ecumenical and with age-relevant skills and interests, that is committed to the overall concept of the centers. Church and synagogue property is used for office space and major programs and services. Duplication of services is a problem that Shepherd's Centers seek to avoid. The centers encourage partnerships with other agencies serving older adults, always giving credit and recognition where due. Congregations, participants, friends, businesses, civic organizations and clubs, United Way, public funds, and foundations are the funding sources for the Centers. The Shepherd's Center concept is a new social model with a healthy view of life after retirement. The idea is applicable to any ethnic, economic, or cultural group of older adults (Maves and Bock 1990).

One of the many programs offered by the Shepherd's Centers is the Adventures in Learning program. The program utilizes older adults as both teachers and students, planners and participants. Classes are normally held weekly, biweekly, or monthly. The purpose of the educational program is to provide an environment where older adults may share their knowledge, talents, skills, and new interests with their peers. A committee of volunteers makes the program decisions regarding curriculum, faculty, marketing, and evaluation. This committee is composed of faculty and students with background experience in education, public relations, administration, the arts, health, and clerical services. Most of the teachers are older adults who volunteer their time, knowledge, and skills. The educational program allows students to choose their own subjects. If the student finds a course that does not meet his or her needs, the student may then try a different class. Many classes may require advanced registration due to space limitations (Maves and Bock 1990).

Students participate in the Adventures in Learning program for the joy of learning without the pressures of tests, grades, and academic credits. Courses are organized on an academic semester or quarter basis with classes being held during the daylight hours. Some Centers are closed during the month of August and between sessions. During the long breaks, some Centers offer alternative programs, such as short-term classes, picnics, trips, or fairs to provide an opportunity for those who count on the friendship and stimulation of the Center's activities. Registration fees are kept low, with a maximum of fifteen dollars for a full quarter of classes. All classes are held on one day of the week in the same location; usually a church or synagogue. Hour-long courses are offered in current events, history, philosophy, literature, religion, and art; needlework, crafts, or painting; exercise, yoga, nutrition, or health information; and travelogues.

Noontime fellowship is an important part of the Adventures in Learning program. Students, teachers, and volunteers share a meal and conversation. During this noontime forum, the program coordinator makes announcements, recognizes teachers, celebrates accomplishments, and welcomes and introduces new participants in the program. Musical entertainment, a theatre presentation, an address by a community leader, or a guest speaker on a topic of interest to the students rounds out the program. The planning committee of the Adventures in Learning program remains interfaith. Protestant, Catholic, and Jewish persons serve on the committee (Maves and Bock 1990).

Workplace Education

Workplace education or training programs are not a new phenomenon. For years, preservice and in-service training for workers has taken place in the private and public sectors. However, traditionally these programs have been reserved for younger workers because older worker were forced to retire at or before age sixty-five.

Social policy has promoted retirement instead of employment for older adults. The past twenty-eight years reflect a slight trend in new policy formation that encourages continuing participation of older adults in the labor force rather than early retirement. People are beginning to believe that working beyond traditional retirement age will help older adults experience self-worth while continuing to contribute to society (Moody 1988).

These trends are evident in federal laws, such as the Age Discrimination in Employment Act (ADEA) of 1967, which prohibits hiring or firing on the basis of age. In the following decade, further advances were made in laws which focused specifically on the older worker. In 1978, the mandatory retirement age for older workers was pushed back to seventy and, in 1986, mandatory retirement at any age was eliminated for almost all workers (Long 1990).

As shown in Table 2.2, the U.S. Bureau of Labor Statistics reports that in 1989, males in the civilian work force fifty-five to sixty-four years of age totaled 6.8 million or 67.2 percent and males sixty-five and older totaled 2.0 million or 16.6 percent. Females in the civilian labor force fifty-five to sixty-four years old totaled 5.1 million or 45.0 percent and women sixty-five and older totaled 1.4 million or 8.4 percent. By the year 2000, males in the civilian labor force fifty-five to sixty-four years of age will total 7.8 million or 68.1 percent and males sixty-five and older will total 2.0 million or 14.7 percent. Females fifty-five to sixty-four years of age will total 6.1 million or 49.0 percent and females sixty-five years and older will total 1.4 million or 7.6 percent (U.S. Bureau of the Census 1991).

As shown in Table 2.3, the U.S. Bureau of the Census (1980) reports that white males eighty-five years and older constituted 4.2 percent of the labor force and white females eighty-five years and older constituted 1.5 percent of the labor force. Nonwhite males eighty-five years and older constituted 4.3 percent of the labor force. Nonwhite females eighty-five years and older constituted 3.0 percent of the labor force (Rosenwaike 1985).

Today, employees are facing new problems. The Committee for Economic Development (CED), a private, nonprofit, and nonpartisan research and education organization made up of 250 top business executives and university presidents, has stated that the United States has now entered a time when there are fewer young job entrants into the workforce and an increasing older adult population. The CED contends that business and policy makers must develop qualified workers to fill the increasing number of knowledge- and technology-driven jobs (U.S. Senate Special Committee on Aging 1991b). The tight labor market will provide incentives for employees to encourage older workers to remain in the workforce. By the year 2000, over 50 percent of the workforce will be thirty-five to fifty-five years of age (Moody 1986). One trend that is contributing to this projection is the number of women having children after age thirty-five. We will have more sixty-year-old mothers of college-aged young adults, which may keep women and men in the workforce longer to pay college costs and other expenses of their children (Long 1990).

With the changes in laws regarding age and employment, higher costs of living, the reduced labor market of younger workers, and an increasing elderly population, some corporations are now designing and implementing retraining programs for older workers. McDonald's Corporation has an educational program, McMasters, that provides skills training and job placement for persons fifty-five and older. Eighty to one hundred employees are trained annually per McMasters program. General Electric has established a special Technical Renewal Program in its Aerospace Electronic System Department. This program provides training to engineers to update their skills in order to stay current with the new technology.

The private sector is not alone in its pursuit of training the older worker. A local government program has been established in Union City, New Jersey, that trains older adults to take care of children in training centers. The program has been accredited by the National Association for the Education of Young Children (NAEYA), an accrediting organization of childcare programs. A unique program in Boston, Operation ABLE (Ability Based on Long Experience), is a consortium effort between industry, government, and private foundations. The program provides computer training programs to prepare older workers to successfully compete in the workplace (U.S. Senate Special Committee on Aging 1991b).

Many older workers are still choosing to retire before the age of seventy, but business and industry have major training responsibilities for those who wish to remain in the work force (Peterson 1990); however, these responsibilities are

Table 2.2
Civilian Labor Force and Participation Rates by Race, Hispanic Origin, Sex, and Age,
1970–1989, and Projections, 2000

Race, sex and age	Civilian Labor Force (millions)						
	1970	1975	1980	1985	1988	1989	2000
Total[1]	82.8	93.8	106.9	115.5	121.7	123.9	141.1
White	73.6	82.8	93.6	99.9	104.8	106.4	119.0
Male	46.0	50.3	54.5	36.5	58.3	59.0	63.3
Female	27.5	32.5	39.1	43.5	46.4	47.4	55.7
Black[2]	9.2	9.3	10.9	12.4	13.2	13.5	16.5
Male	5.2	5.0	5.6	6.2	5.5	5.7	8.0
Female	4.0	4.2	5.3	5.1	6.6	6.8	8.5
Hispanic[3]	(NA)	(NA)	6.1	7.7	9.0	9.3	14.3
Male	(NA)	(NA)	3.8	4.7	5.4	5.6	8.3
Female	(NA)	(NA)	2.3	3.0	3.6	3.7	6.0
Male	51.2	56.3	61.5	64.4	66.9	67.8	74.3
16-19 years	4.0	4.8	5.0	4.1	4.2	4.1	4.4
16 and 17 years	1.8	2.1	2.1	1.7	1.7	1.6	1.9
18 and 19 years	2.2	2.7	2.9	2.5	2.4	2.5	2.5
20-24 years	5.7	7.5	8.6	8.3	7.6	7.5	6.9
25-34 years	11.3	14.2	17.0	18.8	19.7	19.9	16.6
35-44 years	10.5	10.4	11.8	14.5	16.1	16.6	20.2
45-54 years	10.4	10.4	9.9	9.9	10.6	10.9	16.4
55-64 years	7.1	7.0	7.2	7.1	6.8	6.8	7.8
65 years and over	2.2	1.9	1.9	1.8	2.0	2.0	2.0
Female	31.5	37.5	45.5	51.1	54.7	56.0	66.8
16-19 years	3.2	4.1	4.4	3.8	3.9	3.8	4.4
16 and 17 years	1.3	1.7	1.8	1.5	1.6	1.5	1.8
18 and 19 years	1.9	2.4	2.5	2.3	2.3	2.3	2.6
20-24 years	4.9	6.2	7.3	7.4	6.9	6.7	6.7
25-34 years	5.7	8.7	12.3	14.7	15.8	16.0	15.1
35-44 years	6.0	6.5	8.6	11.6	13.4	14.0	18.6
45-54 years	6.5	6.7	7.0	7.5	8.5	9.0	14.4
55-64 years	4.2	4.3	4.7	4.9	5.0	5.1	6.1
65 years and over	1.1	1.0	1.2	1.2	1.3	1.4	1.4

Source: U.S. Bureau of Labor Statistics, *Employment and Earnings*, monthly; *Monthly Labor Review* (November 1989); and unpublished data.
Note: For civilian noninstitutional population 16 years old and over. Annual averages of monthly figures. Rates are based on annual average civilian noninstitutional population of each specified group and represent proportion of each specified group in the civilian labor force. Based on *Current Population Survey*. NA: Not available.
[1]Beginning 1975, includes other races not shown separately.
[2]For 1970, African-American and other.
[3]Persons of Hispanic origin may be of any race.

often unmet. To assist those older workers that wish to remain in the work force, the AARP has developed workshops and a booklet, *Using the Experience of a Lifetime*, which provides an in-depth look at creative programs and opportunities for older workers (U.S. Senate Special Committee on Aging 1991b).

Race, sex and age	Participation Rate (percent)						
	1970	1975	1980	1985	1988	1989	2000
Total[1]	60.4	61.2	63.8	64.8	65.9	66.5	69.0
White	50.2	61.5	64.1	65.0	66.2	66.7	69.5
Male	90.0	78.7	78.2	77.0	76.9	77.1	76.6
Female	42.5	45.9	51.2	54.1	56.4	57.2	62.9
Black[2]	61.8	58.8	61.0	62.9	63.8	64.2	66.5
Male	76.5	71.0	70.6	70.8	71.0	71.0	71.4
Female	49.5	48.9	53.2	56.5	58.0	58.7	62.5
Hispanic[3]	(NA)	(NA)	64.0	64.6	67.4	67.6	69.9
Male	(NA)	(NA)	81.4	80.3	81.9	82.0	90.3
Female	(NA)	(NA)	47.4	49.3	53.2	53.5	59.4
Male	79.7	77.9	77.4	76.3	76.2	76.4	75.9
16-19 years	56.1	59.1	60.5	56.8	56.9	57.9	59.0
16 and 17 years	47.0	48.6	50.1	45.1	46.1	46.3	48.9
18 and 19 years	66.7	70.6	71.3	68.9	68.1	69.2	69.7
20-24 years	83.3	84.5	85.9	85.0	85.0	85.3	86.5
25-34 years	96.4	95.2	95.2	94.7	94.3	94.4	94.1
35-44 years	96.9	95.6	95.5	95.0	94.5	94.5	94.3
45-54 years	94.3	92.1	91.2	91.0	90.9	91.1	90.5
55-64 years	83.0	75.6	72.1	67.9	67.0	67.2	68.1
65 years and over	26.8	21.6	19.0	15.8	16.5	16.6	14.7
Female	43.3	46.3	51.5	54.5	56.5	57.4	52.5
16-19 years	44.0	49.1	52.9	52.1	53.6	53.9	59.5
16 and 17 years	34.9	40.2	43.6	42.1	44.0	44.5	49.8
18 and 19 years	153.5	58.1	61.9	61.7	62.9	62.5	69.0
20-24 years	57.7	64.1	68.9	71.8	72.7	72.4	77.9
25-34 years	45.0	54.9	65.5	70.9	72.7	73.5	82.4
35-44 years	51.1	55.8	65.5	71.8	75.2	76.0	84.9
45-54 years	54.4	54.6	59.9	54.4	69.0	70.5	76.5
55-64 years	43.0	40.9	41.3	42.0	43.5	45.0	49.0
65 years and over	9.7	8.2	8.1	7.3	7.9	8.4	7.6

SUPPORT OF OLDER LEARNERS

In the 1990s, there is no central system which supports or monitors educational activities for older adults. Programs have developed around the preferences of administrators and/or the needs of the local community. This process has responded to the immediate needs of the older adult learner but has not provided program categories or models that could be easily described or replicated in other sites. The federal government has encouraged the public and private sector employers and community organizations to offer educational opportunities that will assist older adults in holding or gaining contributive roles in society (Peterson 1987; Manheimer 1987–1988).

To date there are a number of major federal statutes which authorize the provision of federal assistance for adult and continuing education. Much of

Table 2.3
Labor Force Participation Rates of Persons 85 Years and Over by Race and Sex, 1950–1980 (percentage of extreme aged in labor force)

Race and sex	1950	1960	1970[a]	1980
White				
Male	6.6	6.9	6.6	4.2
Female	1.2	1.9	3.2	1.5
Nonwhite				
Male	9.8	8.0	8.8	4.3
Female	2.1	3.1	5.7	3.0

Sources: U.S. Bureau of the Census, 1953a: table 118; 1964: table 194; 1970 Census Public Use Sample; 1980 Census Public Use Microdata Sample.
[a] Ages 85 to 99 years only.

the federal assistance is channeled through the appropriate state agency, which in turn disperses the funds at the local government level. The following is a brief description of a few of the programs available.

The Older Americans Act authorizes the state agencies on aging to provide education and training to adults sixty and older in the areas of consumer education, continuing education, health education, preretirement education, financial planning, and other education and training services. The Adult Education Act provides a means by which all adults (young and old) may obtain basic educational skills (U.S. Senate Special Committees on Aging 1991b).

In addition to federal policy, many states have implemented tuition-fee waiver policies (for a complete listing of states and policies, see Appendix E). Some research has been devoted to studying tuition-fee waiver programs available to older adults (see Appendix E for a state-by-state analysis of policies). According to the research, the minimum age requirement varies from sixty to sixty-five. Many institutions allow seniors to enroll for credit, others specify audit only, and many limit enrollment on a space-available basis only. Moyer and Lago have found that cost is neither a barrier nor an incentive to participation in education programs by older adults (Leptak 1987).

Twenty-nine states have established some sort of guideline within their statutes on the subject of tuition-fee waiver programs. Nine additional states have state policies to waive or reduce tuition, mostly on a space-available basis. Alabama, Arizona, Colorado, District of Columbia, Iowa, Maine, Mississippi, Missouri, Nebraska, Pennsylvania, Vermont, West Virginia, and Wyoming have remained silent both in their statutes and in their written state policies (U.S. Senate Special Committee on Aging 1991b).

As the number of older adults increases along with an interest in educational pursuits, the continuing development of knowledge about the older learner will assist institutions of higher education in planning appropriate educational opportunities for this segment of our population.

In summarizing, many leading adult educators and gerontologists believe that education plays an important role in helping older adults to solve problems—both their own and those of others in their communities. Some researchers contend that education can foster older adults' self-reliance and independence by increasing their self-esteem and strengthening their mental and physical health. Education enables the older adult to cope with many practical and psychological problems in a constantly changing world. Others emphasize later life as a special time for deeply reflective learning and a form of practical wisdom that can benefit all generations. Education also helps to strengthen their contribution to society. Many older people strive for expression and learning, which is provided by education (Swindell 1991).

Current U.S. elderly are the best educated and most prosperous generation of older adults in the nation's history. Older adults are mixing work, leisure, education, and personal growth in new ways. According to some experts, in the years ahead older persons' accomplishments will be even more surprising (Thorson and Waskel 1990).

How, then, does a society prepare for the exciting challenges brought to education by new waves of retirement-age persons? This chapter has reviewed some of the emerging trends and organizations. Our next chapter looks at and compares the characteristics of some of the most innovative forms of education for seniors while exploring a new paradigm of the older learner.

NOTE

A portion of this chapter is based on D. Moskow-McKenzie, "Lifelong Learning," in *Older Americans Almanac*, edited by R. J. Manheimer (Detroit: Gale Research, Inc., 1994).

REFERENCES

American Association of Retired Persons (AARP). 1991. Resourceful Aging: Today and Tommorrow. Conference proceedings. Vol. 5. Lifelong Education. Washington, D.C.: AARP.

American Library Association (ALA). 1987. "Guidelines for Library Service to Older Adults." *RQ* 26(4): 444–447.

Baltes, P. B. 1993. "The Aging Mind: Potential and Limits." *The Gerontologist* 33(5): 580–594.

Brahce, C. I., and W. W. Hunter. 1990. "Leadership Training for Retirement Education," In *Introduction to Educational Gerontology*. Edited by R. H. Sherron and D. B. Lumsden. New York: Hemisphere.

Butler, R. 1963. "The Life Review: An Interpretation of Reminiscence in the Aged."
    Psychiatry 26: 65–76.
Casey, G. M. 1984. *Library Services for the Aging*. Vol. 33. Hamden, Conn.: Library
    Professionals Publications.
Charles, R. R., and C. Bartunek, eds. 1989. "Community College Programs for the
    Older Adult Learner." ERIC Document Reproduction Service No. ED 322 977.
Chautauqua Institution. 1992. "55 Plus" Program for Older Adults brochure. Chau-
    tauqua, N.Y.: Chautauqua Institution.
Clayton, V. P., and J. E. Birren. 1980. "The Development of Wisdom Across the Life
    Span: A Reexamination of an Ancient Topic." In *Life-Span Devleopment and
    Behavior*. Vol. 3. Edited by P. B. Baltes and O. G. Brim. New York: Academic
    Press.
Cross, K. P. 1981. *Adults as Learners*. San Francisco: Jossey-Bass.
Dewey, J. 1938. *Experience and Education*. New York: Macmillan.
Doucette, D., and C. Ventura-Merkel. 1991. *Community College Programs for Older
    Adults—A Status Report*. Washington, D.C.: American Association of Retired
    Persons.
Elderhostel Institute Network (EIN). 1991. *The Institute Movement and Elderhostel:
    A National Overview*. Durham, N.H.: Elderhostel Institute Network.
Erikson, E. 1964. *Insight and Responsibility*. New York: W. W. Norton.
Evangelauf, J. 1992. "Enrollment Projections Revised Upward in New Government
    Analysis." *The Chronicle of Higher Education* 38(20): A1(2).
Fischer, R. B. 1991. "Higher Education Confronts the Age Wave." *Educational
    Record* 15: 14–17.
Fischer, R. B., M. L. Blazey, and H. T. Lipman, eds. 1992. *Students of the Third Age—
    University/College Programs for Retired Adults*. New York: Macmillan.
Fisher, P. P. 1989. *Creative Movement for Older Adults: Exercises for the Fit to Frail*.
    New York: Human Science Press.
Gelfand, D. E. 1984. *The Aging Network: Programs and Services*. 2d ed. New York:
    Springer.
———. 1988. *The Aging Network: Programs and Services*. 3d ed. New York:
    Springer.
Goggin, J. M. 1991. "Elderhostel: The Next Generation." *Aging Today* (February/
    March).
Hales, C. 1985. "How Should the Information Needs of the Aging Be Met? A Delphi
    Response." *The Gerontologist* 25(2): 2.
Hales-Mabry, C. 1990. *Serving the Older Adult, Special Populations in the Library*.
    New York: Haworth Press.
Hart, J. 1992. *Beyond the Tunnel—The Arts and Aging in America*. Washington, D.C.:
    Museum One Publications.
Hendrickson, A. 1973. *A Manual on Planning Educational Programs for Older
    Adults*. Tallahassee, Fla.: Department of Adult Education.
Hospital Audiences, Inc. (HAI). 1992 *HAI News* (Spring).
Kaminsky, M., ed. 1984. *The Uses of Reminiscence: New Ways of Working with Older
    Adults*. New York: Haworth Press.
Knowles, M. 1980. *The Modern Practice of Adult Education: From Androgogy to
    Pedagogy*. New York: Cambridge Books.

Krout, J. A. 1989. *Senior Centers in America*. New York: Greenwood Press.
Labouvie-Vief, G. 1980. "Adaptive Dimensions of Adult Cognition." In *Transitions of Aging*. Edited by N. Datan and N. Lohmann. New York: Academic Press.
Laslett, P. 1991. *A Fresh Map of Life, The Emergence of the Third Age*. Cambridge, Mass.: Harvard University Press.
Leanse, J. 1978. "A Blend of Multi-Dimensional Activities." *Perspective on Aging* 7: 8–13.
Leptak, J. 1987. "Older Adults in Higher Education: A Review of the Literature." Ohio State University: Department of Education: Policy and Leadership. ERIC Document Reproduction Service No. ED 283 021.
Lipman, H. T. 1992. "Instructional Program Design." In *Students of the Third Age— University/College Programs for Retired Adults*. Edited by R. B. Fischer, M. L. Blazey, and H. T. Lipman. New York: Ace/Macmillan.
Long, H. B. 1981. "Taverns and Coffee Houses: Adult Educational Institutions in Colonial America." *Lifelong Learning: The Adult Years* 4: 14–16.
———. 1990. "Educational Gerontology: Trends and Developments in 2000–2010." *Educational Gerontology* 16: 317–326.
Lowy, L., and D. O'Connor. 1986. *Why Education in the Later Years?* Lexington, Mass.: Lexington Books.
Mackintosh, E. 1988. *Humanities Programming for Older Adults*. Washington D.C.: Federation of State Humanities Councils.
Manheimer, R. J. 1984. "Developing Arts and Humanities Programming with the Elderly." In *Adult Services in Action*. Vol. 2. Chicago: American Library Association.
———. 1987–1988. "The Politics & Promise of Cultural Enrichment Programs." *Generations* 12(2): 26–30.
———. 1992. "Creative Retirement in an Aging Society." In *Students of the Third Age— University/College Programs for Retired Adults*. Edited by R. B. Fischer, M. L. Blazey, and H. T. Lipman. New York: Macmillan.
Maves, P. B., and K. Bock, eds. 1990. *Organizational Manual for Shepherd's Center*. Kansas City, Mo.: Shepherd's Center of America.
Meyers, F. 1987. *The Handbook for Learning in Retirement Organizations*. Los Angeles: The Association for Learning in Retirement Organizations.
Moody, H. R. 1976. "Philosophical Presuppositions of Education for Older Adults." *Educational Gerontology* 1: 1–16.
———. 1986. "Late Life Learning in the Information Society." In *Education and Aging*. Edited by D. A. Peterson, J. E. Thornton, and J. E. Birren. Englewood Cliffs, N.J.: Prentice-Hall.
———. 1987. "Education as a Lifelong Process." In *Our Aging Society: Paradox and Promise*. Edited by A. Pifer and L. Bronte. New York: W. W. Norton.
———. 1988. *Abundance of Life: Human Development Policies for An Aging Society*. New York: Columbia University Press.
———. 1990. "Education and the Life Cycle: A Philosophy of Aging." In *Introduction to Educational Gerontology*. 3d ed. Edited by R. N. Sherron and D. B. Lumsden. New York: Hemisphere.
National Council on the Aging (NCOA). 1991a. *Discovery through the Humanities Introductory Handbook*. Washington, D.C.: National Council on the Aging.
———. 1991b. Discovery through the Humanities Program brochure. Washington, D.C.: National Council on the Aging.

Older Adult Service and Information System (OASIS) 1991. Older Adult Service and Information System—OASIS Fact Sheet and Brochure. St. Louis: OASIS.
———. 1992. Summer brochure. St. Louis: OASIS.
O'Donnell, K. M., and W. D. Berkeley. 1980. "Elderhostel: A National Program." *New Directions for Higher Education* 29.
Peterson, D. A. 1981. "Education for the Aging." *Lifelong Learning: The Adult Years* 4: 16–18.
———. 1983. *Facilitating Education for Older Learners*. San Francisco: Jossey-Bass.
———. 1987. "Adult Education." In *The Encyclopedia of Aging*. Edited by G. L. Maddox. New York: Springer.
———. 1990. "A History of the Education of Older Learners." In *Introduction to Educational Gerontology*. 3d ed. Edited by R. H. Sherron and D. B. Lumsden. New York: Hemisphere.
Renaissance Society, The. 1992. The Renaissance Society C.S.U.S. brochure. California State University, Sacramento.
Riley, M. W., and J. W. Riley. 1987. "Changing Meanings of Age in the Aging Society." In *Our Aging Society: Paradox and Promise*. Edited by A. Pifer and L. Bronte. New York: W. W. Norton.
Romaniuk, J. G. 1983. "Development of Educational Programs for Older Adult Learners." *The Gerontologist* 23(3): 313–318.
Rosenwaike, I. 1985. *The Extreme Aged in America—A Portrait of an Expanding Population*. Westport, Conn.: Greenwood Press.
Scanlon, J. 1978. *How to Plan a College Program for Older People*. Washington, D.C.: Academy for Educational Development.
Schaie, K. W. 1975. "Age Changes in Adult Intelligence." In *Aging—Scientific Perspectives and Social Issues*. Edited by D. S. Woodruff and J. E. Birren. New York: D. Van Nostrand.
Shepherd's Centers of America. 1991. *Meeting the Challenge and Opportunity of an Aging Society*. Kansas City, Mo.: Shepherd's Centers of America.
Swindell, R. F. 1991. "Educational Opportunities for Older Persons in Australia: A Rationale for Future Development." *Educational Gerontology* 35(2): 176–177.
Thorson, J. A., and S. A. Waskel. 1990. "Educational Gerontology and the Future." In *Introduction to Educational Gerontology*. 3d ed. Edited by R. N. Sherron and D. B. Lumsden. New York: Hemisphere.
Timmermann, S. 1979. "Older Learners in an Aging Nation: Projections and Guidelines for Planners and Policymakers." Abstract in *Dissertation Abstracts International*.
Turock, B. 1982. *Serving the Older Adult—A Guide to Library Programs and Information Sources*. New York: R. R. Bowker.
U.S. Bureau of the Census. 1991. *Statistical Abstract of the United States 1991*. Washington, D.C.: U.S. Department of Commerce.
U.S. Senate Special Committee on Aging. 1991a. *Aging America, Trends and Projections*. Washington, D.C.: U.S. Senate Special Committee on Aging, the American Association of Retired Persons, the Federal Council on the Aging, and the U.S. Administration on Aging.

U.S. Senate Special Committee on Aging. 1991b. *Lifelong Learning for an Aging Society* (Serial No. 102-J). Washington, D.C.: U.S. Senate Special Committee on Aging.

Ventura, C., and E. H. Worthy. 1982. "Education for Older Adults: A Synthesis of Significant Data." ERIC Document Reproduction Service No. ED 303 607.

Weinstock, R. 1978. *The Graying of the Campus.* New York: Educational Facilities Laboratories. Pamphlet no. 29.

3

The Transformation of Older Learner Programs

As reflected in Chapters 1 and 2, the number and quality of educational programs for older adults has sharply increased during the past twenty years. While how-to program descriptions, single-focus studies of particular programs, and general research on the benefits of education for seniors are increasingly available, there are fewer broad-based investigations of newly emerging programs for older learners or of the organizational forms they have taken. This chapter draws on a 1992–1993 national study of five organizational models of older adult education, forms that give further testimony to an emerging paradigm that links leisure and virtue in retirement.

THE CHANGING PICTURE

Summarizing key factors from Chapters 1 and 2 that led up to the present situation of older adult education, we can attribute the growth of older learner programs to several factors:

- Recommendations that emerged from the 1971 White House Conference on Aging gave emphasis to positive outcomes of education for seniors (McClusky 1971) and to 1973 amendments to the Older Americans Act which encouraged the rapidly expanding network of multipurpose senior centers to include education as part of their mission. However, little federal money was directly appropriated to promoting education for seniors.

- New programs that began to arise through state and local initiatives such as tuition-free policies enabled older adults to audit or take courses for credit on a space-available basis at public colleges and universities.

- Funding from the two national endowments, Arts (NEA) and Humanities (NEH), supported hundreds of projects that attracted older adults to senior centers and public libraries including NCOA's nationally-distributed reading and discussion group series, the Senior Center Humanities Program (later renamed Discovery Through the Humanities).

- On the more pragmatic side, vocational instruction was made available to seniors through passage of the Senior Community Services and Employment Act (Title V of the Older Americans Act).

- The senior population experienced growth, especially that portion coming into retirement with prior high school and college-level educational experience and new expectations to lead an active and involved later life.

Whatever the cause, the percentage of people over fifty-five formally enrolled in courses tripled between 1973 and 1983 (U.S. Department of Education). These figures do not capture the thousands of people like those mentioned in Chapter 1, the Elizabeth Houstons or the Earl and Marabeth Hitchcocks, who have become significantly involved in informal education.

While there is no new data comparable to the 1984 statistics, continued expansion of programs is reflected in the AARP's Directory of Older Adult Education Programs, which has doubled in size over the last ten years. However, a review of the types of institutions serving as hosts for these programs tells an additional story. Tuition-free college programs draw rather few participants and are not widely publicized (O'Connor 1991). In some states the provisions have been rescinded (e.g., Wisconsin in 1992) or are now left to the discretion of individual community college districts. Private and public foundation money for older adult education peaked and declined somewhere in the mid-1980s.

What have augmented or replaced these transitory programs are hundreds of new, community-based institutions, situated at colleges and universities, senior centers, churches and synagogues, and even department stores. Though many of these program models were first introduced in the 1970s or earlier, rapid expansion came in the mid-1980s and continues on an upward trajectory. While Elderhostel, which started in 1975, invites seniors to travel to a distant educational campus to enjoy an already established curriculum and, therefore, is not generally community-based or senior-led, its expansion to 1,200 locations attracting over 300,000 seniors annually also reflects the success of fee-based programs with intellectually challenging courses.

FIVE MODELS OF OLDER ADULT EDUCATION

Of those serving local seniors in their communities, five models have shown distinctive growth, stability, and innovation during the past two to three decades.

1. College- and university-based LRIs, like the NCCCR's College for Seniors, which invite members to share in administrating, governing, and teaching and now number over two hundred with twenty-five new institutes starting each year.

2. Department store-based OASIS institutes, located in some twenty-eight department stores owned by the May Company of St. Louis and attracting over 125,000 people yearly to arts, humanities, health promotion, and volunteer service programs
3. Shepherd's Centers, volunteer-driven coalitions of religious congregations providing services and programs, now boast almost 100 local sites that include the intellectually-stimulating Adventures in Learning program.
4. Community colleges which have attracted thousands of seniors among their constituencies since the early 1970s; in many states, they supplied classes through senior centers at little or no cost. A shortage of state funds in the late 1980s limited or reduced the number of these offerings, but special courses targeted to seniors continue. Some community colleges are shifting to LRI-type member-directed institutes.
5. Senior centers, which have long provided a wide variety of educational programs ranging from nutrition and consumer education to arts and crafts. As might be expected of some 12,000 sites across the country, the professional quality of instruction has been uneven. In a fairly recent trend, some senior centers are moving toward more substantive educational programs that go beyond a recreational level, as exemplified by Senior Neighbors of Chattanooga.

Older adult education programs established during the last two decades depart from earlier models that tended to offer episodic programs dependent on the contingencies of outside funding. Instead, they are financially viable, evolving organizations with track records that reach back five, ten, fifteen years, or longer. LRIs, OASIS sites, and Shepherd's Center programs are securely established in host institutions with relatively stable funding through membership fees and in-kind institutional support.

Many of these organizations have embraced the concept of senior empowerment: Participants play leadership roles as board members, teachers, administrators, or curriculum planners. Human capital in the form of volunteerism is their greatest asset, since most of these organizations could never afford the expertise and resourcefulness that their members provide freely. With the securing of infrastructure, these organizations are gaining cumulative experience, leadership, and visibility.

An additional trend beginning to emerge from some of these organizations is senior involvement in community service programs and intergenerational projects. For example, programs like the one in Asheville view community service and intergenerational programs as a way of augmenting their members' learning and personal growth goals. OASIS has developed a reading tutorial program that participants bring to local schools to work with third graders.

Though these educational programs involve a small percentage of today's older persons, they may be harbingers of the near future as increasingly better-educated people who value learning make the transition to retirement. Others may follow in the footsteps of people like Elizabeth Houston and the Hitchcocks who embrace the threefold relationship of lifelong learning, leadership, and community service—a new retirement paradigm linking leisure and virtue.

A NATIONAL RESEARCH PROJECT
ON OLDER ADULT EDUCATION

Until recently, there has been little systematic effort to study the emergence and evolution of this spectrum of educational programs for seniors. Traditionally, besides older adults' intellectual functioning and learning abilities (see Chapter 2), research examining education for seniors has tended to focus on the motivation and goals of older learners (Londoner 1971, 1978; Boshier and Riddell 1978; Bova 1981; Kingston and Drotter 1983; Wirtz and Charner 1989; Bynum and Seaman 1993; Danner, Danner, and Kuder 1993) or on curriculum planning, policy, and designs for older adult educational programs (Beckman and Ventura-Merkel 1992; Fischer, Blazey, and Lipman 1992; Meyers 1987; Peterson 1983; Romaniuk 1983; Sprouse and Brown 1981; Weinstock 1978; Scanlon 1978; Glickman et al. 1975; Academy for Educational Development 1974; Hendrickson 1973).

These publications, with the exception of Sprouse and Brown studying community learning centers, have focused on educational programs for seniors in the university or college setting. Little or no comparative research has been devoted to the organizational phases undertaken by senior centers, Shepherd's Centers, OASIS institutes, LRIs, and community college programs. Most planners seem to operate by contacting existing programs, attending seminars and workshops sponsored by either aging network organizations such as the NCOA, the American Society on Aging (ASA, which in 1992 established the Older Adult Education Network), the Association for Gerontology in Higher Education (AGHE), or the AARP; or by attending those sponsored by adult education organizations such as the National University Continuing Education Association (NUCEA), the Association for Continuing Higher Education (ACHE), or the EIN (EIN 1991).

Even the EIN, whose business is that of sponsoring replication workshops and training conferences for institutes, had only begun to conduct research on member institutes' curricula in 1993. While most individual institutes and related programs evaluate their participants' degree of satisfaction with courses, few assess their own organization's progress, community impact and positioning, limits to growth, failures, and disappointments (Verschueren 1991). To date, OASIS National has not conducted a systematic organizational study nor has anyone conducted research on its development (Mann 1991). The last time NCOA undertook to study its Discovery Through the Humanities program was in 1981 (Liroff 1991).

Comprehensive treatments of policy and philosophy of seniors' education are found in several anthologies edited by Lumsden (1985) and Sherron and Lumsden (1990), in Lowy and O'Connor (1986), and in Peterson (1983). However, little or no comparative research has been devoted to studying the types of organizations supporting the interests of older learners (e.g., senior centers, Shepherd's Centers, OASIS institutes, LRIs) or how the organizations have developed infrastructures, policies, staffing patterns, and curriculum. And only recently have studies been published examining the trend toward greater participant leadership, community involvement, and the impact of these programs on host institutions.

The critical result of the lack of synthesized information is that planners of individual programs are often unaware of their own options and choices, or even that they are making choices that commit them to a particular educational philosophy or organizational structure. Planners often have difficulty making comparisons among programs because they lack standardized criteria and language. Even at conferences and workshops, program representatives often fail to identify the difficulties and obstacles of the institutional growth process; instead, they highlight positive experiences ("cheerleading") while overlooking negative ones. Moreover, there is little in the literature of older adult education that assesses how these educational organizations promote new roles and norms for older adults (for an exception see Cusack 1994; Manheimer and Snodgrass 1993) and what this might mean for other institutions increasingly affected by growing numbers of healthy, active people who enter retirement with unprecedented expectations and contributory potential.

Building on the existing literature and beginning an exploratory investigation of the areas where no current information exists, the NCCCR launched a national study, Identifying Critical Pathways in Organizing Educational Programs for Older Adults, to document this new phenomenon. The study, funded by AARP's Andrus Foundation, examined the emergence of community-based, participant-influenced, educational programs for seniors. Besides a detailed research report (NCCCR 1993), another product of the study was a Planning Guide to Organizing Educational Programs for Older Adults (Moskow-McKenzie and Manheimer 1994).

The decision to focus on these types of educational programs for seniors was based on the researchers' observation that the biggest visible growth in new programs was occurring among these institutions; moreover, that emphasis on participant leadership and power sharing paralleled changing attitudes toward aging and the elderly.

Methodology of the Study

The purpose of the national study was to add to the body of research literature by surveying 430 organizations that have been conducting intellectually challenging, substantive, educational programs for seniors that are community-based, draw to varying degrees on older adult leadership, and are developmental rather than vocational in purpose. Selected for study were 137 LRIs that were, as of 1992, members of the umbrella organization, EIN, or listed in the AARP's directory of older adult educational programs; 28 OASIS programs; 91 Shepherd's Centers; 72 community colleges with educational programs designed specifically for older adults as identified by the LICC and the AARP; and 109 multipurpose senior centers identified by the NCOA's National Institute of Senior Centers (NISC) state delegates as having structured educational programs.

The study involved variations in sampling since it was relatively easy to send surveys to all EIN member institutes while it was more difficult to identify those of the 12,000 senior centers or 1,200 community colleges that were providing substantive educational programming that also involved seniors in some degree of leadership. No list exists of senior centers that offer intellectually challenging programming or that might involve members in important leadership roles. Even when state representatives of NISC were asked to identify centers that met the criteria, some were hard pressed to find any examples in their respective state, while others could immediately think of several.

As part of the research methodology, a stage model of organizational development was formulated, derived in part from David Peterson's (1983) fifteen planning phases of educational programs for older adults. Termed by researchers in this study as a *Critical Pathways Taxonomy*, it identified major steps or choice-points that senior educational organizations take as they plan, assess, implement, modify, evaluate, and refine such programs. A brief definition of the fifteen stages is as follows.

Critical Pathways Taxonomy: Fifteen Stages

1. Inception—origin of the program and institutional goals and motivations
2. Assessment—determination of the need, desire for, and feasibility of the program
3. Planning—method of planning, make-up, and authority of planning committee
4. Organizational positioning—administrative placement in host institution
5. Rationale—justification, benefits, mission, and purpose of program
6. Funding and resources—expenses, revenue sources, and institutional support
7. Participants—targeted population, socioeconomic characteristics, and degree of inclusiveness
8. Governance—representation and method by which program direction is decided
9. Program content and pedagogy—curriculum design, staffing, and teaching methods
10. Strategy—short-term or long-range focus and societal impact
11. Scale—goal for size of program, number of program units, involvement in community, and intergenerational projects
12. Delivery—location and number of sites, cosponsors, and use of distant learning technology
13. Evaluation—criteria of success and procedures for determining
14. Continuity and growth—growth goals, size limits, and institutional development
15. By-products—publications, exhibits, recognition events, and new programs

Each of these steps involves nodes of choice which in turn generate a set of questions that planners consciously or unconsciously answer through decision making. The validity, order, and accuracy of the taxonomy was confirmed by a majority of the survey respondents. The survey questions derived from the taxonomy provided the basis for cross-comparisons. Table 3.1 summarizes the stages, choices, and types of questions used in the survey.

The taxonomy was applied through the use of a self-administered questionnaire based on the fifteen steps and nodal choice points. Types of questions asked are indicated in Table 3.1. The print survey was supplemented by a telephone interview schedule derived from the preliminary findings and directed to forty-seven programs defined as exemplary based on criteria of distinctiveness and replicability. The data collection was completed with four case studies of geographically and organizationally diverse programs. The on-site visits to outstanding programs included multiple-source interviews which provided an opportunity to confirm research findings and gain in-depth understanding.

Of the 430 programs approached, 260 responded by filling out the fourteen-page questionnaire (see Table 3.2 for a breakdown of responses by institutional type).

RESEARCH FINDINGS

Detailed results of each taxonomy stage can be obtained from the final report submitted to the Andrus Foundation (NCCCR 1993). Here we limit our discussion to the most salient findings that would be of interest to older adult educators as well as to the broader audience of experts in the field of aging, researchers, planners, and other interested parties. Accordingly, we will discuss and explore the fifteen stages and their various options and illustrate some of the findings through particular examples drawn from the telephone survey.

When and How Programs Started

The study showed that 1982 was the median year for establishment of the programs surveyed. This date reflects two trends. First, growth in the 1970s of senior center and community college programs was influenced by the mandates of the Older Americans Act (especially in the 1973 amendments) and by policy changes that encouraged community colleges to offer tuition-free courses for seniors. Second, program start-ups for the three other organizational models are more recent. While the first LRI was established in 1962 at the New School for Social Research in New York, it was not until the early 1980s, when several national conferences were devoted to the institute concept, that LRIs began to spread. LRIs have shown an even stronger growth rate since 1990. Of the 151 EIN members in 1994, 121 (80 percent) were established

Table 3.1
Critical Pathways Taxonomy

Stage	Nodes of Choice	Sample Derived Questions
Inception	• Institution initiated • Response to community needs • Response to request of older learners • Response to changes in institutional regulations • Special opportunity (gift, fund, etc.)	Did the program arise from motivation within the organization or from outside forces? Was it in response to the demands of older learners, institutional leaders, changes in regulations, response to a community problem, need, desire, or because of a special opportunity?
Assessment	• Formal feasibility study • Use of focus groups • Institutional review of mission • Leadership incentive	How was feasibility for the program determined and by whom? Were formal techniques utilized such as surveys and focus groups? To what extent were local leadership and personal imagination a primary moving force?
Planning	• Outside consultant • Use of paid staff • Involvement of older adults as volunteers • Combined approach • Investigation of existing programs	Who were the planners for determining program feasibility -- staff, recruited representative volunteers, a combination, a hired consultant? How were planning responsibilities assigned and coordinated? Were other programs studied as possible models and, if so, how was the appropriateness of these models determined?
Institutional Positioning	• Designated as affiliated institute • Placed under department or division • Designated as department or division • Informal program status • Independent	Under what supervisor, department, division or program area was the program placed and why? Did this placement give the program added strength or did it put the program on the "fringes" of institutional concern? Were advocates for the program sought and cultivated? How successfully?
Funding & Resources	• Determination of start-up costs • Projected financial requirements, long-term • Determination of fee-driven approach • Determination of free provision based on grants, gifts and/or institutional revenue • Balance of volunteer vs. paid staff • Role of partnerships in funding	How were resource needs (e.g. space, overhead, promotion, financial management) determined and how were they acquired? What options were considered as far as cost analysis of the program (e.g. fees, grants, gifts, in-kinds provided through partnerships) and how did this influence the targeted market for the program? How did first budget formulations compare with actual program costs? What was the balance between volunteer services and those of paid staff?
Scale	• Launched as pilot project or full start • Projected ideal size: small group, small community scale, larger institutional scale, division into satellites to maintain scale • Conceived as single-program or multiple-program focus (e.g. leadership, community outreach, community service)	Did the program begin with a pilot or small scale project? What was the projected ideal participant size of the program? What factors were considered as far as scale was concerned -- e.g. small community model, large institution, small sub-groups? How did the scale change and what were the consequences?
Governance	• Participant governed through by-laws • Institution governed or mixed (balance) • No governance, program not autonomous	What by-laws or governing principles were developed and by whom? How did the host institution exercise interest (and control) in the program? To what extent was the program autonomous and were there conflicts over issues of governance and authority? How were these resolved?
Strategy	• Conceived as short-term or long-term • Determination of ideal fulfillment • Mechanism for evaluation and redirection	Was the program thought of as short-term or long-term? Was there an ideal toward which it was expected to grow? How was progress measured? If certain directions proved unfeasible, how were redirections determined? How were failures assessed and corrected?

Table 3.1 (continued)

Stage	Nodes of Choice	Sample Derived Questions
Rationale	• Determination of mission (by whom?) • Justification to host institution • Justification to community • Articulation of benefits to participants, host institution, community • Philosophy of program: value and purpose	How was the program's mission determined and by whom? Did it change over time? How was the existence of the program justified to the host institution and its clientele and staff, to the community, to potential funding sources, to civic and government leaders? How were the potential benefits of the program articulated and communicated to the various constituencies?
Participants	• Identification of target audience • Predicted or divergent audience response • Acknowledgement of excluded groups • Decision to recruit minority participants, other socio-economic groups, geographical diversity (urban, suburban, rural) • Intergenerational approach (with other age groups -- children, youth, old-old)	Was a target audience for the program selected in advance and marketed to? Was the audience which actually responded favorably or were there surprises? Was there awareness of principles of self-selectivity or pre-selective dispositions? Was there an attempt to recruit minority participants, people of different socio-economic backgrounds, diverse age groups among seniors, the physically impaired (e.g. blind, deaf, wheelchair bound)? Were the limits of participating groups acknowledged and was an attempt made to conduct further outreach?
Program Content and Pedagogy	• Determined by participants (curriculum committee) • Determined by staff or combination • Influence of other program models • Influence of available resource people • Expert-led or study circle or both • Use of prepackaged modules (Great Decisions, National Issues Forum, Discovery through the Humanities)	How and by whom was the content of the program determined? Was there a philosophy of curriculum development based on other program models? Was the content dictated by available resources such as volunteers, pre-packaged programs, local available experts? Did the content change over time and, if so, why?
Delivery	• Central location (senior center, department store, college campus) • Satellite program locations • Cosponsor locations • Use of distant learning technology	Was the program delivered in one location or several? How was linkage to the host institution utilized? How was the program promoted and what proved most successful?
Evaluation	• Formal evaluation procedure • Determination of success criteria • Documentation of achievements • Identification of barriers and failures • Communication of evaluation results	How was the success of the program determined -- evaluations, word of mouth, participant numbers, etc.? What were the criteria of success -- increased self-esteem, better informed citizenry, increased social contact, political empowerment, intellectual stimulation, and so on? Was there an effort to document the history, accomplishments and impasses of the program? Were successes highlighted to the participants, the host institution, the outside community?
Continuity and Growth	• Issues of in-group vs. new members • Development of senior leadership • Principles of program expansion • Limits to growth	Was there emphasis on recruiting new participants and retaining old ones? Did an in-group image begin to form and was this a problem? Were volunteer leaders and advisors encouraged to seek ambitious program expansion?
By-products	• Production of publications • Exhibits, seminars and workshops • Recognition events • Satellite and outreach programs	What spin-offs were generated by the program -- exhibits, publications, new projects, satellite programs?

Table 3.2
Breakdown on Survey Response

	OASIS	SHEPHERD'S CENTER	LRI	COMMUNITY COLLEGE	SENIOR CENTER	ALL
MAILED	21	91	137	72	109	430
COMPLETED	16	51	95	43	55	260
% COMPLETED	75%	56%	69%	59%	50%	60%

since 1989 (EIN 1994). OASIS National was founded in 1982 with the first year of funding coming from the U.S. Department of Health and Human Services. Since that time twenty-eight OASIS institutes have been established in twenty-one cities throughout the United States with funding by a variety of sources supplementing the May Company's contribution. In 1972, the Shepherd's Center Adventures in Learning program was first initiated, but the big expansion of Shepherd's Centers came during the 1980s (Shepherd's Centers of America 1991).

The data suggest that older adult education is still primarily a local phenomenon aided by several national networks rather than the result of legislation or public policy. The emergence of a relatively better educated and more affluent retiree population may help to explain the strong, positive response to these programs, since it is well documented that prior educational attainment is the key determinant of educational participation in later life (Cross 1981). As discussed earlier, in 1970 the median level of education among the elderly was 8.7 years. In 1989, the median level of education among seniors was 12.1 years (U.S. Senate Special Committee on Aging 1991). By the year 2000, that number will reach 12.4 years. In 1979, 8.5 percent of those sixty-five and older had graduated from college. In 1992 it was 12 percent, and by 2009, 20 percent of seniors will be college graduates. These factors would suggest continued growth in older adult education.

Participant interest in older adult educational opportunities could explain the rapid growth of programs in recent years. However, by and large, potential participants were not the direct initiators of these programs. Instead, it was institutional leaders. Seventy percent of respondents reported that host organization leaders who perceived a need for the programs were the primary moving forces. Over half of the programs (57 percent) indicated that an organizational directive or change in goals was involved. Relatively few programs were directly initiated through requests from older adults, though many were influenced by requests or inquiries from seniors.

The right chemistry for creating a learning program for seniors appears to include an organizational champion for the idea, awareness of a potentially interested clientele, some familiarity with existing model programs in other locations, and the nurturing support of one of several national organizations.

Determining the Need for Older Adult Education

Despite being systematic in other aspects of planning, most (70 percent) of the programs studied did not use a structured needs assessment such as a formal feasibility study, focus groups, or market analysis to determine demand or appropriate fees. However, several senior centers and Shepherd's Centers (1990) reported using the findings of community-wide surveys conducted by institutions of higher education or local government departments, such as parks and recreation, on the needs of older adults. For example, the Shepherd's Center in Little Rock, Arkansas, used the findings from an educational needs assessment of persons fifty-five and older conducted by the University of Arkansas. This assessment included questions pertaining to educational needs, desired location of program and schedule of activities, types of courses to be offered, transportation needs, and willingness to pay for courses. Another example is the Elsie J. Stuhr Leisure Center in Beaverton, Oregon. This senior center distributed 2,000 questionnaires to churches, motor vehicle registrants, and senior groups to assess older persons' (age fifty-five-plus) educational needs and interests.

The general tendency was for programs to use informal means of assessment: usually sounding out local leaders in the education system, aging network, and representative seniors. Fifty-eight percent of the programs used an informal survey approach, which included talking with other educational program leaders, seniors, and staff of agencies serving the elderly. Lacking a systematic and comprehensive method of assessment, this approach runs the risk that perceived need may not always fit the broader range of seniors' actual interests.

The Planning Process and Inclusion of Older Adults

All program types used a planning group in the first year, and most reported they continued to use a planning group, usually referred to as a curriculum or advisory committee, for the duration of the program. Especially notable is the 78 percent who said they involved older adults in planning committees. However, the role of seniors in planning, and subsequently, managing, programs varied considerably by program host type (see Figure 3.1).

The broad make up of representation on planning committees is exemplified by the Retirement Institute at Westchester Community College in New York state. The thirty-member committee included older adults, corporate representatives, individuals from potential funding sources, and faculty and staff from the college.

Figure 3.1
First-Year Planning Group Composition

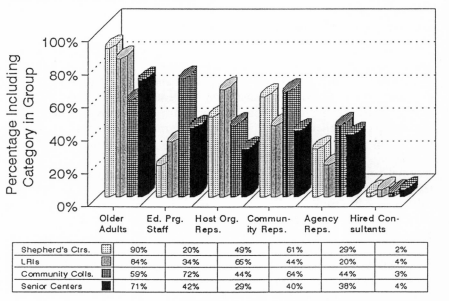

		Older Adults	Ed. Prg. Staff	Host Org. Reps.	Community Reps.	Agency Reps.	Hired Consultants
Shepherd's Ctrs.		90%	20%	49%	61%	29%	2%
LRIs		84%	34%	65%	44%	20%	4%
Community Colls.		59%	72%	44%	64%	44%	3%
Senior Centers		71%	42%	29%	40%	38%	4%

Categories of Representation

Source: D. Moskow-McKenzie and R. J. Manheimer, *A Guide to Developing Educational Programs for Older Adults* (Asheville, N.C.: UNCA University Publications, 1994).

Senior centers, community colleges, and OASIS institutes reported that planning committees are more likely to serve in an advisory capacity with the host organization making the final program decisions. The Shepherd's Center Adventures in Learning program and the LRIs were more likely to use committees to plan curricula, recruit teachers, and publicize and evaluate programs. Use of ongoing planning groups varied somewhat by program type (see Figure 3.2).

Noteworthy is the fact that twelve of the forty-seven organizations participating in the telephone survey reported using a written plan of action. For example, the Johnson City (Tennessee) Senior Center developed an initial plan of goals, objectives, and action steps and reviewed the plan on an annual basis.

LRIs were the most frequent users of written plans, and LRI members had considerable input. According to Arthur Peterson, director of Eckerd College's Academy of Senior Professionals (ASPEC), the St. Petersburg–based program grew out of an initial proposal written in the 1970s that led to formation of four think tanks with older adults, college administrators, and community representatives joining in to discuss economics, the environment, fate, culture,

Figure 3.2
Use Ongoing Planning Group

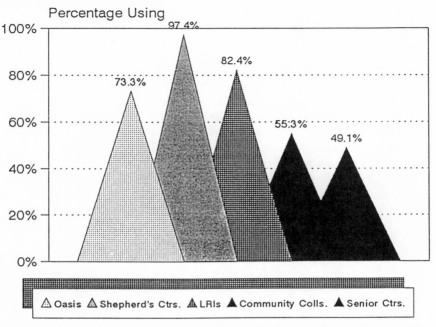

Source: D. Moskow-McKenzie and R. J. Manheimer, *A Guide to Developing Educational Programs for Older Adults* (Asheville, N.C.: UNCA University Publications, 1994).

and values in higher education. This broad, philosophical approach helped the group draft the plan that eventually enabled them to find funding for and establish the program. The ASPEC group periodically revisits and updates their organizational plan.

Some planning groups made use of paid consultants. While these were relatively rare, costs for consultants were reported to range from a low of $3,000 to a high of $30,000 for a one-year period. In addition to using paid consultants, 69 percent of the programs reported studying other educational program models, with 80 percent of LRIs having studied other LRIs.

The average length of time for moving from a first meeting of the planning committee to actually offering the program was six months. The EIN leaders suggest to fledgling groups that they plan on about this length of time for establishing an LRI. Activities during the six-month period include the following: (1) formation of a planning committee made up of stakeholders (people who are committed to the program and its future); (2) securing of host organization support; (3) assessment conducted to determine need, level of interest, and fee structure; (4) securing of needed start-up funding, resources, and space; (5) determination of curriculum, teaching methods (e.g., lecturing, study circles, seminars, and workshops), and instructional and administrative staffing; and (6) launching of promotional campaign (e.g., marketing approach, publicity, and mechanism for registering participants).

Organizational Positioning

All of the programs included in this study were part of a larger host organization. One-fourth of the respondents reported benefitting from the host organization's name and reputation, which added legitimacy and sometimes prestige to the program. One out of four said that administrative and financial support were provided by the host organization. Over three-fourths (76 percent) of the respondents reported the host institution's attitude toward the educational program was "very supportive."

An instance of the supportive role played by host-institution leadership was communicated by the executive board chairman of the University of Texas at El Paso's Center for Lifelong Learning. Herbert Schwartz reported that support of the University president, Diana Natalicio, provided "clout and reflects itself throughout all levels of the hierarchy" (NCCCR 1993). The Center for Lifelong Learning was attached for administrative purposes to the Division of Professional and Continuing Education. Division staff provided such services as bookkeeping, telephone communication, and classroom assignments. The host institution also provided office space, close parking, classrooms, and a lounge area free of charge.

In addition to the positive effect the host organization had on programs, many reported a reciprocal effect. For example, Lawrence A. Ianni, Chancellor of the University of Minnesota, Duluth, lauded the school's University for Seniors program for its public service role to area older adults. Echoed by numerous other higher-education administrators, many of the LRI-type programs provide high-profile examples of universities' commitment to their communities while doing so on small budgets with extensive volunteer resources. Additionally, these programs have attracted a few large and a great many smaller financial contributions from their quasi-alumni older students.

Several problems in connection with the positioning of these programs also were identified. Some LRIs and community college-based programs reported problems with excessive bureaucracy, low status in the host organization, and imposed requirements such as fee structures and certain types of mandated courses. Fischer, Blazey, and Lipman (1992) warn planners of LRIs to be aware of the budget control that educational institutions must exert in order to administer their fiduciary responsibility.

Another problem reported across all types of educational programs was inadequate office and classroom space. For example, Evelyn Chasan of the Adult Learning Institute at Columbia Greene College in New York reported that classroom space is available to the Institute only after the regular college needs are met and that financial arrangements must adhere to the college's system.

Rationale

An integral aspect of the planning process is formulation of an organizational sense of purpose and mission. This so-called "mission statement" also forms part of the rationale for the program's existence, who it benefits and serves, and its institutional relationship. Mission statements were commonly found (82 percent) among the programs surveyed, and in 58 percent of the cases, it was the original planning committee that formulated the written statement of purpose. In other cases the function of writing a mission statement was left to the program's board of directors, host organization leaders, the program staff, or participants themselves.

Mission statements are not cast in stone. One key reason identified for changing mission statements concerned ideological shifts in attitudes toward the senior population and the type of programming deemed appropriate. Telephone survey responses revealed that, especially among senior centers, need was found for changing the mission statement to reflect new emphasis on actively involving and intellectually stimulating curriculum and activities where earlier there had been more focus on sedentary, passive programs on primarily an entertainment level. Senior center respondents talked about their need to attract younger, healthy retirement-age individuals. They saw a need to change the institutional image from programs perceived as serving the frail and old-old to one that communicated greater diversity of age and ability. Inclusiveness of both the frail and well, those in advanced and those in younger years, as well as people of diverse educational backgrounds was identified by senior center personnel as a crucial issue for now and the future.

Amplifying this situation, Bobbe Nolan of the Wilmington (Delaware) Senior Center reported her Center's research that senior centers will be serving two disparate populations: very elderly people with multiple needs who require personalized, in-home services; and young aging people who desire information, referral, job placement or advice, and educational opportunities. The Wilmington Center currently serves a middle age-range (sixty-five to eighty-five) population that is in relatively good health. This group will shrink by attrition as, for their area, the birth dearth of the Great Depression era will mean fewer people in the next wave of retirees.

Residential patterns will also affect the Wilmington Center's population. Inner-city senior centers will be serving an increasingly elderly, widowed, low-income, and minority population, while suburban centers will see more couples, people who drive, fewer minorities, and individuals with higher educational levels. According to Nolan, "younger seniors" (fifty-five to sixty-five) are still in the workplace, do not view themselves as elderly or identify with the term senior, and would avoid coming to a senior center unless they are seeking information on how to care for an aging parent or other relative. The Wilmington Senior Center was considering finding a new name to avoid the problem of people associating them with adult day care and to reflect a more upbeat image. Changes in mission statement and rationale that would reflect a new emphasis are being considered.

Funding and Resources

Over half (56 percent) of the programs were started on donated institutional services, funding, and volunteers. Through connection to a host organization, the start-up barrier of securing advanced funding and resources was sharply reduced. The average actual first-year operating expenses for all programs, except OASIS, was $4,600. The primary cash funding sources were course or membership fees. In addition, a substantial amount of in-kind contribution often came from host institutions' provision of office and classroom space and some support-staff time. For many programs, volunteers create the greatest amount of human capital. Figure 3.3 shows first-year expenses by program type, and Figure 3.4 shows sources of funding. (OASIS is not included in Figure 3.4 because it operates through a national funding mechanism.) Note the low dependency on foundation support generally and relatively low support from government agencies. In the case of LRI programs, many were

Figure 3.3
Actual First-Year Expenses

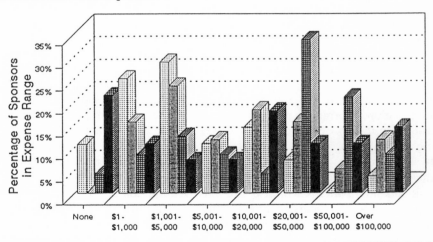

	None	$1-$1,000	$1,001-$5,000	$5,001-$10,000	$10,001-$20,000	$20,001-$50,000	$50,001-$100,000	Over $100,000
Shepherd's Ctrs.	11%	25%	29%	11%	14%	7%	0%	4%
LRIs	0%	16%	23%	12%	18%	16%	5%	12%
Community Colls.	4%	8%	13%	8%	4%	34%	21%	8%
Senior Ctrs.	21%	11%	7%	7%	18%	11%	11%	14%

Expense Ranges

Source: D. Moskow-McKenzie and R. J. Manheimer, *A Guide to Developing Educational Programs for Older Adults* (Asheville, N.C.: UNCA University Publications, 1994).

Figure 3.4
First-Year Funding Sources

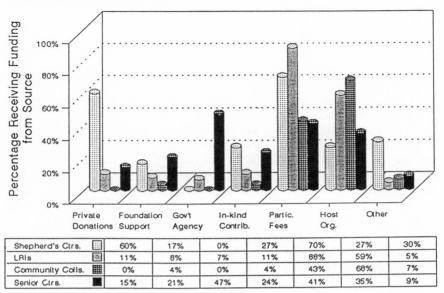

		Private Donations	Foundation Support	Gov't Agency	In-kind Contrib.	Partic. Fees	Host Org.	Other
Shepherd's Ctrs.		60%	17%	0%	27%	70%	27%	30%
LRIs		11%	8%	7%	11%	88%	59%	5%
Community Colls.		0%	4%	0%	4%	43%	68%	7%
Senior Ctrs.		15%	21%	47%	24%	41%	35%	9%

Funding Sources

Source: D. Moskow-McKenzie and R. J. Manheimer, *A Guide to Developing Educational Programs for Older Adults* (Asheville, N.C.: UNCA University Publications, 1994).

launched with the provision that they would be financially self-sufficient after the first year. Shepherd's Centers accomplish their balanced budget through reliance on volunteers. In the world of education, at any level, these programs are remarkable for how much they accomplish on relatively few dollars. As programs grow, their need for added space and support staff does create new problems. In several instances, LRIs have raised substantial amounts of money to help fund new buildings which they share with the campus.

Some of the programs reported having inadequate funds and needing additional funding sources. The educational programs hosted by public institutions of higher education and publicly funded senior centers indicated the stability of their programs was often in question because of funding cuts within the host organization. Many of the programs reported initiating fundraising activities to cover the budget shortfalls.

In addition to cash and host-institution in-kind funding, partnerships with other organizations played an important role. Forty-five percent of the programs benefitted from sponsorships or partnerships with other organizations and businesses. For example, OASIS institutes jointly sponsor wellness programs with local hospitals and offer classes jointly with other organizations serving seniors.

Overall, programs surveyed demonstrated relatively more stable funding and secure organizational positioning than programs twenty years ago because the host institutions embraced meeting the educational needs of older adults as part of their mission.

Participants

How would participants benefit from joining educational programs offered through the various centers? Only about one-third of the respondents reported a need to justify their programs to the host institution, a funding agency, or other outside inquirer. The two most frequently mentioned benefits were life-long learning and community service opportunities. Other responses included not only benefits for participants but ways in which participants would benefit others through the program. These included better informed citizenry, intellectual stimulation, sources of donations, volunteers on campus, socialization, intergenerational opportunity, seniors as key communicators with the community, increased state funding, good public relations, support for milage funds, as a benefit to the region, and vocational training.

Recruitment of participants was another dimension of great importance. The data collected suggest that very few programs were using creative or aggressive methods for recruiting minorities or disabled persons and diverse age groups to the educational program. The exceptions were the programs making special efforts to recruit minorities through contacting minority community agencies, using public service announcements in Spanish, targeting particular neighborhoods to receive fliers, using minority photographs in marketing publications, contacting the Urban League and the National Association for the Advancement of Colored People (NAACP), and distributing newsletters to low-income housing projects. The programs offering courses in nursing homes, a variety of courses at various times throughout the day, and preretirement seminars were aggressively marketing to diverse age groups.

Programs that recruit members of younger-age groups through contacting public schools and colleges, offering intergenerational programs, and contacting girls and boys clubs appear to be using creative recruitment techniques. Using sliding fee scales, offering scholarships, and not charging fees may be considered aggressive techniques in the recruitment of persons from various socioeconomic backgrounds. Creative recruitment techniques such as involving the agencies serving the blind and using audiotaped newsletters of the educational program should be replicated by educational programs wishing to serve the blind or visually impaired. Providing interpreters, using assistive listening devices, and contacting deaf support groups are aggressive methods for recruiting the deaf or hearing impaired. Providing building accessibility is a start, if not a requirement of all government funded agencies, but providing transportation for the wheelchair bound or persons with limited mobility through coordination with public transit services is an aggressive recruitment technique.

Ann O'Hanlon of the Rosa Keller Campus at the University of New Orleans reported developing a special outreach project designed to recruit minorities to their educational program. This particular program also makes a special effort to disseminate information about the educational program to people representing various socioeconomic backgrounds.

How Programs Are Governed

Fifty-six percent of the programs in this study had formal governance/bylaws with senior participants playing major decision-making roles in determining program content, setting policy, scheduling activities, and leading or teaching educational offerings. The OASIS sites, Shepherd's Centers, and LRIs invited participants to make the major decisions concerning the programs, while community college and senior center administrative staffs were responsible for the major decision making in their organizations (see Figure 3.5). The host organization for all program types, with the exception of LRIs, was reported responsible for determining the form of governance and the establishment of fees, suggesting that even though these programs reported being

Figure 3.5
Major Decision Makers Regarding Program

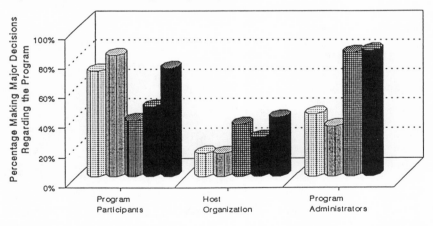

		Program Participants	Host Organization	Program Administrators
Shepherd's Ctrs.		71%	16%	42%
LRIs		82%	16%	34%
Community Colls.		38%	35%	84%
Senior Ctrs.		47%	27%	85%
Oasis		73%	40%	

Decision-Making Groups

Source: D. Moskow-McKenzie and R. J. Manheimer, *A Guide to Developing Educational Programs for Older Adults* (Asheville, N.C.: UNCA University Publications, 1994).

senior-led, control and authority was shared to varying degrees with the host organization. Further research should be undertaken to determine the impact and implication of seniors sharing power and control of these programs.

Forty-eight percent of the respondents rated the participants' involvement in determining content of program as being very significant; 39 percent rated the participants' involvement in leading or teaching educational offerings as being very significant. Half of the LRI respondents reported the participants' involvement in leading or teaching educational offerings and scheduling activities as being very significant (see Figure 3.6).

Staffing, Curriculum, and Pedagogy

The majority of educational programs for seniors operate on small, often inadequately funded budgets. Administrative staff, overhead (in situations where the program must pay for space, heat, light, electricity, etc.), printing costs, and teaching (where paid) make up, in descending order, the largest portions of most program expenditures. The key for many programs lies in the utilization of volunteers.

Forty-three percent of the respondents reported 76 to 100 percent of the work for the educational program is completed by paid staff (see Figure 3.7).

Figure 3.6
Significant Participant Involvement in Various Aspects of Program

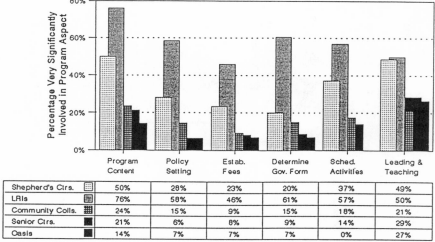

		Program Content	Policy Setting	Estab. Fees	Determine Gov. Form	Sched. Activities	Leading & Teaching
Shepherd's Ctrs.		50%	28%	23%	20%	37%	49%
LRIs		76%	58%	46%	61%	57%	50%
Community Colls.		24%	15%	9%	15%	18%	21%
Senior Ctrs.		21%	6%	8%	9%	14%	29%
Oasis		14%	7%	7%	7%	0%	27%

Program Aspects

Source: D. Moskow-McKenzie and R. J. Manheimer, *A Guide to Developing Educational Programs for Older Adults* (Asheville, N.C.: UNCA University Publications, 1994).

Figure 3.7
Comparative Workload Distribution between Paid Staff and Volunteers

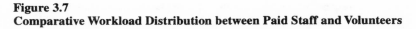

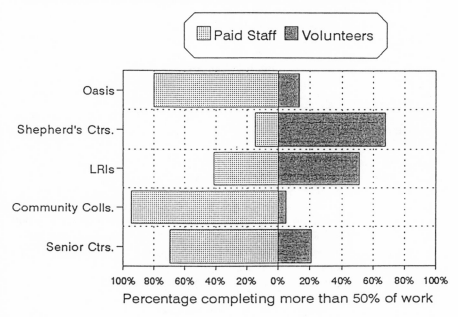

Source: D. Moskow-McKenzie and R. J. Manheimer, *A Guide to Developing Educational Programs for Older Adults* (Asheville, N.C.: UNCA University Publications, 1994).

Over half of the OASIS sites, community colleges, and senior centers reported that paid staff are responsible for 76 to 100 percent of the work required by the educational program. Eighty percent of the programs are using 1 to 5 paid employees with a median of 4.1. Thirty-one percent of the programs are using volunteers for 1 to 25 percent of the work required by the educational program and 27 percent of the programs are using volunteers for 76 to 100 percent of the work. The number of volunteer staff ranged from a low of 1 to a high of over 100 with a median of 10.

The curricula of the various types of programs exhibited wide diversity. During the first year, many of the educational programs began offering wellness, life enrichment (including packaged curricula programs such as National Issues Forum, Great Decisions, and Discovery through the Humanities), or liberal arts courses based on the assumed needs of the elderly. The programs then expanded to include vocational/technical courses, community service, mentoring, and intergenerational programs. Courses offered by the programs, with an emphasis on the liberal arts, include history, current events, computers, languages (Spanish, French, German, Norwegian, Yiddish, Hebrew,

Japanese, Hawaiian, and Chinese), psychology, art, music, religion, literature, political science, wellness, recreation, hobbies, self-help, geography, astronomy, archaeology, creative writing, and ecology.

The respondents reported attempting to incorporate into the programs the skills and expertise of these seniors: the well elderly working with the frail seniors, tutoring and/or mentoring with various age groups, and seniors playing leadership roles in the community. Seniors were included in the planning of these programs as well as determining their content.

These programs used a variety of teaching methods with older adults. The expert-led or lecture approach was the most popular or, at least, the most common method. Lecture methods usually included time for questions and some discussion. When program directors were asked in the telephone survey how teaching methods were determined, some asserted that the experience of their teachers and direct intuition were deemed a sufficient basis. An exception, Kathy Wilkins of the Shepherd's Center of Little Rock, reported that her research indicated that the majority of her Adventures in Learning participants preferred active discussion group involvement as opposed to being passive during lecture classes. The students enjoyed discussion groups with peer leadership that complemented lectures, or they were engaged in study circles utilizing rotating leadership.

This is another area in which a more professional approach (familiarity with the research literature on older learners) may be wanting. Further research is needed to examine the disparity between adult educator experts' findings on the need for experience-based, participatory education and the trend in many programs to what may be a cultural and generational bias toward the expert-led, lecture format.

Strategy

While it seems to be less true today, programs that were started in the 1970s and 1980s were more likely to be considered temporary or pilot projects subject to renewal or further expansion. But 70 percent of the respondents indicted that their program was planned from the start to be long term. This reflects a closer relationship to the host institution which views the programs as part of its mission.

The Senior Enrichment Program at Delta College, University Center, Michigan, is an example of a time-limited project that grew long term. Delta College began offering free classes to seniors in the early 1970s. Subsequently, the college received a five-year grant from the Advanced Institutional Development Program to start an older adult educational program. The program grew quickly from 500 students to 1,000 with over eighty-five classes offered. Consequently, it outgrew the available staff and classroom space. Between 1981 and 1986, the college set aside funds to carry on the program. Then, in 1986, the college decided to charge seniors 25 percent of tuition for credit classes while noncredit courses remained free.

Another example, the Salinas (California) Union High School District launched an Older Adults Program on a pilot, six-month basis with initial funds and space provided by the school district. Strong interest in the program led to the establishment of a long-term program.

Numerous other programs were launched on a one- or two-year trial-period basis to determine need and feasibility.

Scale

How large should a program be? This issue has been raised in a variety of ways. For some, the question concerns having enough participants to justify the program's existence or to meet a minimum budget requirement. For others, scale is a question of how large a program can become before a sense of community is lost. Still others found it necessary or desirable to diversify programming by adding multiple focuses such as community service and intergenerational opportunities.

A common target number for first-year programs was approximately 100 participants. This enrollment or membership size permitted programs to demonstrate perceived value, establish a working budget, and offer a wide enough scope of classes. Over half (54 percent) of the programs reported offering ten courses during the first year. At the time of data collection (1992–1993), these programs had an average annual enrollment of 350 participants and an average of twenty-five courses or activities in each semester or session.

Increases in size of programs were influenced by factors such as improved course quality, effective publicity and recruitment techniques, increases in the number of senior persons in the area, and growing interest in older adult education. Where decreases were reported, the most common reasons were transportation problems and ineffective recruitment techniques.

Diversification of program focus changes the scale of an educational organization for older adults. Increasingly, programs in senior centers and LRIs were taking on additional functions, such as community service components, leadership classes, and intergenerational projects. In so doing, the programs spilled over into other community settings and often involved partnerships with other organizations.

The Senior Neighbors program of Chattanooga (mentioned in Chapter 1) was contacted by a private school in the area and requested to provide a gerontologist to speak to students about myths of aging. Senior Neighbors in turn proposed a full-year program which would bring older persons to meet with the children. The school readily accepted the proposal. When word of the success of the year-long program got around, other schools contacted the center and requested similar programs involving older adults. In addition, Senior Neighbors launched a summer art program which involves center members and teenagers (eleventh and twelfth graders) enrolled in the University of Tennessee at Chattanooga's Upward Bound program.

The 60+ Club at California State University at Bakersfield (CSUB) initiated a volunteer program, the Action Network, in addition to their peer learning and teaching classes. The retiree members work with university departments to carry out specific projects such as organizing and labeling laboratory equipment or helping to run a component of CSUB's video production studio.

A third example is the OASIS Institute's Intergenerational Tutoring Program which prepares hundreds of seniors, through a twelve-hour training class, to tutor children in grades one through three in reading. The tutoring program was designed by the OASIS National Office and disseminated to their twenty-nine member sites who in turn work with local school districts to implement the training, place the tutors, and convene monthly meetings in support of the tutors' skills and motivation.

The scale of a program can thus be a matter of size, complexity, or scope. A program may have one focus or many—one entry door or several leading both from and to the community.

Delivery

Decisions regarding the scale of a program relate directly to time frame, scope, geographic locations, and means of communication. Over half (51 percent) of the reporting programs operated in five- to ten-week course periods with the median of eight weeks. These shorter (when compared to colleges and universities) intervals reflect seniors' preference for briefer commitments and greater flexibility in scheduling of personal time.

Just over one-third (35 percent) of programs used off-site or satellite locations. The five most frequently reported were college or universities settings, churches and synagogues, a private agency such as a YMCA or a hospital, a public agency such as a senior housing complex or library, and senior centers. Community colleges and senior centers were the most likely to use off-site locations. For example, Portland Community College's Senior Citizen Program provides classes in school buildings, churches, senior housing facilities, local libraries, YMCA buildings, hospitals, shopping malls, and senior centers.

Use of electronic media in support of instructional means was not especially common. LRIs and senior centers were the most frequent users of videotapes. Those LRIs and community colleges with access to teleconferencing facilities were the most likely to take advantage of the resource. The study did not include the national network of senior computer users, SeniorNet, which is discussed in Chapter 5.

Evaluation

Over 85 percent of the programs surveyed in this national study reported using some method for evaluating the success or failure of the overall program. Most frequently (77 percent), success was determined by counting numbers of participants. Other methods were the use of formal evaluation instruments (59 percent) and word-of-mouth reports (63 percent). Most frequently, the results of evaluations were communicated to the host institution, faculty, and participants (in that order). Rarely did programs communicate evaluation findings to the general community.

The majority of programs (78 percent) did evaluate courses, usually by using a printed evaluation form. Criteria of success included increased self-esteem of participants, better informed citizenry, increased social contact, intellectual stimulation, number of participants, size of program, involvement of participants, and acceptance by the host organization. Other success criteria included participant enjoyment, sense of belonging, program diversity and innovation, and quality of instruction.

Evaluation may also involve documentation. About half the programs reported documenting in print form their history, changes, and accomplishments. Few (less than 18 percent) documented impasses their program had encountered.

Continuity and Growth

It is not enough to have a faithful following of older adult members in educational programs. There is need for interesting and challenging activities to retain current participants and to attract new ones. Otherwise, as numerous program directors reported in telephone conversations, a program may develop a comfortable in-group or be perceived as "cliquish," thus deterring new membership. New participants were found to be important to the vitality of many of the programs surveyed (63 percent). Some 68 percent of the programs reported that each year about one-fourth of their membership was new members.

Over half (51 percent) of the programs reported that more than three-quarters of attendees were continuing participants who stayed with the program between two and ten years with a median of five years. Many of these programs, senior centers in particular, have populations that are aging in place and are considering marketing to a younger senior population.

Many of the programs are planning to or have changed their name. Reasons for name changes centered on creating a more positive institutional image in keeping with changing attitudes of older adults or toward them from younger members of society. Name changes may reflect aspects of institutional development in the brief history of older adult education, as the following example illustrates.

The Lifelong Learning Society at Florida Atlantic University was originally organized in the 1970s as the Society of Older Scholars, a program designed to encourage seniors' enrollment in credit courses leading to bachelor or master's degrees. But in 1980 the Florida Board of Regents instituted a policy by which state residents sixty and over could enroll in courses tuition-free, but not for credit, on a space-available basis. At once, great interest surfaced for the Society and the courses made available. The program became known as the 60+ Audit program, while the Society came to be known as the Society of Older Students. Then, in 1988, in order to lay greater stress on "learning" and less on "older," the association was renamed the Lifelong Learning Society.

By-Products

Forty percent of the programs reported having spin-offs or by-products as a result of the educational program. These spin-offs included exhibits (e.g., art shows and sales), recognition events (e.g., outstanding volunteers), performance groups (e.g., choral, dance, and theater) and intergenerational projects. For example, June Stiern, Chair of the Instructional Television Committee of the 60+ Club at CSUB reported a 60+ committee was formed to work with the CSUB Instructional Television Organization in the planning, preparing, and televising of programs of a public service nature.

OASIS, exemplifying tutoring–mentoring programs, offers an intergenerational tutorial program through its national office for its centers to implement in their various communities. Through the OASIS Intergenerational Tutoring Program, the combined resources of older adult tutors, local school districts, and the OASIS organization make it possible for hundreds of third graders to build their confidence and reading skills.

Many programs offering poetry, creative, or autobiographical writing classes provide opportunities for members to publish their work. For example, *Recollections* is a publication of the Seniors' Studies at Ryerson Polytechnical Institute in Toronto, Canada, that grew out of a writing class. The magazine-format publication was funded in part by a grant from Canada's Department of Health and Welfare.

Other educational programs for seniors have established dance and acting companies that tour locally and nationally. Senior Neighbors of Chattanooga has a choral group that performs at locations throughout the community and an ensemble of members has formed the Ripe and Ready Players, a performance group that has been featured at national conferences where they present original theatre scenes developed from reminiscences, improvisations, creative brainstorming, and high-spirited debate.

DETERMINANTS OF SUCCESS

No single cluster of factors can be derived from the research findings that would automatically provide the formula for success—where success means innovation and continuity of program development, growth or planned stability of enrollment numbers, institutional stability, senior empowerment, and some degree of shared leadership. Informally, however, we can identify some of the most important keys to viability and quality growth:

- A clear sense of institutional goals and mission
- Strong links to host institution with good avenues for communication
- Encouragement of senior leadership and well-coordinated use of volunteers
- Adequate financial planning using multiple funding sources with long-range budgetary expectations
- Openness to new clientele and continuing efforts to evaluate existing programs and anticipate possible new ones
- Ties to and knowledge of older adult education networks from which new ideas and research findings could be gleaned
- A willingness to be as outward as inward looking to put the educational program in the context of larger institutional and community issues

PROSPECTS FOR THE FUTURE

The institutional types reviewed in the NCCCR's 1992–1993 national research project demonstrated evolving infrastructures, curricula, governance, and participant involvement. With the exception of senior centers, most organizational development took place outside the network of aging organizations, perhaps because primarily the well elderly are served by these programs and the aging network is more focused on service delivery to the frail and at-risk. The future of older adult education is both promising and perplexing. Even with the relatively flat growth of the older adult population during the 1990s, certain types of programs have multiplied across the country. Programs based in colleges and universities are growing at a rapid pace, though they often exist at the margins of power and resource allocation. These programs have proven to be valuable community service arms of their host institutions, which may help ensure their survival, but are generally nonprofit centers (a liability in the eyes of many campus administrators).

Availability of funding is also a factor. Elbert Cole, president and founder of the Shepherd's Center movement, reported that newly forming groups were caught between choosing to launch community eldercare programs with funds made available from a major foundation, or the wellness, productive-aging type of Shepherd's Center program that does not readily attract funders and operates largely on volunteer power.

The growth of older learner programs, not unlike adult education in general, is somewhat unpredictable because it is not the result of a coordinated national effort, government policy, or public expenditure of money. Umbrella organizations like the EIN, now with almost 200 LRI members, and Shepherd's Centers of America conduct workshops and offer support services to groups that want to establish programs. In 1992, the ASA formed an Older Adult Education Network membership group and introduced a valuable newsletter and the NCOA has its Arts and Humanities Committee. Still, older adult education seems to be driven more by the changing demographics of an aging society than by the intention of any particular group. Various state and national organizations are bringing their own particular strengths to help enhance growth and leadership.

The successes of consumer-driven types of programs, with their course or membership fees, and of higher education-based programs raise a critical question: Are the only people who benefit those who can afford to pay for these programs, are comfortable on college campuses, and have access to quality offerings? Has participation in older adult education been left to factors of the marketplace? The answer is clearly yes. And within that marketplace there is also competition among program types. Senior centers, for example, have lost many potential younger seniors to Shepherd's Centers and OASIS Institutes.

The drift toward taking on volunteer community service projects as an outgrowth of senior educational programs suggests that participants hold a broad view of self-actualization. Being of service to members of other generations and taking leadership positions in community organizations points to a different concept of personal fulfillment—communal belonging. This is particularly critical in light of societal concerns about justice between generations as reflected in national health-care policy debates and perceived conflicts over scarce funds for at-risk youth and at-risk elderly.

How will other social institutions respond to the new generation of retirees who have unprecedented goals, expectations, resources, and creative and contributory powers? Lessons can be learned from educational organizations trying to meet the wants and needs of the new seniors.

REFERENCES

Academy for Educational Development. 1974. *Never Too Old to Learn*. Washington, D.C.: Academy for Educational Development.

Beckman, B. M., and C. Ventura-Merkel. 1992. *Community College Programs for Older Adults: A Resource Directory of Guidelines, Comprehensive Programming Models, and Selected Programs*. Laguna Hill, Calif.: League for Innovation in the Community College and the American Association of Retired Persons.

Boshier, R., and Riddell, G. 1978. "Education Participation Scale Factor Structure for Older Adults." *Adult Education* 28: 165–175.

Bova, B. M. 1981. Motivational Orientations of Senior Citizens Participating in the Elderhostel Program. Paper read at the National University Continuing Education Association Regional Meeting. ERIC Document Reproduction Service No. ED 206 927.

Bynum, L. L., and M. A. Seaman. 1993. "Motivation of Third-Age Students in Learning-In-Retirement Institutes." *Continuing Higher Education Review* 57 (1&2): 12–22.

Cross, K. P. 1981. *Adults as Learners*. San Francisco: Jossey-Bass.

Cusack, S. A. 1994. "Developing Leadership in the Third Age: An Ethnographic Study of Leadership in a Seniors' Center." *Journal of Applied Gerontology* 13(2): 127–142.

Danner, D. D., F. W. Danner, and L. C. Kuder. 1993. "Late-Life Learners at the University: The Donovan Scholars Program at Age Twenty-Five." *Educational Gerontology* 19(3): 217–239.

Elderhostel Institute Network (EIN). 1991. *The Institute Movement and Elderhostel: A National Overview*. Durham, N.H.: Elderhostel Institute Network.

———. FAX communication to author. September 1994.

Fischer, R. B., M. L. Blazey, and H. T. Lipman, eds. 1992. *Students of the Third Age—University/College Programs for Retired Adults*. New York: Macmillan.

Glickman, L., B. S. Hersey, and I. I. Goldenberg. 1975. *Community Colleges Respond to Elders—A Sourcebook for Program Development*. Washington, D.C.: Institute of Education, Department of Health, Education, and Welfare.

Hendrickson, A. 1973. *A Manual on Planning Educational Programs for Older Adults*. Tallahasse, Fla.: Department of Adult Education.

Kingston, A. J., and M. W. Drotter. 1983. "A Comparison of Elderly College Students in Two Different Geographic Areas." *Educational Gerontology* 9: 399–403.

Liroff, S. R. (manager, Older Adult Education, NCOA). Letter to author, April 1991.

Londoner, C. A. 1971. "Survival Needs of the Aged: Implications for Program Planning." *International Journal of Aging and Human Development* 2: 113–117.

———. 1978. "Instrumental and Expressive Education: A Basis for Needs Assessment and Planning." In *Introduction to Educational Gerontology*. 2d ed. Edited by R. H. Sherron and D. B. Lumsden. Washington, D.C.: Hemisphere.

Lowy, L., and D. O'Connor. 1986. *Why Education in the Later Years?* Lexington, Mass.: Lexington Books.

Lumsden, D. B., ed. 1985. *The Older Adult as Learner, Aspects of Educational Gerontology*. New York: Hemisphere.

Manheimer, R. J., and D. Snodgrass. 1993. "New Roles and Norms for Older Adults through Higher Education." *Educational Gerontology* 19: 585–595.

Mann, M. (director of OASIS). Letter to author, 1991.

McClusky, H. Y. 1971. Education: Background Issues. Paper presented at the White House Conference on Aging, February. Washington, D.C.: Government Printing Office. ERIC Document Reproduction Service No. ED 057 335.

Meyers, F. A. 1987. *The Handbook for Learning in Retirement Organizations*. Los Angeles: The Association of Learning in Retirement Organizations.

Moskow-McKenzie, D., and R. J. Manheimer. 1993. Organizing Educational Programs for Older Adults: A Summary of Research. Asheville, N.C.: North Carolina Center for Creative Retirement.

———. 1994. *A Guide to Developing Educational Programs for Older Adults*. Asheville, N.C.: UNCA University Publications.

North Carolina Center for Creative Retirement (NCCCR). 1993. Identifying Critical Pathways in Organizing Educational Programs for Older Adults. Final Report submitted to the AARP Andrus Foundation. Asheville, N.C.: University of North Carolina at Asheville.

O'Connor, D. 1991. "Free Tuition for Elders: Intentions and Effects of the Massachusetts Policy." *Journal of Aging and Social Policy* 3(1/2): 57–72.

Peterson, D. A. 1983. *Facilitating Education for Older Learners*. San Francisco: Jossey-Bass.

Romaniuk, J. G. 1983. "Development of Educational Programs for Older Adult Learners." *The Gerontologist* 23(3): 313–318.

Scanlon, J. 1978. *How to Plan a College Program for Older People*. Washington, D.C.: Academy for Educational Development.

Shepherd's Centers of America. 1990. *Organization Manual for Shepherd's Centers*. Kansas City, Mo.: Shepherd's Centers of America.

———. 1991. *Adventures in Learning*. Kansas City, Mo.: Shepherd's Centers of America.

Sherron, R. H., and D. B. Lumsden, eds. 1990. *Introduction to Educational Gerontology*. 3d ed. New York: Hemisphere.

Sprouse, B. M., and K. Brown. 1981. *Developing Community-Based Learning Centers for Older Adults*. Madison, Wis.: Faye McBeath Institute on Aging and Adult Life.

U.S. Department of Education, National Center for Education Statistics. Integrated Postsecondary Education Data System. "Fall Enrollment, 1987" Survey.

U.S. Senate Special Committee on Aging. 1991. *Aging America, Trends and Projections*. Washington, D.C.: U.S. Senate Special Committee on Aging, the American Association of Retired Persons, the Federal Council on the Aging, and the U.S. Administration on Aging.

Verschueren, J. (director, Elderhostel Institute Network). Letter to author, March 1991.

Weinstock, R. 1978. *The Graying of the Campus*. New York: Educational Facilities Laboratories. Pamphlet no. 29.

Wirtz, P., and I. Charner. 1989. "Motivations for Educational Participation by Retirees: The Expressive–Instrumental Continuum Revisited." *Educational Gerontology* 15(3): 275–284

4

The Impact of Institutional Policies on Older Adult Education

In 1990, graduate student Stephany Schlachter traveled from Illinois to Washington, D.C., as part of her dissertation research. The reason for her trip was to question congressmen, consultants, advocacy group directors, and various federal officials about their attitudes toward purposes and policies related to education, particularly of older adults. Assured of confidentiality, these officials responded to Schlachter's questions without fear of jeopardizing their positions should they happen to say something that might not be considered politically correct. From their responses, Schlachter deduced some basic assumptions about government leaders' values that shape older adult education policies.

A strong proponent of education admitted:

Public policy reflects, I think, all constituents' concerns with balancing the budget. So we all say, I mean we sit here and say, gosh we can use ten times what we have now just for adult education programs. They reach three million people out of a projected twenty-some million, depending on who you talk to. And you know that's a priority, and you say, well then you shouldn't let budget constraints dictate public policy if all these people should learn. It's not just us. It's [the Department of Health and Human Services], it's [the Department of Labor], it's all these groups and someone has to draw the line in saving the public interest. We can only afford to spend X amount of money unless the public wants to pay more and no one wants that. So . . . it's a balancing, it's always a balancing. (Schlachter 1991)

Another supporter of education concurred with this view that policy decisions often are based primarily on economic and pragmatic criteria rather than on philosophic and pedagogic concerns about equity.

It's true that a lot of elders are better off than ever before and it's true that a lot of elders are poor, and . . . in near poverty. . . . Policymakers at every level and certainly at the federal level, in an era of budget stringency, must set priorities. And their setting of priorities is often painful . . . So that what you see is a shifting of resources away from the middle class, at least the public dollars and maybe the other sources. (Schlachter 1991)

In part, the future of older adult education will be shaped by policymakers' assumptions about older people and public values of education as a tool for making life better for all Americans, regardless of age. Apparently it will be significantly influenced by the economic stability and educational leadership of the country. Advances in older adult education have also occurred outside the purview of governmental policies and legislation. How do nongovernmental institutions and policies compare to those at the federal and state government levels? How will the future of older adult educational policy be decided?

This chapter explores the contexts in which contemporary public policy decisions are made that affect educational programs targeted for older adults. We look at the following areas: (1) the different views of older adults, older adult educational programs, and the effects of national trends; (2) the stakeholders and their motivations in policy decisions related to older adults; and (3) the institutional policies related to older adult education established by federal and state governments, educational institutions, national aging associations, and other organizations that have played a role in education for older adults.

PUBLIC POLICY AND THE GREYING
OF THE UNITED STATES

The rapid growth in the number of older adults in the United States during the twentieth century (see Chapter 1) has affected many elements in our modern culture (Table 4.1 and Figure 4.1). Trends that begin to reverse the effects of negative attitudes toward the elderly, ageism (Binstock 1990), and the youth-oriented culture of the sixties affect areas as diverse as architecture and interior decorating to clothing design and advertising. Automobile manufacturers, banks, hospitals, and grocery stores utilize the expertise of older adult focus groups in understanding the needs and wishes of their age cohort. In the political arena, older adults have developed a large and sometimes powerful lobby through participating in state senior legislatures or in national advocacy organizations such as the AARP. Retirement communities and life-care facilities, as well as condominiums and patio homes, represent major housing trends. Yet many retirees find that their golden years are still tarnished with financial, medical, or social concerns. America looks toward a new century with not only the potential but also the problems of an aging society.

Table 4.1
Growth of the Older Population, 1900–1990 (thousands)

Year	Total number (all ages)	65 years and over Number	Percent
1900	75,995	3,080	4.1
1910	91,972	3,949	4.3
1920	105,711	4,933	4.7
1930	122,775	6,634	5.4
1940	131,669	9,019	6.8
1950	150,697	12,269	8.1
1960	179,323	16,560	9.2
1970	203,302	19,980	9.8
1980	226,546	25,550	11.3
1990	248,710	31,079	12.5

Source: U.S. Bureau of the Census, 1900 to 1940, 1960, and 1980 from 1980 Census of Population, PC80-B1, 1990 from 1990 Census of Population and Housing, Series CPH-L-74.
Note: Figures for 1900 to 1950 exclude Alaska and Hawaii. Figures for 1900 to 1990 are for the resident population. Data for 1900 to 1990 are April 2 census figures.

Life Course Change and Older Adult Education

Demographers predict that more people living past sixty-five will produce "an older population on a scale never before experienced in the United States" (NCOA 1994). As the baby boomers age and begin to reach sixty-five in less than twenty years, we can expect a bulge in that age group combined with the increased life expectancy and decreased fertility rates, causing a "squaring of the population pyramid" (Pifer and Bronte 1986). (See Figures 4.2, 4.3, and 4.4; also see Chapter 1.)

The rate of growth of the aging population is as dramatic as the sheer volume (Tauber 1992). The over-sixty-five population has nearly doubled since 1960 and is projected to double again by 2030 (see Table 4.1). As illustrated by Figure 4.1, the projected growth in the older population is expected to raise the median age of the United States population to thirty-six by the year 2000 and to forty-two by the year 2040 (U.S. Senate Special Committee on Aging 1989).

Not only are the absolute number and percentages of older people large, but the questions of accommodating the needs of the older population are formidable. In 1992, older adults accounted for 12.7 percent of the population;

Figure 4.1
Median Age of the Population: 1950–2050

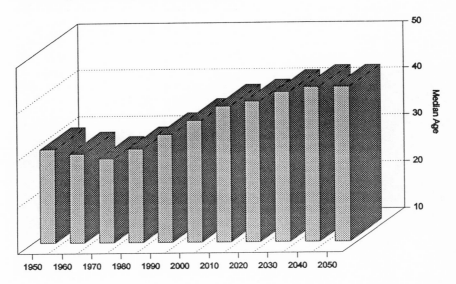

Sources: U.S. Bureau of the Census, *Statistical Abstract of the United States: 1985* (Washington, D.C.: U.S. Government Printing Office, December 1984); idem, "Projections of the Population of the United States, by Age, Sex, and Race: 1988 to 2080," by Gregory Spencer. *Current Population Reports*, Series P-25 No. 1018 (January 1989).

only 12 percent of those are in the labor force, often as part-time employees (Fowles 1993). The percentage of older people who have completed high school has risen from 28 percent to 60 percent since 1970; despite the rising percentage, only about a third of minority older adults have completed high school (Fowles 1993).

Those providing services and benefits to the older population, including Medicare and Social Security, wonder if resources will match demand. Some suggest that our policies ought to be based on "trying to maximize the satisfaction and value of the retirement years" (NCOA 1994) rather than trying to provide services that foster dependency and perhaps extend the length but not necessarily the quality of life. Others argue that we can never provide or afford enough services to meet the needs of all older adults, but we can maximize appropriate services for particular older adults. Thus, public policy should target those with the greatest need. Still others question the basic premise of providing for older adults at the expense, as they see it, of younger generations, especially considering the depth of needs in other age groups, particularly children. The realities of an aging population raise complex social and political issues.

Figure 4.2
Population by Sex and Age: 1975 (in millions)

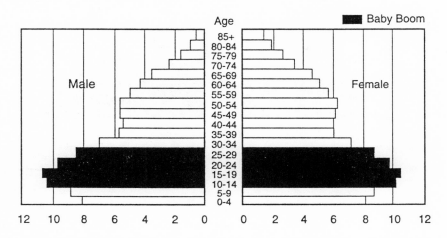

Source: U.S. Bureau of the Census. "Estimates of the Population of the United States, by Single Years of Age, Color, and Sex: 1970 to 1981." *Current Population Reports*, Series P-25, no. 917 (Washington, D.C.: U.S. Government Printing Office, 1982). From Ronald J. Manheimer, ed., *Older Americans Almanac: A Reference Work on Seniors in the United States*, North Carolina Center for Creative Retirement, University of North Carolina at Asheville. Copyright © 1994 by Gale Research, Inc. Reprinted with permission of the publisher.

The Political Context

Politics and policy decisions respond to changing demands; therefore, changing social, political, and economic issues affect public policy. At least two recent trends in the social, political, and economic realm are cu·· ·ntly affecting public policy related to older Americans. The first is overall economic improvement: Benefits such as Social Security, the major source of income for 37 percent of older people in 1990 (Fowles 1993), have "helped to reduce the proportion of elderly persons in poverty from about 35% three decades ago to 12.2% today" (National Academy on Aging 1994). The second is the composite change of the federal budget: The trend in the last three decades is toward more money being spent on older people. "Today, expenditures on aging are well over 30% of the budget" compared to about 25% thirty years ago (National Academy on Aging 1994).

Both trends reflect primarily economic concerns. The public sentiment of the early 1960s that public resources were plentiful and that all segments of society, including older people who were considered deserving, should reap benefits has been replaced by a new approach. Current thinking reflects anxiety about scarce resources and generational equity issues: Are all segments of the society cared for as well as older people? Will those currently paying

Figure 4.3
Population by Sex and Age: 2010 (in millions)

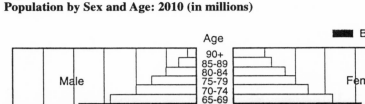

Source: U.S. Bureau of the Census. "Estimates of the Population of the United States, by Single Years of Age, Color, and Sex: 1980 to 2080." Gregory Spencer. *Current Population Reports*, Series P-25, no. 1018 (Washington, D.C.: U.S. Government Printing Office, 1989) (middle series projections). From Ronald J. Manheimer, ed., *Older Americans Almanac; A Reference Work on Seniors in the United States*, North Carolina Center for Creative Retirement, University of North Carolina at Asheville. Copyright © 1994 by Gale Research, Inc. Reprinted with permission of the publisher.

for benefits to older people be afforded those same benefits when they retire? Should older people receive benefits solely based on age or should services benefit only those who cannot pay for them?

Some gerontologists see one solution to the issue of equitable distribution of benefits and services by offering the *generational investment paradigm*, meaning that today's middle-ager is not only the adult child of an older person but also is tomorrow's elder. Hence, all generations will eventually benefit from decent treatment of the older generation.

Old age programs and other social programs (such as public education) might be better understood within a generational investment paradigm, in which they play an integral part in the system of reciprocal contributions that generations in any society make to one another. In this context, for example, Social Security and Medicare can be seen more clearly as mechanisms through which the generations invest in one another, and share in the fruits of that investment. (National Academy on Aging 1994)

At least in the short term, interest in older Americans remains strong. Not only are they a growing segment of the population, they are a politically ac-

Figure 4.4
Population by Sex and Age: 2030 (in millions)

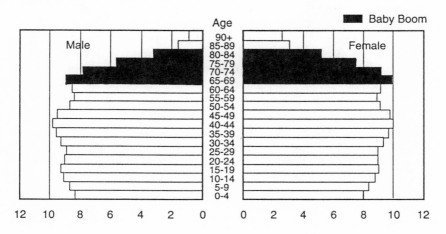

Source: U.S. Bureau of the Census. "Estimates of the Population of the United States, by Single Years of Age, Color, and Sex: 1988 to 2080." Gregory Spencer. *Current Population Reports*, Series P-25, no. 1018 (Washington, D.C.: U.S. Government Printing Office, 1989) (middle series projections). From Ronald J. Manheimer, ed., *Older Americans Almanac: A Reference Work on Seniors in the United States*, North Carolina Center for Creative Retirement, University of North Carolina at Asheville. Copyright © 1994 by Gale Research, Inc. Reprinted with permission of the publisher.

tive group with considerable income: median net worth at $73,500 in 1988, well above the national average of $35,800 (Fowles 1993). In the long term, with the aging of the baby boom looming closer, the National Academy of Aging's recent report, among others, suggests an urgency to older adult policy considerations.

A New Phenomenon: Older Adults as an Industry

Predictably, numerous institutions have responded to the aging of America. Chambers of commerce, universities, area agencies on aging, and state government departments of tourism and economic development have organized numerous conferences and seminars on marketing to the over-fifty population. Television and radio stations program for an older audience. Health-care providers expand facilities to fill the demands of an aging population. Local, state, and federal governments establish agencies to serve the older constituents. And indeed, both public and private educational institutions provide courses, training, and programs for older learners.

Chapter 2 and Chapter 3 describe many of the current organizations and programs providing educational services to older adults and responding to the needs and interests of this growing, vocal, and significant group. Have these programs developed in response to the demands of older learners? Have they developed because institutions saw opportunities to expand into this growing and sometimes affluent market? Or have such programs developed in response to federal, state, or local mandates to provide equal access to all segments of the population or to serve older learners as a specially deserving or underprivileged group? The answers to these questions are both yes and no, depending on the program itself and who gives the answer.

For example, in a large southern city a multipurpose senior center has been providing various services and programs to mostly poor elderly for fifteen years. When the center begins a reading and discussion program of local authors, coordinated by a volunteer, some participants think that this new program arose in response to their suggestion to the center's program council for additional programs and activities. The center's paid staff regards the new offering as an effort to go beyond such existing services as providing meals, transportation, and health screening services. In their view the new program contributes to recreational and educational activities that will attract younger members to their aging membership. The local Area Agency on Aging, which provides funding for several of the programs of the center, sees the new offering as a way to satisfy the area plan requirements by developing comprehensive services for helping to keep older adults independent and by reaching out to rural and low-income elderly who will be transported to the program.

As this example shows, various groups may have different objectives in the development of older adult education programs. One such program can be attributed to a number of influences and can fulfill assorted purposes. Successful programs encourage diversity by fostering both community and institutional support and by responding to interests and needs of current and potential participants.

While educational programs achieve a variety of purposes claimed by different interest groups, what is the role of public policy in encouraging or discouraging maintenance of existing educational programs or developing new ones? Considering the proliferation of organized educational programs for older adults over the last twenty years may underscore the importance of public policy or may suggest, instead, the predominance of market response to the demands of older learners.

The influence of market demand, rather than the impetus of public policy, is corroborated by the recent study of 260 community-based participant-influenced educational programs for older adults (see Chapter 3) which indicates the rapid growth since the 1970s of locally initiated, fee-based programs. Only a few of these programs indicated their inception grew from a public policy, such as state-level tuition-waiver policies or as an act of the state legislature, as in the case of the NCCCR (NCCCR 1993).

Older Adult Education: Not One but Many Policies

Examining the current public policies related to education of older adults necessitates initial clarification. First, the history and definition of older adult education in Chapters 1 and 2 clarifies who are older adults and what qualifies as educational programs within the scope of this book. Grasping the scope of public policies on older adult education demands appreciation of the diversity of older adults as a subcategory of the larger population. Can older adults be categorized? Do older adults have the same needs, concerns, and values? What characteristics do they share other than chronological age? An excerpt from the Final Report of the 1981 White House Conference on Aging states:

There appears to be a misconception among some that the aged in America are: victims of poverty; abandoned by their families . . . ; living in deteriorated housing; victims of inflation; prisoners in their homes and neighborhoods; isolated from family, friends, and society; forced into premature retirement. . . . Indeed, emphasis on the problems of the elderly has obscured the single most extraordinary fact about the great majority of the elderly Americans: They are the wealthiest, best-fed, best-housed, healthiest, most self-reliant older population in our history. (Department of Health and Human Services 1982)

This statement of extremes suggests that older Americans are at least as diverse as any other age group; services, programs, and policies need to take into account this diversity rather than considering all older adults to have the same interests and needs (Moody 1985; Yeo 1982). Some states, such as North Carolina, have explicit policy goals to reach all older citizens, well and at-risk, by "achieving an equitable distribution of state and federal resources and promoting the development of a minimum set of supportive services, rights and protections, and opportunities for all older adults" (Division of Aging 1991). Other states target services only to the poor, frail, and at-risk senior population.

Next, although local, state, and federal policies do exist which support the ideal of enabling older adults to participate in forms of lifelong learning (e.g., through tuition waivers for college courses), these policies refer to different types of older adult education, often without definition of responsibility, impact, and funding. For example, the 1976 Lifelong Learning Act, which was passed by Congress, outlined numerous issues related to education of older adults. For a variety of political reasons, the act was never funded. Does absence of funding nullify the ideals set forth in the policy? Further, different groups have a stake in older adult education and related policies but view older adults and their education differently. For example, some educational organizations claim or accept responsibility for education which targets a certain group of citizens, older adults being one of them. Aging organizations, on the other hand, claim or accept responsibility for older adult programs that happen to be educational. Turf conflicts can arise, according to Manheimer (1987–1988), who indicates that many older adults participate in learning programs in locations as different as shopping malls, nursing homes, libraries, and churches that may compete with each other. Because of their locations, these programs may be classified as informal and devalued by colleges and universities as not truly educational. Alternatively, educational institutions may open programs to older learners, but, because of lack of attention to costs, access, scheduling, and learning needs of seniors, few may choose to participate.

Finally, since both education policy and aging policy address issues of older adult education, these factors combine to produce not *a* public policy, whether local, state, or federal, but *several* public policies of older adult education. This lack of uniformity makes it difficult for users or potential users to assess educational opportunities and for providers or potential providers to assess obligations to older learners and possible funding sources.

MOTIVATIONS OF MAJOR STAKEHOLDERS IN OLDER ADULT EDUCATION POLICY

Public policy reflects the values, concerns, attitudes, and images held by the larger society. As such, policy is organic; various parts form integral elements of the whole even while the parts, viewed separately, may appear disparate. Policy related to education of older adults is no exception: State policies entitling tuition waivers to citizens by virtue of their age may seem incompatible with federal policy preventing age discrimination; a state university's policy to permit its LRI to charge seniors a membership fee to attend institute classes may seem incompatible with the state policy to grant those same citizens tuition waivers when enrolling in the undergraduate program.

Understanding older adult education policy necessitates appreciation of the different groups with strong interest in or influence over that policy. In addition to older adults, those in public service, such as elected officials and civil servants, educators, and aging specialists influence adult education policies.

Older Adults

Older adults have a vital interest in public policy that affects their lives and opportunities. Their interest is primarily with practical matters of their own needs: what they as consumers desire to be offered or provided. As previously noted, older adults are a large and diverse group. Not only can their interests not be easily characterized, but even defining who they are is difficult for those who make policy. Some federal policymakers use age forty to designate older workers in relation to retraining needs and related job discrimination concerns. The Department of Labor uses age fifty-five for its programs. Many policymakers cite age sixty since this is used in the Older Americans Act and by the NCOA—a "provider-focused group" (Schlachter 1991). The AARP used age sixty as its original criterion but several years ago dropped the membership requirement to age fifty, probably to broaden the membership base. Most policymakers do not seriously consider educational needs for older adults once they have reached age seventy.

Older adults have indirect and limited influence on policy because, as a group, they are not a clearly defined or active political constituency even though as individuals they vote more regularly than do individuals in other age groups. Despite the effectiveness of organizations such as the AARP that lobby for older adults, these organizations select the issues on which they take stands based on what they perceive to be of primary importance; usually education is not a selected concern. "Although the older adult lobbying groups represent a large enough constituency to have an impact on legislators, these groups have not designated education as an 'issue'" in the way Social Security and Medicare have become issues based on how they "better reflect the values of their constituencies" (Schlachter 1991).

Government Representatives

A second group of stakeholders is elected officials and others in state and federal government responsible to the people. One interest of this group is rights of citizens, such as equal access, nondiscrimination, and provisions that enable a better society for all. They are responsive to and influenced by the general electorate, organizations, and advocacy groups, as well as private business. The concerns and attitudes of representatives of this group related to older adult education are the subject of the study cited at the beginning of this chapter which samples and analyzes opinions and perceptions about older people, their values, and their potential (Schlachter 1991). According to this study, "education for older adults is not an important topic on Capitol Hill," being considered by Congressmen as a "minor assignment" (Schlacter 1991).

A second interest of this group is the economic impact of any given policy decision; in this case policies related to education for older people. According to the Schlachter (1991) study, policymakers were most interested in the functions of education, not for the general benefit to older people, but for the potential economic benefit to the country in job retraining, retaining older workers, adult literacy, and volunteerism. Many have called for expanded opportunities for older people to serve as community resources through volunteer services (Quirk 1991). Of course, policymakers were interested in enabling seniors to maintain economic independence without welfare or unemployment compensation.

Moody (1988) categorizes four views of older adult education: rejection of older adults, provision of social services for dependent older adults, encouraging older adults to participate in mainstream activities and to be self-sufficient, and providing for self-actualization and growth of older people. Policymakers are currently moving from a social service to a participation model; they have not yet embraced self-actualization. Perhaps their emphasis on education of older people as support for labor is not surprising, since policymakers perceive that "as labor goes, so goes the country" (Schlachter 1991). If education of older people is tied to the success of the economy, then, necessarily, it is important in the eyes of policymakers. Government sector policymakers have interest in youth education, job retraining, and literacy education because those affect, most directly, the economics of the country.

Therefore, job retraining is considered an important segment of older adult education for this group of policymakers. With the U.S. work force growing older and more older workers retiring, Workforce 2000 predicts labor shortages (U.S. Department of Labor 1989). Corporate downsizing of recent years could impact these predictions. Retraining older workers could solve certain types of labor market shortages, according to some policymakers, despite policies that encourage retirement, such as Social Security benefits and tax breaks for seniors. Yet retraining and employing older adults raises questions related to those who volunteer or work without pay. Should older volunteers receive the same training as those who work for pay? If not, is volunteerism then a type of exploitation of older people? On the other hand, if older volunteers are offered training and retraining, then could their work be considered stealing jobs away from others, including younger workers?

Some funding of work-related education of older people focuses on training them to provide tutoring and social supports for children in their development as future qualified workers (Schlachter 1991). Training seniors in preschool child care is one new job area (Smith, Mack, and Tittnich 1993). Other growing employment areas are retail sales (department stores and telephone marketing) and the food industry.

Many policymakers need to quantify the returns on programs. General education is difficult to quantify, so programs in retraining and literacy, which are more easily quantified, are easier to promote. This factor may account for the lack of funding for the more general provisions in the Lifelong Learning Act (Schlachter 1991). Although the 1971 White House Conference on Aging asserted that education is a basic right, policymakers have not felt a need to guarantee programs but, rather, allow older people the right to pursue education if they so desire and can pay.

In summary, public policy related to educating older people is based on labor force concerns (economics), investment in human capital, and the questions of equity and access (competition for scarce resources). "No one would argue that education for older adults is not a good thing. But when this need is placed in the forum of other competing needs, it is more difficult to make a clear case in support of older adults" (Schlachter 1991). Lowy and O'Connor (1986) put it this way:

Indeed, if there were not the problem of scarcity in the social system, education of older adults would hardly need justification any more than any other societal program or benefit. However, the choice to devote more resources to education of older people in order to meet the various needs of a growing elder population invariably involves some tradeoffs. The availability of another program, service, or benefit must be reduced or eliminated altogether if a new opportunity—the large-scale education for older adults—is to demand a larger share of society's resources.

While policymakers are happy to encourage older adults to continue to learn, they are only willing to pay for economically beneficial programs. Those who consider that older adults themselves benefit from educational programs usually believe they should pay for their own education, especially considering the relatively low rate of participation (6.7 percent according to the Department of Education) (Schlachter 1991). Policymakers believe that businesses investing in their own workers through retraining should pay the costs themselves. Some policymakers believe that education of older people benefits the individual, business, and the society at large and that public/private partnerships should pay. Most policymakers believe that those that have the ability to pay for their own education should and that what money there is should go to job retraining, literacy, or programs to "help those who are unable to help themselves" (Schlachter 1991).

Federal policymakers consider educational policy and financing to be the responsibility of state or local governments. They, like state and local policymakers, endorse the concept of education for older adults, but do little to plan educational policy since other concerns, such as social and health problems, take precedence.

Practitioners: Educators

A third group concerned with the educational opportunities available to older adults are educators. These include the following groups: (1) educational administrators involved with policy matters and funding issues; (2) academicians who research and analyze the theory and implications of education; and (3) practitioners who teach courses, design curricula, administer programs, and run educational institutions. Although these three groups of educators are affected by educational policy decisions, oftentimes they do not talk to each other and do not present a coherent voice for education to the public and policymakers. For example, practitioners such as teachers may value education as intrinsically good as well as for its role in solving societal problems, such as teaching students skills that make them employable or teaching students parenting skills. An administrator could object to the same programs as not being cost-effective. Similarly, some adult educators might not want to schedule daytime continuing education classes that would accommodate senior citizens, and yet, some administrators may value the role of older adult education in solving institutional problems such as decreased enrollments or the need to diversify revenue sources. Educators' approaches to education reveal their professional training, experience, and bias.

Public Education, Adult Education, and Older Adult Education. At one time, people considered that life followed a linear course—childhood, youth, adulthood, old age—with certain functions associated with each age. Childhood was characterized by dependency and growth, youth by education, adulthood by work and family, and old age by dependency and death. Education (primary, secondary, and postsecondary) was for the young, with its primary purposes being socialization, enculturation, and preparation for raising families and entering the work force. Vast local, state, and federal systems developed to direct the primary, secondary, and postsecondary public education of America's young people.

Education for those other than the young became necessary for those who were not qualified for particular work or who needed courses for job advancement or retraining. Businesses, unions, and professional organizations often sponsored or delivered such continuing education. In addition, many colleges and technical schools entered the business of adult or continuing education, expanding beyond the particular need of job training. Such adult education was usually patterned after its host or sponsoring educational institution and in response to perceived needs of the target audience. In other words, adult education in colleges tended to be instructor-led classes following academic disciplines, while adult education in trade unions tended to be hands-on skill development classes with practitioners as instructors.

Knowles (1977) pointed out that whereas adult education in England and Sweden developed primarily to educate workers, in the United States the proliferation of programs, associations, and networks related to adult education have developed with various directions and purposes, such as within trade unions to train workers and maintain membership clout or within women's organizations to promote higher paying jobs for members. While such expansion provided many options for older learners, it also complicated evaluation and assessment of the programs and the policies that applied to them. By 1960, adult education had become an "integral part of the American way of life" in areas as different as business and industry, extension services, labor unions, libraries, museums, religious institutions, health and welfare agencies, and other government agencies in addition to colleges and universities (Knowles 1977). In 1955, the U.S. Office of Education established an Adult Education Section.

Dramatic changes in education paralleled the turbulent changes in the United States during the 1950s, 1960s, and 1970s. School integration, open classrooms, and new math were the backdrop for a period of rapid growth in adult education. Increased industrialization and application of new technologies created the need for additional job training and retraining. The G.I. Bill enabled many of those returning from military service to enroll in colleges. Community colleges and technical institutions experienced rapid growth. Public television and radio developed with financial support from private foundations and the federal government. Such dramatic expansion of adult education opportunities foretold an expansion of older adult educational opportunities.

Most educators consider older adult education a branch of adult education developed in response to perceived needs of that particular audience in particular locations. At one community college, for instance, the director of adult education noted that those enrolling in extension courses, such as investment or bridge, had to pay a fee covering the cost of the course; 80 percent of those enrolled in extension courses were over fifty-five. Meanwhile, students who were over fifty-five and taking academic courses, such as history and literature, enrolled tuition-free; yet only 4 percent of those enrolled in academic courses were over fifty-five. Since this administrator wanted to increase college enrollment by attracting more older adults, his solution was to offer more investment and bridge classes. Although these additional classes might indeed fill with more older people, other classes might also appeal to them. Barriers such as the schedule of the classes or methods of instruction may affect participation as much as cost and subject matter. In fact, because older people represent as much or more diversity than any other age group, educational offerings for them should reflect that diversity. The proliferation of programs over the last twenty-five years targeted for older adults does exhibit variety. LRIs, Elderhostel, educational travel programs, senior center programs, and literacy programs all offer different types of learning experiences. Yet despite, or perhaps because of, the growth in numbers and popularity of such older adult education programs, they represent a collage or patchwork of efforts rather than a systematic development (Eklund 1969).

Continuous Education or Lifelong Learning. Some educators refer to the conglomeration of programs for older adults as evidence of the commitment by our educational system to lifelong learning. Is older adult education synonymous with lifelong learning? Older adult education implies educational programs for a particular age group and for a particular purpose, whereas lifelong learning implies a cradle to grave approach to learning more than learning by a particular group. In other words, people can be lifelong learners at eighteen or eighty by continuing to apply learning to new situations. Many believe that although we have lifelong learners in America, our public education system, which is based on transfer of knowledge rather than on problem-solving and use of knowledge, does not encourage institutional commitment to lifelong learning.

Historically, educators have based educational systems on the prevailing human development theory of life stages (see Chapter 2) which considers the first phase, birth to twenty or twenty-five, to encompass the period of education. Certainly current older adults were schooled under such a system and are less likely to have had the benefit of formal educational programs throughout their adult lives. Furthermore, to change the entire educational system toward a system of lifelong learning would require emphasis on learning as a process. Eklund (1969) was prescient to suggest that such a change would be possible only with a "revolutionary redesign and overhaul of the existing educational system."

When learners are taught skills necessary to seek new knowledge as their needs and situations change, they are prepared to be continuous, lifelong learners. When seen in this way, older adult education may be considered an outcome of a policy of lifelong learning. Lowy and O'Connor (1986) say that essential to such a policy is having older adults willing and able to learn and with access to programs.

Commitment to Older Adult Education. Even twenty-five years ago, Eklund (1969) observed that "the education of mature adults is being recognized as an obligatory function of most education institutions." Do educational institutions accept this function? Can such an obligation translate into substantive programs? Focusing on higher education, Eklund (1969) emphasized the need for a comprehensive and coordinated approach utilizing "an unqualified philosophical base which attests to the merit and justification of adult education, and which influences federal and state legislatures, college and university governing boards, administrations, and particularly faculties to accept and demonstrably support the coequality of continuing educational services." Should the system of public education take on older adults when the problems of educating the youth seem insurmountable? Services to adults and older adults by higher education systems are not coequal with services and programs for young adults, but in the last twenty-five years continuing education programs have dramatically expanded. In the 1970s, the Administration on Aging encouraged the AACJC "to develop an awareness of the needs of older Americans and to explore ways in which these community-oriented institutions might contribute to an improvement in the quality of life in the nation's elderly population" (Korim 1974).

In addition to considering the responsibility of institutions of higher education, alternatives need to be available for noncollege educated adults who may not be comfortable in the college or university setting. Many adults do not live close enough to colleges or universities to attend them. Alternatives can include programs provided by local secondary schools, churches, employers, senior centers, and the like.

How can educational institutions, public or private, justify allocation of resources to education of older adults? How significant is the role of education in addressing the various problems often associated with aging? Perhaps only when the education of older people is linked with the solution of problems for other age groups will communities and the education hierarchy willingly provide resources for their education. "Old people's ever-increasing numbers and days represent a growing resource whose potential is too precious to neglect; and, conversely, whose neglect is too great a social and economic loss to countenance" (Eklund 1969). Do those who make and fund educational policy consider education of older adults an important investment as well as an essential element in the larger picture of the country's public education system? Few practicing educators hold public office and can influence policy from the inside. Even educational advocacy groups separate into those who create the programs and those who create the policy.

Practitioners: Gerontologists and Aging Specialists

A fourth group concerned with the educational opportunities for older adults are gerontologists and aging specialists. Some value the function of education as filling needs of older people. Many aging specialists are practitioners dealing directly with older adults. Like practicing educators, how they approach older adult education depends on their professional orientation, training, and bias. While educators tend to focus on curricula and methods, aging specialists usually focus on life-course stages and tasks. This section highlights the general view of older adult education held by those in aging fields.

An Aging Society, Problems, and Potential. Organizations with responsibilities for the elderly have generally looked at factors that differentiate the elderly from other age groups rather than at what the age groups have in common. Focusing on how older people are different from younger people emphasizes the losses and needs in old age: losses in income and health, needs in housing, transportation, and legal matters. Few consider education a primary concern or need for the elderly. In the early 1970s, some, including Peterson (1985) and Moody (1976), posited that such a view was shortsighted. McMahon (1979) extended the argument to include training older adults as community leaders:

A compelling need exists for social policy and programming which will recognize the needs of the elderly for small-scale social programming and informal educational opportunities. Along with this goes a need for reinvolvement in community life. Policy which will improve the capabilities of senior citizen groups to provide programming toward fulfillment of these needs which will promote the development of community leadership capacities in these groups and which will train the leaders of these groups toward these ends should be of the highest priority.

In either case, those active in the field of aging generally view education as a tool to achieve the goal of helping older adults live better lives.

The aging view of older adult education is largely derived from the social service model, the medical model, or a combination of the two. The social service model considers older adult education as a social activity for seniors. These are group activities that keep people busy with positive activities including learning activities, volunteer roles, and intergenerational experiences. Experts believe such activities can ward off social disengagement often associated with aging (Manheimer 1994). The medical model considers older adult education a part of the broad plan for promoting physical and mental health.

Activities can include dissemination of information about medical problems, nutrition, and health-related issues which can either help the elderly understand the physical decline in old age, or, perhaps, slow the decline. In either case, this aging view focuses on ways to keep older people active, involved, and connected to the mainstream of society; educational programs are a tool to achieve this end.

In accordance with the aim of group interaction and social engagement, aging specialists endorse the benefits of formal educational programs for older adults. The rapid growth of such programs at colleges, universities, senior centers, churches, and community centers is often regarded by aging specialists as promoting the therapeutic benefit of mental and social involvement by older people. Some studies, however, show that older learners have a "preference for self-directed, independent educational activities and informal learning programs . . . [rather than] the more formal programs offered at institutions of higher education" (McMahon 1979). These results suggest that older learners find benefit in learning even without the added benefits of social engagement and activity.

Influence of Stakeholders

Policy does not evolve directly in proportion to the wisdom and interests of these four stakeholder groups, but their actions and values do influence the decisions of policymakers. In return, public policies also influence the stakeholders. The next sections will examine various types of public policies that directly impact older adult education participants, practitioners, and programs.

GOVERNMENTAL POLICIES BEFORE 1965

A Look Back at Adult Education Policy

During the nation's colonial period the church was the universal provider of adult education, while education in general was available primarily to the elite who could afford it. An explosion of secular knowledge and rapidly developing frontiers in the new world combined to cause a demand that education be separate from the church. The need for workers with new skills and for an educated population prepared for self-government led to the demand that education should be for everyone. In addition to education provided by schools and universities, apprenticeships and agricultural societies helped to train workers. Libraries, civic organizations, and town meetings served to educate the general populace. Thus the tradition of access of adults to education and educational programming has deep roots in the history of this country.

During the nineteenth century the groundwork was laid for public policy supporting education for adults. The Lyceum and Chautauqua movements (see Chapter 2), for example, not only linked adult learners in various communities and states, but also provided responses to the needs of an increasingly industrialized and urbanized country. In helping to raise public support for tax-supported public schools, the Lyceums established the adult education movement as a political force (Peterson 1990).

The population expansion and the political stimuli have combined during the twentieth century to cause a great expansion of adult education opportunities. The slightly older, more urban, better educated population with a raised standard of living demanded increased educational activities. The rapidly changing world, including changes in the technological, economic, political, and cultural climates, has necessitated opportunities for adults to learn and relearn. The revolution in the world of communication is an example. At the beginning of this century, the telephone revolutionized the way people conducted business. As we approach the next century, we are learning new business techniques in response to the capabilities of fiber optics and the information highway. Such innovations require educational programs for users.

PUBLIC POLICY RESPONDS TO OLDER AMERICANS

In modern America, older people are claiming more and more public resources because their numbers are increasing, they have needs, and they want their fair share. They want to grow old with dignity and respect while maintaining their individual rights, as do other Americans. Yet distribution of public resources to older people often comes under fire from those who do not value the aging and the contributions that older people make to our society or who find the costs too high. Often other needy groups, such as children, the poor, minorities, and the disabled, are pitted against older people for resources. Older people who lobby for what they see as a right and need of their age group are sometimes characterized as "greedy geezers" trying to get for themselves at the expense of other groups in need, such as children. Several current scholars dispute such generational equity arguments as being, instead, the result of "a more general assault on the welfare state that has been going on in the U.S., Britain, and elsewhere. The aim is to cut social benefits of both current and future retirees and of the young as well as of the old. It is . . . part of an effort to reverse history and shift the 'burden' of dependency from the public sphere to families once again" (Myles 1994).

While most policymakers do not consider older adult education to be a critical social need in this country, their view may be narrow enough to prevent consideration of the costs of not supporting educational programs for older people. Whether considering the personal benefits to older people themselves, such as being connected, creative, and productive, or the benefits to the larger society, such as their contributions as engaged citizens helping to solve problems, older adult education may be worth the investment. Why do few governmental policies exist that address older adult education? Glanz (1994) suggests such programs are not supported because investing in programs that benefit the aged is controversial. The controversy continues because policies that support older adults can be seen as not supporting children or other age groups. Also, many Americans continue to question the value of educating older people.

The active role of older adults as an organized and politically active special interest group pressing for benefits began in the early years of the Great Depression with those who supported the Townsend Movement. This pre–Social Security proposal by Francis E. Townsend for pensions to 60-year-old retirees was supported by clubs created across the country to lobby congressmen. Although the proposal failed to pass Congress, its legacy was the Social Security Act of 1935 which focused specifically on old-age pensions (see Table 4.2). Con-

Table 4.2
Older Adult Education: Key Legislation and Events

1935	Social Security Act
1950	National Conference on Aging
1951	Committee on Aging and Geriatrics
1956	Federal Council on Aging
1961	White House Conference on Aging
1964	University of Kentucky tuition waiver program
1965	Higher Education Act (HEA)
1965	Older Americans Act (OAA) amended in 1967, 1969, 1973, 1975, 1977, 1978, 1981, 1984, 1987, 1992 Administration of Aging established in Department of Health, Education and Welfare
1966	Adult Education Act
1967	Age Discrimination in Employment Act (ADEA) amended in 1978, 1986, 1990
1971	White House Conference on Aging
1972	Fund for Improvement of Post Secondary Education
1973	Area Agencies on Aging established
1976	Lifelong Learning Act (Public Law 94-482) amendment to HEA 1965
1981	White House Conference on Aging
1990	Age Discrimination Employment Act
1995	White House Conference on Aging

gress widened its interest in the needs and concerns of older citizens beyond pensions when appropriating funds in 1947 "to study problems facing older people" (Dobelstein 1985), which led to the development of the National Conference on the Aging (1950). This conference led to establishment of the Committee on Aging and Geriatrics (1951) charged with coordinating federal programs, particularly health and social services for older people. A few years later came the establishment of the Federal Council on Aging (FCA) and allocation of resources in 1956 to the Department of Health, Education, and Welfare (DHEW) for a staff on aging. Their functions included coordinating activities of government agencies related to aging. Some states followed suit, establishing similar departments to focus on aging issues.

About the same time, the White House Conference on Aging Act (1958) proposed "to convene a national forum of the most knowledgeable people in the field of aging to distill their combined experience into a blueprint for action on aging" (U.S. Congress Special Committee on Aging 1958). Following this act, the White House Conference on Aging (1961) convened to hear reports from state conferences. The typical calls included the need to improve services for older people, to increase retirement income, and to improve housing. But the 1961 Conference "was noteworthy for its major health debates" (Bass, Kutza, and Torres-Gil 1990). The sentiment was that "older persons were not getting their fair share of public resources and services" (Dobelstein 1985). Two results of the Conference were the emphasis on the need for Medicare legislation and the development of the Older Americans Act. Prior to passage of the Older Americans Act, the Administration on Aging (AOA) was proposed as a new division within DHEW (1963) but failed to pass.

Older Americans Act

The Older Americans Act and Medicare were passed in 1965 as Title XVIII to the Social Security Act. The Older Americans Act (see Appendix D) did establish the AOA within the DHEW and emphasized coordination and planning of existing resources as an alternative to developing new service programs, on the assumption that through such efforts the elderly might receive a fair share of social resources" (Dobelstein 1985). The assumption was that better coordination and planning would allow "shifts in resource allocation" in local communities in order to provide better for older people (Dobelstein 1985). To help with this coordination and planning, Areawide Agencies on Aging (AAA) were established within states, thus forming a new level of governmental administration in addition to the tradition hierarchy of federal, state, and local and county governments. Federal funds to administer Older American Act programs were passed through the states (State Units on Aging) to the AAAs for planning and coordinating within their jurisdictions. Yet, because the AOA administrator's authority was limited, the "AOA had no practical authority to direct the product of any aging programs that might be offered in the typical local community. AOA's independence from DHEW was exclusively dependent on the amount of interest Congress showed in aging programs, and this interest, in turn, was a product of the growing effectiveness of the newly developing voluntary organizations (interest groups) of aging people, like AARP" (Doblestein 1985).

Meanwhile, the administration of the AOA was adapted in the 1970s to area planning, encouraging AAAs to be multijurisdictional. Since government cooperative activities were undertaken by Councils of Government (COG) across the country, in many places the COG was designated as the AAA of Title III of the Older Americans Act. In some cases this presented a problem of isolating the issues from the mainstream of public discussion (because COGs have limited jurisdiction for most public functions).

The Older Americans Act "did not provide services; rather it provided a structure in which older people and their advocates could compete for existing resources" (Dobelstein 1985). With issues being decided at the substate and local level, the effect of this change was to lessen the effectiveness of the political power of older people. Because the AAAs and COGs were politically fragmented from the local, state, and federal political systems, aging policy became fragmented. And yet, while diffusing the political power of older people, this structure increased the provision of resources for older people at the local level.

Why has the Older Americans Act been touted as a major influence on programs for older adults initially passed by Congress in 1965? Many of these "legislative initiatives and programs (were) formulated at the federal level and implemented by state and local government" (Gelfand 1988). Initially these programs were designed to benefit all individuals within the group defined as older adults. Present emphasis is focused on programs for specific subpopulations within the larger category.

The objectives of the 1965 Older Americans Act (Title I) were to entitle and assist older adults in gaining equal opportunity with other age groups for such rights as adequate income, suitable housing, services, physical and mental health, freedom, and dignity.

One outcome of the Older Americans Act was the establishment of the AOA (Title II) to carry out Older Americans Act provisions. Theoretically, the AOA coordinates aging programs across all government agencies and departments (Maynard 1994).

A significant part of the Older Americans Act is contained in the section entitled Grants for State and Community Programs in Aging (Title III), which sets up a design that makes individual states responsible for aging services. Each state is to establish a statewide plan for serving the elderly with AAAs designated to be responsible in specific geographic areas. Services include various supportive services (health, housing, transportation, etc.), nutrition programs, and senior centers. Training and research is covered in Title IV.

Title V is Community Service Employment. Title VI is Grants for Native Americans.

The 1961 White House Conference on Aging influenced the language and substance of the Older Americans Act which "has been amended 10 times; the 1971 White House Conference on Aging influenced the 1974 and 1975 amendments" (Gelfand 1988).

EFFECTS OF THE OLDER AMERICANS ACT: NATIONAL POLICIES AFTER 1965

In 1965, the idea of passing legislation and developing and funding programs for the elderly was evolving. What most Americans thought they knew about the elderly was that they were poor, frail, in need of care, and deserving of public aid and support. In fact, in 1965, turning sixty-five meant the beginning of old age. Few elderly lived beyond eighty-five. One-third of the elderly were below the poverty level for the country. In the 1960s and early 1970s, during Lyndon Johnson's Great Society and Richard Nixon's New Federalism, social programs were acceptable socially and politically. In particular, programs for older Americans were acceptable. "Prior to the late 1970s the predominant stereotypes of older persons in American society were compassionate. Elderly persons were seen as poor, frail, socially dependent, objects of discrimination and, above all, *deserving*. For some forty years—dating from the Social Security Act of 1935—American society accepted the notion that all older persons are essentially the same and worthy of some form of governmental help" (Binstock 1991). This was the climate which helped to create the Older Americans Act—a nationwide network of services for older persons who were exempted from the means test (income and asset screening) usually applied to other age groups and to other Americans to determine eligibility for public assistance.

New Policy Trends Emerge

The social context that fostered such policies came to an end about fifteen years ago. "Since then, the social policy retrenchment has been in vogue, and the general political environment—previously supportive of almost any policy proposals to benefit aging persons—has become increasingly hostile to older people" (Binstock 1991). Furthermore, the percentage of funding for older Americans has either remained static or has decreased. Because both the number and the percentage of older persons are expected to grow steadily over the next fifty years, politicians and others express increasing concern over the growing costs of governmental expenditures on older people. In his analysis of the twenty-five years following the passage of the Older Americans Act, Binstock (1991) states that as "the climate of American politics and public discourse has become increasingly hostile to older persons," the aging of Americans is seen as an even larger problem.

Yet he also cites the positive accomplishments of the Older Americans Act, including means for identifying the needs of older adults, programs and services to meet those needs, establishment of a federal and state system focused on older adults, and many career professionals trained in aging issues. Perhaps its greatest contribution is as the "symbolic embodiment of our attitude and commitment" to older people and public policy addressing aging issues (McConnell and Beitler 1991).

Future federal policies related to older adult education will continue to focus on needs as a method for deciding which programs and services should be provided to which older persons. Fewer programs and services will be available to all older people; rather, public older adult education policies will address literacy, job retraining, and volunteer programs.

Policy Consideration Given to Older Adults

One legacy of the Older Americans Act is recognition that older adults are a significant group of Americans. Whether they are considered as deserving and needy, as "greedy geezers," or as active contributors, they are considered. Differing needs and interests of separate generations spark generational equity debates that focus on whether older adults, often on fixed incomes, should pay through taxes for services to unemployed younger people; whether younger workers should pay through taxes for services to the elderly; or whether the government should balance services making certain that various age groups receive their fair share (Kutzah 1991).

Subsequent legislation and forums dealing with the issues of older adults are considered the legacy of the Older Americans Act. The 1971 White House Conference on Aging "made aging a public issue" as older adults lobbied for their own agenda (Bass, Kutza, and Torres-Gil 1990). During the conference, delegates made over 700 recommendations (to states, the AOA, and Congress) concerned with improving the lives of older people. Some outcomes included the AOA Elderly Nutrition Program, designed to provide for those in greatest need, and creation of the FCA, "which was given broad investigative power over programs administered by AOA" (Dobelstein 1985).

The 1971 conference did help to establish "the credibility of the elderly . . . as advocates for their own needs" (Bass, Kutzah, and Torres-Gil 1990). Four categories of needs were addressed during the conference: coping, expressive, contributive, and influence needs. Whereas previous conferences and legislation had focused on ways to assist older adults in dealing with basic subsistence and health-care needs, public policy had not addressed the needs of older adults to continue to engage in life, give of themselves, and become involved in improving society. The goals of education set forth by the conference included helping older people fulfill lifetime potential, develop abilities to help society, and serve as models for oncoming generations. This conference gave national affirmation to older adults who "potentially constitute one of the nation's largest sources of human experience, skill, and wisdom. The major problem with growing old is not chronological age, but a society that has failed to deal with the aged as functional adults who have potential for an active role in our culture" (Edelson 1978).

Federal Policies on Educating Older Americans

Subsequent to the 1965 passage of the Older Americans Act, the last several decades have seen an increased role for federal and state governments in instituting and providing financial support for education at all levels, including adult and older adult educational programs (Knowles 1977). Significantly, the recognition of the potential of aging led to the acknowledgement of educational need for older Americans and, subsequently, to public policy supporting education of older people. Some policies centered on illiteracy among older adults and the need for educating for life survival skills among the elderly. "In 1970, one out of five people over sixty-five years of age was illiterate and one out of three had no schooling beyond eighth grade. Older people are the most poorly educated segment of the population" (Edelson 1978).

An example of addressing the needs of poorly educated older people is the establishment of the Adult Basic Education Program (part of the Economic Opportunity Act of 1964). Other policies focused on the larger role of education in enriching lives and benefiting society. "Education for all ages must be integrated with such routine pursuits as family life, careers, leisure-time activities, and the necessities imposed by active citizenship" (Edelson 1978). Examples include the Adult Education Act (Title III of 1966 Amendments to the Elementary and Secondary Education Act PL 89-750) and the 1970 Amendments (PL 91-230) which "authorized the establishment of state advisory councils on adult education" (Knowles 1977).

The 1971 White House Conference of Aging was significant in establishing public policy supporting education for older adults. By encouraging both private and public sectors to develop or to expand programs that would help older people prepare for retirement, this White House Conference validated the potential contributions of older people who were no longer working. Significantly, the goals of the White House Conference indicate that education for older people is pivotal to successful aging. According to the White House Conference 1971 report, retirement planning should be a lifelong process that begins in early years.

We need education for older adults as well as about older adults. Although McClusky's background paper (1971) on education issues for the 1971 Conference argues that education for "the state of being old" should begin in elementary school, it proposes that middle age is actually time enough to acquire information necessary to make decisions and establish attitudes toward aging

Table 4.3
Selected Measures of Educational Attainment for People 25+ and 65+, 1950–1989

Year and age group	Percent with:		Median years of school
	High school education	Four or more years of college	
1989*			
25+ years	76.9	21.1	12.7
65+ years	54.9	11.1	12.1
1980			
25+ years	66.5	16.2	12.5
65+ years	38.8	8.2	10.0
1970			
25+ years	52.3	10.7	12.1
65+ years	27.1	5.5	8.7
1960			
25+ years	41.1	7.7	10.5
65+ years	19.1	3.7	8.3
1950			
25+ years	33.4	6.0	9.3
65+ years	17.0	3.4	8.3

Sources: U.S. Bureau of the Census. Unpublished data from the March 1989 Current Population Survey. U.S. Bureau of the Census. "Detailed Population Characteristics." 1980 Census of Population PC80-1-D1, United States Summary (March 1984). U.S. Bureau of the Census. "Detailed Characteristics." 1970 Census of Population PC(1)-D1, United States Summary (February 1973). U.S. Bureau of the Census. "Characteristics of the Population." 1960 Census of Population Volume 1, Part 1, United States Summary Chapter D (1964).
*Excludes people in institutions.

as a means of fulfillment rather than as a limitation. One could argue that intergenerational activities, age-integrated activities, and a national emphasis on the promise of aging should be available to all ages of people. This background paper utilizes material from the 1961 White House Conference in establishing what should be the long-range goals for older adult education.

As a Nation we realize that continued planning and preparation are needed to insure the well-being, the strength, and the happiness of the older adult, his family, and his society. People need to prepare through continuing education as they prepare for earlier periods of life. Older adults can make a substantial contribution to the education of others. It is clear that National leadership is essential, that State leadership must be developed and expanded, and that there must be coordinated efforts among all agencies involved in education of older people (U.S. Senate Special Committee on Aging 1961). (McClusky 1971)

The background paper further proposes for the conference the essential and long-range goals for older adult education.

(1) To help older people grow in the fulfillment of their lifetime potential, thus assuring them the means of attaining a self-respecting level of well-being, freedom to cultivate a good life, and freedom to develop a partnership role in promoting the welfare of society

(2) To assist older people in developing the abilities uniquely available in the later years (e.g., wisdom and contributive abilities) and to assist the society in utilizing the abilities so developed.

(3) To help older people serve as models of lifelong fulfillment for emulation and for the guidance of oncoming generations

(4) To create a climate of acceptance by both older persons and the society of the desirability, legitimacy, and feasibility of the preceding goals

(5) To help society understand the need and provide the support for quality education for everyone of all ages as a continuing opportunity in lifelong learning

(6) As an essential part of this comprehensive program of continuing education (goal 5), to provide specialized programs to meet the particular needs of the older segment of the population, illustrative of which (but not definitive of) are the need for mental and physical health, for adequate income, for adequate housing, for adjusting to and making the most of relations with the immediate and the extended family, for making wise use of leisure time, and especially for preretirement education for dealing with these and related issues

(7) To make special provisions for delivering educational programs to "hidden populations" of older people, usually nonparticipant and isolated from the mainstream of community services (McClusky 1971)

The recommendations were endorsed by the Conference. They are significant long-range goals not only because they represent a rational federal approach to older adult education, but also because they emphasize older adult education as part of a coherent national plan of lifelong learning for all Americans. Older people are not singled out as either particularly needy or privileged but as having significant roles and rights in the larger society. Although they might have particular educational interests and needs, they also have skills and abilities and the responsibility to share them with younger age groups.

Additional Fallout from the Older Americans Act

Subsequent to the 1971 White House Conference on Aging's passage of broad and inclusive goals related to older adult education, the Lifelong Learning Act (Public Law 94-482), enacted as part of the Education Amendments of 1976, stated the federal government's interest in lifelong learning:

Lifelong learning offers hope to those who are mired in stagnant or disadvantaged circumstances—the unemployed, the isolated elderly, women, minorities, youth, workers whose jobs are becoming obsolete. All of them can and should be brought into the mainstream of American life . . . lifelong learning . . . is a necessary step toward making the lives of all Americans more rewarding and productive. (Walter Mondale 1975 quoted in Hartle and Kutner 1979)

But neither policymakers, educators, nor older learners agree on what lifelong learning is. Some think of it as cradle-to-grave learning. Others think of it as educational opportunities for those past the age of compulsory schooling, especially for those typically not served by existing programs. Some consider that any learning, including independent learning, qualifies. Others consider lifelong learning to be formal educational programs.

Despite its involvement in lifelong learning opportunities, the federal government's efforts lack coordination and, therefore, impact. Much of federal involvement in education is in response to issues outside of the educational arena (such as poverty, integration, drug abuse, the trend toward single parent families, economic demand for a skilled labor force, and the legal obligation to provide equal access and opportunities for handicapped) rather then to pedagogical issues. In any case, lifelong learning programs are as diverse as lifelong learners; one cannot equate lifelong learning programs and policy with older adult education programs and policies.

During the 1981 White House Conference on Aging, the Leadership Council of Aging Organizations (LACO) (see Appendix A for listing of current member organizations) played an important role in emphasizing maintenance of Social Security and other human services to the elderly. The Council's decisions are made by consensus and its chairmanship rotates between the three largest organizations: the NCOA, the NCSC, and the AARP (Ficke 1985). The 1981 White Council on Aging urged reinstating previous cuts in human services and preventing future cuts in Social Security.

Amendments to the Older Americans Act (1984, 1987, 1992) have sought to achieve greater flexibility for the AAAs in administering programs and services. Additionally, these amendments have moved toward targeting services to those with special needs (income, racial, ethnic, or status) even while affirming that the Older Americans Act programs be available to all older adults regardless of income level (Manheimer 1994). In addition to debating possible means testing for services, the possibility of fees for services was also considered. Mandatory cost sharing, particularly for in-home care, was opposed as not reflecting the original legislation. States were allowed flexibility in allowing volunteer cost sharing.

Older Americans Act: The Next Generation?

A network of public and private agencies and organizations— the so-called aging network—has developed over the last three decades in response to the goals and provisions of the Older Americans Act. Although the original goals of the Older Americans Act advocate educational opportunities to impact all older adults, the realities of inadequate public funding have forced eligibility limitations (Gelfand and Bechill 1991). Some agencies, such as senior centers, confront the challenge of lack of public funding by targeting services to specific groups, such as the frail elderly. Moody (1988) suggests that public policy should enable rather than fund aging policy, thus avoiding the vicissitudes of public funding.

Moody (1988) also points out the irony of legislation (e.g., the Older Americans Act) that is supposed to benefit older people but actually promotes the "failure model": "For public policy, the consequence is that we have an aging policy that embraces the 'two worlds of aging.' Our aging policies are legitimated by appeals to a negative image of old people as victims. Yet the policies are constructed in such a way that the most needy elderly do not benefit as much as the well-off elderly." His view is that negative stereotypes of aging continue to permeate public policy and public opinion even though most elderly do not fit the model.

Despite the attention given to older adults, especially since the passage of the Older Americans Act, lack of federal coordination of policies and funding have hampered development of universal programs, including educational programs for older adults. At the federal and state levels, older adult education lacks coherent leadership; aging practitioners are not educators, and educators consider older adults to be marginal to their primary purpose.

Some states and institutions of higher education are, however, forging new policies on older adults. According to Moody (1988), even as "colleges and universities are . . . being forced to cope with demographic fluctuations, such as the declining number of 18-year-olds and with the spread of aging, 'tenured-in' faculties . . . institutional survival puts a premium on flexibility and change." Colleges and universities have expanded markets to nontraditional students, including older adults, through flexible programs.

STATE INITIATIVES

State policies related to aging generally fall into four categories: income maintenance (including state supplements to Supplemental Security Income and tax relief), health and long-term care (including state Medicaid programs and nursing home regulations), regulatory protection (including hearing aid sales and funeral home practices), and social services. Educational policies for older people usually fall within this last category.

Tuition-Free Policies

One important public policy affecting older adult education is the tuition waiver (also discussed in Chapter 1 and Chapter 2). According to Long and Rossing (1979), the spread of tuition-waiver programs during the 1970s was a response to the desire of higher education institutions to serve the growing population of older adults. As described in Chapter 1, the University of Kentucky had started such a program in 1964 (see Appendix E for listing of tuition waiver programs). Several other states followed suit in the 1970s, while some states encouraged institutions to develop special courses for older students. This trend to serve older people may have been a factor in the passage of the Lifelong Learning Act as an amendment to the Higher Education Act.

In tuition-waiver legislation, states allow or require publicly supported institutions of higher education to permit senior citizens to enroll in classes at no cost or at a reduced cost, usually dependent on space being available after regular (paid) enrollment is completed. In some states, those enrolling through the tuition waiver policies have to be admitted to the college or university. States may have various other restrictions, such as age eligibility or financial need. In 1993, all but eleven states had tuition-waiver policies (in six of those states individual institutions have tuition-waiver policies), yet in the last twenty-five years, relatively few older adults have enrolled using the tuition-waiver policy.

The reasons for lack of enrollment include the fact that many people do not know about the program, others lack transportation, and still others find the campus environment intimidating. But probably the most important reason is that older people simply do not want the kind of learning offered by conventional higher education. (Moody 1988)

Policymakers can credit themselves with passing legislation that helps older adults and supports education of older adults, and yet opponents say the legislation does not fill the educational needs of older learners (Moyer and Lago 1987). Either they do not want to accept the financial help or they do not want the kind of teaching and classes offered in the regular degree programs and are not interested in academic credit. Chelsvig and Timmermann (1982) assert that encouraging older adults to enroll in academic programs may necessitate special counseling, while other studies (Perkins and Robertson-Tchabo 1981) find that older adults do not need counseling.

According to Chelsvig and Timmermann (1979), another factor limiting participation in tuition-reduction or -waiver programs is lack of publicity about the programs by the institutions offering them. College and university administrators want to maintain only those programs that are self-supporting. Allowing older adults to take classes for little or no tuition is not cost-effective, especially when such students are not included in determining formula funding. For example, Romaniuk (1983) reported that, "No senior citizen admitted under [tuition waiver] provision is counted in any computation of full-time equivalent (FTE) formulae for state funding to the institution." Some states such as North Carolina and Arkansas have amended legislation to permit inclusion of tuition-waiver students in FTE formulae. If states want to encourage greater participation in tuition-waiver programs by older adults then they need to provide incentives for institutions, such as inclusion in formula funding; institutions would then find recruiting older adults to be beneficial.

O'Connor (1991) gives an interesting history of the tuition-waiver policy in Massachusetts. Passed originally in 1977, the Massachusetts law was meant to encourage participation by older people in higher education but without an expectation of large numbers or a diversity of participants. The original law, restricted to space-available only, set the eligibility age at sixty-five and then, just before passage, an amendment was added limiting annual income of those eligible to $12,000.

According to O'Connor (1991), this law was passed at a time that a number of other waivers were being considered, such as those for Vietnam veterans, members of the National Guard, and police officers. "Providing tuition assistance to individuals based on some category of eligibility rather than on the basis of financial need had become a way of modifying the existing tuition structure to accommodate particular groups while avoiding a wholesale re-examination of the effect of tuition in limiting educational opportunities for those not in the targeted groups." The legislators did not consider that a tuition-waiver program had negative effects; in fact, it seemed to be giving benefits but, in reality, the program cost the state little. Further, lost tuition was not factored, since policymakers believed that older people would not pay to attend college anyway.

The 1977 Massachusetts law was amended in 1981 to eliminate the income limits and to lower the age eligibility to sixty. According to O'Connor (1991), few older adults with low income had taken part in the original tuition waiver; the amendment tended to benefit the middle-class older adults who were already enrolling in classes and paying tuition. The legislators believed, however, that the amendments would demonstrate their support of older people while not requiring much of colleges and universities. O'Connor says the result of the amendments is difficult to assess because of lack of data; analysis of existing data shows that "enrollment decreased (during the 1980s) after the 'expansion' of the tuition waiver program."

Perkins and Robertson-Tchabo (1981) earlier reported different results in Maryland, where a tuition waiver was also authorized in 1977. Their data show that during the first year of the program (1977–1978) the College Park campus experienced a 340 percent increase in enrollment of students over age sixty. Their study assessed responses of older people who took advantage of the program but did not assess reactions of policymakers.

Long's (1980) early national study of tuition-waiver programs suggested that the most significant finding was how few states were able to report data such as hours taken, grade point average (GPA), and audit information regarding older adults. Although policies varied from state to state at that time, co-ordinating officials expressed "a general attitude that such programs are window dressing and are not to be pursued with vigor" (Long 1980) despite their public relations potential. Lack of state formula-funding assistance was a negative factor, and the role of the institution in providing counseling and health services needed to be explored. Now, twenty-five years after that study, the same questions and resistance to tuition-waiver programs for older adults remain.

Other State Educational Initiatives in Aging

Each state has an office on aging, either as a separate department or as a component of a larger unit. State offices on aging can provide information and resources for older people, including information on educational opportunities.

State policies related to older adult education may be found in state education plans such as that of California (Gilford 1990). Yet such policies play minor roles in state plans despite a recommendation made twenty-five years ago at the 1971 White House Council on Aging:

Primary responsibility for the initiation, support, and conduct of education programs for older persons must be vested in the existing educational system, Federal, State and local, with active participation and cooperation of specialized agencies. A Division of Education on Aging should be established in the Office of Education immediately, to initiate supportive educational services for the aging. Similarly, all State Departments of Education should designate full-time responsibility to key staff for the development and implementation of programs in education for aging. (Rabe 1977)

Few states have taken steps to realize this vision. Some state plans on aging include older adult education policies. For example, the North Carolina Aging Services Plan addresses education needs and services in a chapter on "A Concept of Comprehensive County-Based Programs for Older Adults."

The same (1971) White House Council on Aging suggested a concept of what programs for older adults might encompass:

Education for older persons should be conducted either apart from or integrated with other age groups, according to their specific needs and choices. Where feasible and desirable, the aged must be granted the opportunity to take advantage of existing programs with both old and young learning from each other. However, alternatives must be provided which emphasize the felt needs of the aged at their particular state in the life cycle. (Rabe 1977)

The suggestion of intergenerational learning was aimed, in part, at dispelling ageism myths on the part of other age groups. State departments of education were to help in improving people's attitudes toward older people as well as in developing curricula and methods designed for older people.

Using public schools as delivery sites for education to older people was also recommended:

The public school, present in all size communities, is the most readily accessible educational resource for older persons. This has special relevancy in light of the transportation problem facing many retirees. A public school program of continuing education is open-ended. Adding new dimensions to existing programs poses no administrative problems if ways can be found to cover the cost of the same. In the final analysis, therefore, state departments of education must find ways of financially helping the local schools to provide life-long learning opportunities for all who wish it, as well as education about aging designed for different sectors of the population. (Rabe 1977)

One can only wonder if the crisis of violence, low-achieving students, and little parental involvement now facing public schools would be diminished if, twenty-five years ago, they had actively involved older adults in education and, in addition, tapped their resources. Putting education for elders in public schools would be efficient, since facilities, educators, and administrators exist there. Such a change would require the leadership of state departments of education.

Some states like New Jersey (New Jersey State Department of Education 1973) targeted specific groups of adults for educational services. Such groups may include functional illiterates, non-English-speaking persons, public offenders, and older adults.

New York adopted an extensive strategy to address educational needs of their aging population as part of a comprehensive aging policy. The six major policy directions are the following (New York State Education Department 1985):

- To provide education and training opportunities for older persons
- To enhance the coordination of services for the elderly
- To involve the elderly as active participants in society
- To educate students at all levels about aging
- To train needed professional, paraprofessional, and informal service providers for older persons
- To increase the research potential of postsecondary institutions to address the needs of the elderly

The first three policy goals focus on educational services directly for older people. The last three involve education about older people. The approach of this plan demonstrates the efforts of several states during the 1980s to develop tangible programs and services, to coordinate different state departments, and to utilize the potential of older people.

In Michigan, an innovative coalition between the Office of Aging Services and the Department of Education is working to expand lifelong learning opportunities for older adults. A 1989 Memorandum of Understanding between these two departments established the Coalition for Older Adult Learning (COAL) with three goals (Dekker 1993):

1. Raising public awareness about the benefits of older adult learning
2. Obtaining and disseminating ideas and information about programs and methods for meeting the lifelong learning needs and preferences of older adult learners

3. Collaborating on networking strategies for interagency coordination and cooperation

Regional Older Learner Forums help older learner service providers and policymakers to identify learner needs, exchange information, and raise public awareness. The coalition provides additional training and information.

POLICIES OF INSTITUTIONS

A number of other public institutions, including libraries, colleges and universities, senior centers, parks and recreation departments, and agricultural extension service programs, formulate aging and educational policy. All of these institutions serve diverse populations, but with a growing number of older adults in the country, they are responding to this special population with programs and policies that vary widely. Some examples of current policies follow.

Libraries

Libraries potentially serve the entire population. Located in small towns, suburbs, and cities, they vary greatly in size, resources, and services; but services to older adults have existed in many libraries for many years. In the late 1950s, the ALA established the Adult Services Division (Turock 1982) and, under it, the Library Services to an Aging Population Committee (see also Chapter 2). The Library Services and Construction Act was amended by Congress in 1964 to allow libraries to alter physical structure to meet the needs of older people and to fund large-print collections (Turock 1982).

In the early 1970s, a wide variety of outreach programs addressed the underserviced elderly and found most of those programs included cooperative planning with other social agencies, utilized mobile units, visited shut-ins, provided mail service, provided large-print and talking books, provided magnifiers and other reading aids, organized group programs, and provided free transportation (Casey 1984; Hales-Mabry 1993). By the early 1980s, the Office of Libraries and Learning Resources (which administers the Library Services and Construction Act) stated "that approximately 75 percent of public libraries in the United States were offering some specific program or service to older adults" (Casey 1984).

By 1987, the ALA (at the recommendation of its Library Services to an Aging Population Committee) adopted Guidelines of a Library Service to Older Adults. The following is a summary of those guidelines designed to meet the needs of an increasing number of older adults.

- Libraries can meet those needs by exhibiting and promoting a positive attitude toward older adults.
- Information and resources on aging and its implications must be promoted to older

adults, their family members, professionals in gerontology, and persons interested in the aging process.

- The library services provided must reflect cultural, ethnic, and economic differences.
- The potential of older adults (paid or volunteers) as liaisons should be utilized in reaching other older adults and as a resource in intergenerational programming.
- Older adults should be employed at professional and support staff levels for general library work and older adult programs.
- Older adults should be involved in the planning and design of library services and programs for the entire community as well as older adults.
- A good working relationship should be promoted and developed with other agencies serving older adults.
- Preretirement and later-life career alternatives programs, services, and information should be made available.
- Library design improvements and access to transportation should be implemented to facilitate library use by older adults.
- The library's planning and evaluation process should incorporate the changing needs of older adults.
- An aggressive funding effort should be implemented and a portion of the library budget committed to older adult programs and services. (ALA 1987; see Appendix F for complete guidelines)

These guidelines represent optimum services and require adequate staff and funding.

A national survey completed in 1988 assessed services of public library systems to adults (Van Fleet 1989). This study found that older adults fared well compared to other special groups such as ethnic minorities or the handicapped. Most of the services to older adults provided by libraries, however, were to those institutionalized or homebound. Statistics show that only 5 percent of older people dwell in institutions. "If librarians limit themselves to those in nursing homes, the greatest number of older adults are neglected" (Van Fleet 1989).

Some library programs address the specific interests of older adults. The NEH has been one source of quality public programs through grants funded by the division of Humanities Projects in Libraries and Archives; these programs often attract many older adults. Examples of NEH-funded projects are several developed by the NCOA, which has conducted numerous library-based reading and discussion programs for older adults. For example, the NCOA's Silver Editions Projects provided support to libraries in five critical areas: money, materials, training, consultation, and evaluation (Liroff and Van Fleet 1992). Participants in Silver Editions were primarily regular library users for which this programs was a new, challenging, and intellectually stimulating experience. Libraries considered the program "a continuation and adaptation of traditional services for people who have used the library for most of their lives" (Liroff and Van Fleet 1992).

Some library organizations are calling for increased commitment to older adults by libraries, believing that library professionals are not adequately trained to address the needs of older adults (Thompson 1988; Chatman 1992). "The library community must undergo an attitude change regarding services for older adults" (Stanley-Dunham 1989). They need to include older people, particularly minorities, in their planning process and increase commitment of dollars and staff. Reportedly, "less than 5 percent of the total older population in this country is reached by library service; and only about 1 percent of library budgets is used for older adult services" (Stanley-Dunham 1989).

Agricultural Extension

The Smith–Lever Act (1914) initiated what became the Cooperative Extension System of today, representing cooperative programs between land-grant universities, agricultural experiment stations, and cooperative extension services. Such programs have both federal (30 percent) and state and local (70 percent) funding (Rasmussen 1989).

The mission of the Extension Service is to achieve a system "that is responsive to priority needs and the Federal interests and policies with quality information, education, and problem-solving programs" (Rasmussen 1989). The mission has been updated to include helping "people improve their lives through an educational process which uses scientific knowledge focused on issues and needs" (Rasmussen 1989). Many people may be familiar with 4-H organizations of the Extension Service, but many other programs exist, serving a wide variety of people. Programs particularly targeted for older adults include nutrition programs.

Colleges and Universities

Older adults attending classes at colleges and universities is nothing new. As previously noted, many states have tuition-waiver policies that may encourage some older people to take courses in the regular curriculum. One recent study of the effects of the physical environment on older learners indicates that many older adults would prefer to attend classes separate from the main campus in order to overcome environmental barriers such as parking, directional signs, lighting, classroom arrangement, and seating. "Although educational and service concerns are of paramount importance, physical access, comfort, and convenience must also be considered" (Moore and Piland 1994). Just as colleges and universities consider athletic and honors programs for other age groups, some colleges address the special needs of older adults.

Continuing education programs at many institutions offer special programs and courses outside the regular course of study and reach many in the community at large, including older adults. Some institutions have established programs specially designed for older learners called LRIs. These programs are often endorsed by the host institution as public service outreach or a way to serve a special population within the community. These LRI programs usually have cooperative agreements with their host institutions concerning space and overhead. Some programs rent space; others have it provided. The programs vary in size, scope, and most other aspects.

One of the original LRI programs is the IRP, which was established in the early 1960s at the New School for Social Research in New York and has served as the model for newer university-based programs. Although the 1987 amendments to the bylaws of the IRP state that it is an integral part of the new School Adult Division, the 500 IRP members, who thought their relationship with the New School was secure, were stunned in early 1994 by the request of the administration to change their long-standing agreement allowing the IRP to exist. This controversy, which arose at an LRI with apparently no previous history of conflict with its host institution, serves notice to all LRI programs that they operate within a larger institutional context and that circumstances change. To consolidate their institutional position, LRI programs are well advised to broaden support, be central to the institution's mission, diversify membership, and communicate contributions to the institution and community.

Utilizing the unique volunteer and leadership abilities of older adults is one way some college and university programs for older adults consolidate their position within their institution. The NCCCR is an example. In addition to its active LRI program, the NCCCR functions as a conduit for involving participants in a wide variety of campus and community activities. One program engages seniors in dialogue with community leaders about current challenges and concerns. Another program matches older people with undergraduate students, and these intergenerational teams work with sixth-grade students in a local middle school. Another program provides teams of older volunteer tutors to local elementary schools.

Clearly a university or college can play a meaningful role in promoting preparation for and direction toward substantial volunteer roles. Other institutions may, similarly, be able to play this role, such as chambers of commerce and community leadership programs . . . by combining lifelong learning with leadership and volunteer programs, . . . [programs are] able to tap an affinity group, cultivate internal leadership, and foster the concept of creativity as one that links reinterpreting the past through continued learning and community service. (Manheimer and Snodgrass 1993)

The University of Wisconsin system represents another example of a university responding to older learners. Following the 1973 directive of the state legislature for the university system to serve students of all ages and its own mission "to develop human resources . . . and . . . extend knowledge and its application beyond . . . campuses" (University of Wisconsin 1993), in 1993 the university completed a study of services to older adults. Recommendations included the following:

- Increasing awareness of an aging society to prepare us all to work and live more effectively

- Increasing educational opportunities for lifelong learning to assure that the University provides educational opportunities for all Wisconsin residents, regardless of age

- Increasing teaching, research, and service to confront important health, economic, and social issues that focus on aging (University of Wisconsin 1993)

Each recommendation included several implementation strategies for the campuses and institutions within the system allowing for major response by the university system to the changing population of the state. To date, no action has been taken on these recommendations.

POLICIES OF NATIONAL AGING AND EDUCATION ORGANIZATIONS

Organizations that focus primarily on the issues of the elderly, whether made up of primarily older adults or of the general population, are multiplying. More than a thousand groups represent particular occupations, such as the NRTA, or general aging issues, such as Gray Panthers and the NCOA. Over five thousand local chapters of the national organizations AARP and NCSC represent primarily middle-class and higher-income working-class older adults (Pratt 1983).

Most current aging issues groups were begun for nonpolitical purposes, and few had national headquarters originally in Washington, although over the last twenty years many have moved there (Pratt 1983). This change suggests the interest shift of the organizations toward policy-making. Although the various groups work independently and for different agendas, they all encourage giving aging programs national status. According to Pratt, these groups currently have limited lobbying effectiveness because of the lack of active commitment to focused political goals by the diverse membership despite their large participation numbers.

Not all organizations that focus on issues of aging have explicit policies related to education of older adults. This section explores educational policies of several larger organizations. Further information on these and other aging organizations can be found in Appendixes A and B.

American Association of Retired Persons

With 33 million members over the age of fifty, the AARP is the largest organization of older adults. Offering a wide range of membership benefits and programs, the AARP also supports older adult education. For many years the organization operated the Institute of Lifetime Learning which, among its functions, prepared mini-series of educational materials on a wide variety of nonaging related topics. This Institute no longer exists; instead the AARP advocates older adult education by promoting aging research through grants to nonprofit organizations, universities, and colleges. The AARP provides information such as a directory of educational programs for older people and encourages partnerships that promote older adult education. The AARP also conducts studies on how older adults of today and tomorrow best learn and applies this knowledge in their own training programs (AARP 1994).

American Society on Aging

The ASA began originally in the 1950s as a regional association of gerontology professionals, the Western Gerontological Society. A national organization since 1985, the ASA continues to represent professionals in the public and private sectors. The ASA's general mission is to improve the lives of older people by developing the abilities and commitment of those who work with them. The ASA promotes education of its members but does not specifically address education of older people in its policies.

In 1992, the ASA established the Older Adult Education Network (OAEN), a membership group for those professionals interested in networking with others and gaining information and skills related to older adult education. By 1995, over 300 people had joined the OAEN.

Elderhostel Institute Network

Elderhostel began in 1975 with a few New Hampshire colleges offering short-term summer educational programs for people over sixty. After twenty years, programs are available year-round in every state and forty foreign countries with close to a quarter of a million people participating.

During this growth period, LRI programs were developing independently at numerous colleges and universities for older adults within their own communities. In 1989, the EIN was launched by Elderhostel as an umbrella organization of member-led ILR programs at colleges and universities. A membership organization of about 180 institutions, the EIN serves to encourage development of new ILR programs and to help existing programs to network and share resources. Its primary mission is to foster expanded educational experiences for older adults. "The Institute Network is a national voice for the whole ILR movement" (EIN 1993).

The National Council on the Aging

Established in 1950, the NCOA is a "national organization for professionals and volunteers, with an across-the-board involvement in all matters affecting the quality of life for older Americans" (NCOA 1979). In early statements on policy, the NCOA promoted lifelong learning with particular mention of opportunities that meet the needs and interests of older people. They encouraged free or reduced tuition at colleges and development of education in non-traditional settings as well.

By 1980, the NCOA had collected its policies on education into a category of "Tapping Older People's Potential." By 1984, the category was entitled "Life Enrichment" and included recommendations for arts and humanities programs as well as recreation and leisure activities aimed at increasing volunteerism and reducing isolation among older people.

By 1988, the NCOA policies on education reflected an awareness of the changes in the political economy and the growing economic, social, racial, and gender diversity among older people. Citing the trend of model programs for older people that ended once funding ran out, the NCOA called for programs for older people to be placed "in the missions and budgets of schools, colleges, and nontraditional sponsors" (NCOA 1988). The NCOA directive issued a call to meet the needs of the diverse population.

How can we work to enhance educational opportunities for lower-income and less-educated elders, as well as disadvantaged younger and middle-aged adults who represent tomorrow's poorest elderly? How can older persons of moderate means who are unfamiliar with education and enrichment programs identify and gain access to lifelong learning opportunities? Educators need public support to address effectively the needs of these potential learners. (NCOA 1988)

Current policies of the NCOA advance the issue of diversity among older people. Educational initiatives, although mentioned specifically, are incorporated into the section on Community-based Services under the Older Americans Act with other topics as legal services, transportation, and social services. The NCOA recommendations related to education for older people focus primarily on instrumental goals, such as remedying adult illiteracy, improving library services, supporting retraining for employment, and increasing opportunities for underserved older people. The NCOA also has a board-level Arts and Humanities Committee to advise on project initiatives such as its NEH-funded Discovery Through the Humanities program (NCOA 1994).

National Recreation and Park Association

The National Recreation and Park Association (NRPA) promotes the importance of parks and recreation to all people by encouraging people to find satisfying activities during their leisure time. The Leisure and Aging Section (LAS) of this organization represents those that work with older adults in senior centers, retirement communities, and recreation centers. The mission of the LAS is to provide leisure and recreational opportunities that will help older Americans stay healthy and active. Education, as part of leisure and recreation programs for older adults, is encouraged particularly through networks and shared resources. Additionally, the NRPA is currently training recreation personnel to be prepared to program for an aging population.

National University Continuing Education Association

The National University Continuing Education Association (NUCEA) consists of college and university members and promotes continuing higher education opportunities. Although primarily concerned with providing information and educational opportunities for continuing education professionals, the NUCEA also promotes support of public policies that will strengthen continuing education. One of the twenty divisions of the NUCEA is Continuing Education for Older Adults.

IMPLICATIONS AND TRENDS IN OLDER ADULT EDUCATION POLICY

Over the last forty years older adult education has come of age so that it is considered by both aging and educational professionals as a separate entity. Governmental policies that have addressed the rights of older Americans have been instrumental in establishing older adult education during these formative years. As older adult education matures and we move into the next century, what role will governmental and other public policy fill? What leadership will professionals in aging and education demonstrate? How will older adults themselves advocate for increased opportunities in education?

The growing number and percentage of older adults in the population continues to influence society in numerous directions. Societal institutions, including governing bodies, educational establishments, businesses, and nonprofits including religious and professional organizations, continue to address the needs and concerns of older people. But current trends suggest some changes in how public policy will address aging Americans.

One important trend in such policies is dictated by economics: Societal institutions have limited resources and must target services and programs to particular segments of the population. In the case of the diverse group of people labeled older adults, categories may include those who are poor, or illiterate, or affluent, or healthy, or who live in a particular region. The concern about the equitable distribution of scarce public resources is fueled by the increased proportion of the federal budget directed toward income and health security for older Americans and their general economic improvement over the last several decades.

Policies related to educational programs for older people will also be prescribed by economics and tight resources. Based on current trends, it seems likely that those who can afford educational programs will be expected to pay for them. While federal policies will insure older adults' rights to education opportunities, federal funding will be allotted to aging programs that benefit the general society rather than only older people. For example, literacy and job retraining programs that include older adults and directly affect the national economy will receive base funding, while so-called leisure learning will have to be paid for by those who benefit. Similarly, state-level policies will primarily target educational programs and services to particular populations of older people in need. Institutional policies will develop additional educational programs and services for older adults who will pay for them. The trend in educational and aging organizations for subgroups with interest in older adult education will continue. In other words, the probable prognosis is for continued fragmented public policies of older adult education. While some bemoan the lack of uniformity in older adult education, others see this as an invitation to resourcefulness, creativity, and inventiveness within institutions and the private sector, and an opportunity to develop without the constraints of bureaucratic leadership of some other educational programs.

Certainly the role that older adults themselves might play in influencing policy remains an unknown factor. This ever-growing, better educated, more powerful, and diverse group has the potential to impact public policy. Will they take responsibility to provide leadership for a grass roots movement demanding coherent policies for universal older adult education opportunities? Will they build coalitions within communities so that by providing for their own educational opportunities, they may help others achieve theirs, especially within intergenerational contexts? Will they be willing to pay for educational programs, either in money or institutional and community service?

As we move into the twenty-first century, public policy is not likely to be the driving force behind older adult education. Older adults could be the catalyst for increasingly diverse educational opportunities for themselves, and those innovations could change the way Americans value older people as well as the way they value education.

REFERENCES

American Assocciation of Retired Persons (AARP). 1994. Older Adult Learning, Phase I: Theory and Principles. Unpublished manuscript.

American Library Association (ALA). 1987. "Guidelines for Library Service to Older Adults." *RQ* 26(4): 444–447.

Bass, S. A., E. A. Kutza, and F. M. Torres-Gil, eds. 1990. *Diversity in Aging.* Glenview, Ill.: Scott, Foresman.

Binstock, R. H. 1990. "The Politics and Economics of Aging and Diversity." In *Diversity in Aging.* Edited by S. A. Bass, E. A. Kutza, and F. M. Torres-Gil. Glenview, Ill.: Scott, Foresman.

————. 1991. "From the Great Society to the Aging Society: 25 Years of the Older Americans Act." *Generations* 15(3): 11–18.

Casey, G. M. 1984. *Library Services for the Aging.* Hamden, Conn.: Library Professionals Publications.

Chatman, E. A. 1992. *The Information World of Retired Women.* Westport, Conn.: Greenwood Press.

Chelsvig, K. A., and S. Timmermann. 1979. "Tuition Policies of Higher Educational Institutions and State Government and the Older Learner." *Educational Gerontology* 4: 147–159.

————. 1982. "Support Services for Older Adult Tuition Programs." *Educational Gerontology* 8: 269–274.

Dekker, D., ed. 1993. *COAL: Coalition for Older Adult Learning Newsletter*. May. Lansing, Mich.: Michigan Office of Services to the Aging.

Division of Aging, North Carolina Department of Human Resources. 1991. *North Carolina Aging Services Plan: A Guide for Successful Aging in the 1990s*. Vol. 2. Raleigh, N.C.: North Carolina Department of Human Resources.

Dobelstein, A. W. 1985. *Serving Older Adults: Policy, Programs, and Professional Activities*. Englewood Cliffs, N.J.: Prentice-Hall.

Edelson, I. 1978. "The Role of State University Systems in Providing Educational Opportunities for Senior Citizens." *Educational Gerontology* 3: 175–187.

Eklund, L. 1969. "Aging and the Field of Education." In *Aging and Society*, Vol. 2. Edited by M. W. Riley and A. Foner. New York: Russell Sage.

Elderhostel Institute Network (EIN). 1993. *Institutes for Learning in Retirement and Elderhostel: A National Overview*. Durham, N.H.: Elderhostel Institute Network.

Ficke, S. C. 1985. *An Orientation to the Older Americans Act*. Washington, D.C.: National Association of States Units on Aging.

Fowles, D. G. 1993. *A Profile of Older Americans 1993*. Prepared by Program Resources Department, the AARP and Administration on Aging, U.S. Department of Health and Human Resources. Washington, D.C.: U.S. Government Printing Office.

Gelfand, D. E. 1988. *The Aging Network: Programs and Services*. 3d ed. New York: Springer.

Gelfand, D. E., and W. Bechill. 1991. "The Evolution of the Older Americans Act: A 25-Year Review of the Legislative Changes." *Generations* 15(3): 19–22.

Gilford, R. 1990. "Meeting the Higher Education Challenges of an Aging Society: A Plan for California." *Educational Gerontology* 16: 373–387.

Glanz, D. 1994. "Older Volunteers and Productive Aging: What Do We Know?" *The Gerontologist* 34(2): 276–278

Hales-Mabry, C. 1993. *The World of the Aging: Information Needs and Choices*. Chicago: American Library Association.

Hartle, T. W., and M. A. Kutner. 1979. "Federal Policies: Programs, Legislation, and Prospects." In *Lifelong Learning in America*. Edited by R. E. Peterson. San Francisco: Jossey-Bass.

Knowles, M. S. 1977. *A History of the Adult Education Movement in the United States*. Huntington, N.Y.: Robert E. Krieger.

Korim, A. S. 1974. *Older Americans and Community Colleges: An Overview*. Washington, D.C.: American Association of Community and Junior Colleges.

Kutza, E. A. 1991. "The Older Americans Act of 2000: What Should It Be?" *Generations* 15(3): 65–68.

Liroff, S. R., and C. Van Fleet. 1992. "Silver Editions II: Humanities Programming for Older Adults." *RQ* 31: 473–476.

Long, H. B. 1980. "Characteristics of Senior Citizens' Educational Tuition Waivers in Twenty-One States: A Follow-Up Study." *Educational Gerontology* 5: 139–149.

Long, H. B., and B. E. Rossing. 1979. "Tuition Waiver Plans for Older Americans in Postsecondary Public Education Institutions." *Educational Gerontology* 4: 161–174.

Lowy, L., and D. O'Connor. 1986. *Why Education in the Later Years?* Lexington, Mass.: Lexington Books.

Manheimer, R. J. 1987–1988. "The Politics & Promise of Cultural Enrichment Programs." *Generations* 11(2): 26–30.

Manheimer, R. J., ed. 1994. *Older Americans Almanac.* Detroit: Gale Research.

Manheimer, R. J., and D. Snodgrass. 1993. "New Roles and Norms for Older Adults Through Higher Education." *Educational Gerontology* 19: 585–595.

Maynard, O. 1994. "Government and the Aging Network." In *Older Americans Almanac.* Edited by R. J. Manheimer. Detroit: Gale Research.

McClusky, H. Y. 1971. Education: Background Issues. Paper presented at the White House Conference on Aging. February. Washington, D.C.: Government Printing Office. ERIC Document Reproduction Service No. ED 057 335.

McConnell, S., and D. Beitler. eds. 1991. "The Older Americans Act after 25 Years, An Overview." *Generations* 15(3): 5–10.

McMahon, A. T. 1979. "Needs for New Emphases in Social and Educational Policy Toward the Elderly." *Educational Gerontology* 4: 101–113.

Minkler, M., and C. L. Estes, eds. 1991. *Critical Perspectives on Aging: The Political and Moral Economy of Growing Old.* Amityville, N.Y.: Baywood.

Moody, H. R. 1976. "Philosophical Presuppositions of Education for Older Adults." *Educational Gerontology* 1: 1–16.

———. 1985. "Philosophy of Education for Older Adults." In *The Older Adult as Learner.* Edited by D. B. Lumsden. New York: Hemisphere.

———. 1988. *Abundance of Life: Human Development Policies for an Aging Society.* New York: Columbia University Press.

Moore, M. L., and W. E. Piland. 1994. "Impact of the Campus Physical Environment on Older Adult Learners." *Educational Gerontology* 20: 129–138.

Moyer, I., Jr., and D. Lago. 1987. "Institutional Barriers to Older Learners in Higher Education: A Critique of Fee-Waiver Programs." *Educational Gerontology* 13: 157–169.

National Academy on Aging. 1994. *Old Age in the 21st Century: A Report to the Assistant Secretary for Aging, U.S. Department of Health and Human Services, Regarding His Responsibilities in Planning for the Aging of the Baby Boom.* Syracuse, N.Y.: Syracuse University.

National Council on the Aging (NCOA). 1979. "Public Policy Agenda 1979–1980." *Perspective on Aging* 8(1): 7–20.

———. 1988. "Public Policy Agenda 1988–1989." Perspective on Aging 17(2): 28–30.

———. 1994. "Policy Responses: The Implications of Population Aging." *Perspective on Aging* 22(1): 19–25.

New Jersey State Department of Education. 1973. Adult and Continuing Education: Stage 1: Issue Identification. Trenton Division of Research, Planning, and Evaluation. ERIC Document Reproduction Service No. ED 091 538.

New York State Education Department. 1985. Educational Elements of a Comprehensive State Policy on Aging. Albany Office for Policy Analysis. ERIC Document Reproduction Service No. ED 278 825.

North Carolina Center for Creative Retirement (NCCCR). 1993. Identifying Critical Pathways in Organizing Educational Programs for Older Adults. Final report submitted to the AARP Andrus Foundation. Asheville, N.C.: University of North Carolina at Asheville.

O'Connor, D. 1991. "Free Tuition for Elders: Intentions and Effects of the Massachusetts Policy." *Journal of Aging and Social Policy* 3(1/2): 57–72.

Perkins, H. V., and E. A. Robertson-Tchabo. 1981. "Retirees Return to College: An Evaluative Study at One University Campus." *Educational Gerontology* 6: 273–287.

Peterson, D. A. 1985. "A History of Education for Older Learners." In *The Older Adult as Learner*. Edited by D. B. Lumsden. New York: Hemisphere.

———. 1990. "A History of the Education of Older Learners." In *Introduction to Educational Gerontology*. 3d ed. Edited by R. H. Sherron and D. B. Lumsden. New York: Hemisphere.

Peterson, R. E., and Associates. 1979. *Lifelong Learning in America*. San Francisco: Jossey-Bass.

Pifer, A., and L. Bronte. 1986. *Our Aging Society: Paradox and Promise*. New York: W. W. Norton.

Pratt, H. J. 1983. "National Interest Groups among the Elderly: Consolidation and Constraint." In *Aging and Public Policy: The Politics of Growing Old in America*. Edited by W. P. Browne and L. K. Olson. Westport, Conn.: Greenwood Press.

Quirk, D. A. 1991. "An Agenda for the Nineties and Beyond." *Generations* 15(3): 23–26.

Rabe, H. F. 1977. "State Departments of Education and State Offices for Aging as Resources in Relationship to Education for Aging." In *Learning for Aging*. Edited by S. Grabowski and D. W. Mason. Adult Education Association and ERIC Clearinghouse of Adult Education.

Rasmussen, W. D. 1989. *Taking the University to the People: Seventy-Five Years of Cooperative Extension*. Ames, Iowa: Iowa State University Press.

Romaniuk, J. G. 1983. "Development of Educational Programs for Older Adult Learners." *The Gerontologist* 23(3): 313–318.

Schlachter, S. S. 1991. "Education for Older Adults: An Analysis of National Public Policy." Ph.D. diss., Northern Illinois University.

Sherron, R. H., and D. B. Lumsden, eds. 1990. *Introduction to Educational Gerontology*. 3d ed. New York: Hemisphere.

Smith, T. B., C. Mack, and E. Tittnich. 1993. *Generations Together: A Job-Training Curriculum for Older Workers in Child Care*. Syracuse, N.Y.: Syracuse University Press and Generations Together.

Stanley-Dunham, J. 1989. "Designing Library Services for the Aging: Toward the 21st Century." *Wilson Library Bulletin* 63: 10–14.

Taeuber, C. 1990. "Diversity: The Dramatic Reality." In *Diversity in Aging*. Edited by S. A. Bass, E. A. Kutza, and F. M. Torres-Gil. Glenview, Ill.: Scott, Foresman.

———. 1992. *Sixty-Five Plus in America*. Prepared by U.S. Bureau of the Census. *Current Population Reports, Special Studies*. Washington, D.C.: Government Printing Office.

Thompson, D. G. 1988. "Serving Older Adults in North Carolina Public Libraries: A Survey." *North Carolina Libraries* 46: 163–180.

Turock, B. 1982. *Serving the Older Adult—A Guide to Library Programs and Information Sources*. New York: R. R. Bowker.

University of Wisconsin. Working Committee on Services for Seniors. 1993. Report of the Working Group on UW-System Services for Older Adults. Madison: University of Wisconsin.

U.S. Congress, Congressional Budget Office. 1991. *The Economic and Budget Out-look: Fiscal Years 1992–1996*. Washington, D.C.: U.S. Government Printing Office.

U.S. Congress Special Committee on Aging. 1958. *Hearings on the Elderly Bill*. Washington, D.C.: U.S. Senate.

U.S. Department of Health and Human Services. 1982. *Final Report: The 1981 White House Conference on Aging*. 3 vols. Washington, D.C.: Department of Health and Human Services.

U.S. Department of Labor. 1989. *Key Policy Issues for the Future: Report of the Sec-retary of Labor*. A report of the Older Worker Task Force. Washington, D.C.: De-partment of Labor.

U.S. Senate Special Committee on Aging. 1989. *Aging America: Trends and Projections*. Washington, D.C.: U.S. Government Printing Office.

———. 1991. *Lifelong Learning for an Aging Society* (Serial No. 102-J). Washing-ton, D.C.: U.S. Senate Special Committee on Aging.

Van Fleet, C. 1989. "Public Library Service to Older Adults: Survey Findings and Implications." *Public Libraries* 28: 107–113.

5

Older Adult Learning in the Technological Age

More than eighty older adults trudged through a cold and windy fall rain to attend a noontime lecture by Kern Parker, Director of University Computing at the University of North Carolina at Asheville. The subject: the information highway. Parker explained how information is digitized and why fiber optics carry information more effectively than copper wires. He talked about the possibilities of distance learning and telemedicine. And they asked questions. How do digitized cameras work? What speed modem works best for sending electronic mail (e-mail)? How does the Internet work? Can e-mail send messages overseas? What is Gopher? Is Mosaic better than Gopher? What programs are needed to work with a modem? What information is available on CD-ROM for the home computer? Who will control the information superhighway?

Parker was amazed. He had expected older adults to be afraid of technology. He had heard stories of retirees spending $2,000 on computers just to save pennies on postage by communicating electronically with friends in other states. But here were older men and women exploring the various realms of telecommunications and trying to keep up with their grandchildren. He wondered if those in his audience had used computers on the job before retiring, or was this interest a new retirement activity?

On the same campus, fifty older adults were enrolled in College for Seniors computer classes taught by a former mechanical engineer, Bob Janowitz, who had learned about computers in retirement. Janowitz found that his students wanted to learn about computer uses for a variety of reasons: writing stories and letters, filing taxes, managing finances, and just keeping up with the times. Asked if older adults have a difficult time learning about computers, Janowitz answered that they are good students because they are enthusiastic and eager to learn.

Are older adults utilizing computer technology in their educational endeavors? Do they have more difficulty learning new technologies than younger people? Is computer technology appropriate to older adult learning styles? Can computer technology offer advantages to older adult learners? Are the experiences of Kern Parker and Bob Janowitz with older learners isolated phenomena or indications of future trends in older adult education? ·

EDUCATION IN THE COMPUTER AGE

Computers have revolutionized many aspects of our lives over the last fifty years. The storage, retrieval, and management of information by the computer has changed the ways that we do business, communicate, and amuse ourselves. Ironically, educators have been slow to recognize the potential of computer technology in the classroom. In fact, it is often the demands of the changing labor force requiring more technical skills that catalyzes changes in educational systems. Ultimately, computer technology will have a major impact on education involving new ways of learning and teaching in addition to new curricula (Pogrow 1983).

Traditionally, education has been primarily text-based: Students are presented material to be learned in textbooks and in lectures; mastery is assessed through written tests. Students less adept with text are less successful in learning with such methods. The visual information provided through computers offers some alternatives, at least as supplements to text-based material. Teachers who have been trained predominately using text-based teaching and learning may be resistant to changing or expanding teaching techniques or may devalue different learning styles.

Most educators want computer technology to be used to create new learning opportunities rather than to provide drill-and-practice tutorials that were early associated with computer-assisted instruction (CAI). Prepackaged information with right or wrong answers that gives the impression that learning is an accumulation of remembered facts does not qualify as a desirable use of technology. Some educators are exploring applications of intelligent computer-assisted instruction (ICAI) which allow students to take an active role in their education and encourage problem-solving skills (McClintock 1988). Others are using interactive computer applications that facilitate individual or group learning. Many encourage students to use a variety of computer functions to supplement classroom activities and to allow students to use various learning styles.

SENIORS AND TECHNOLOGY

The rapid technological advances in our lifetime are having dramatic influences on our society. At the same time, the aging of our population is affecting our attitudes, values, and how we live. These two trends, technology and aging, are impacting the economy, labor force, education, and recreation. What is the impact of pervasive technological advances on older adults? In particular, has computer technology affected older adult education? Societal attitudes about aging and technology are crucial elements in answering these questions. Prevalent ideas that computers are for the young can affect the viewpoint of older adults toward the technology as well as limit the opportunities open to them.

Senior Technophobes?

Some have stereotyped older people as unable to adapt to changes; however, people who have experienced technological changes brought about by airplanes, telephones, and television are also accepting changes such as space travel, satellite data, and telecommunications networks. Even in the short term, technology that was considered new twenty years ago, such as bank automated teller machines (ATMs) and video recorders, is in common use by all ages now, although it does tend to move into rural areas more slowly than into urban and suburban areas.

Several studies on older people's reactions to new technologies report that use of technology is inversely proportional to age but directly proportional to level of education and income (Brickfield 1984; Kerschner and Hart 1984; Zandri and Charness 1989; Adler and Furlong 1994). In other words, those with higher income and education levels are more apt to embrace new technology. Kerschner and Hart (1984) report that men are more receptive than women to new technology. Adler and Furlong (1994) report that college-educated men in suburban and urban areas are most likely to be familiar with technological advances such as the information superhighway (see Figure 5.1). However, a study by Ansley and Erber (1988) does not support the stereotype of older adults as any more resistant to computer technology than younger-aged groups.

Technological advances affect the general public most dynamically when adapted to common usage. Such adaptations as microwave ovens and motion-sensor lights are often associated with improved quality of life because they make life easier. Seniors accept technology applications, such as cruise control and automatic door locks on cars, that are used by the general population but are reluctant to use applications that make them feel different from others. Not wanting to be labeled old, seniors may reject a voice-operated electronic device to turn on lights, lock doors, and dial the phone. Other examples include closed captioning decoders for television, pill boxes with alarms, and emergency signaling devices (Bowe 1988).

Of course, computer technology is widely used by the general population, so negative stigma should not be associated with computer use by older adults. A study by Jay and Willis (1992) found that older adults' attitudes toward computers is influenced effectively by direct computer experience. The

Figure 5.1
Familiarity with Information Superhighway by Subgroup (percentage at least "somewhat familiar")

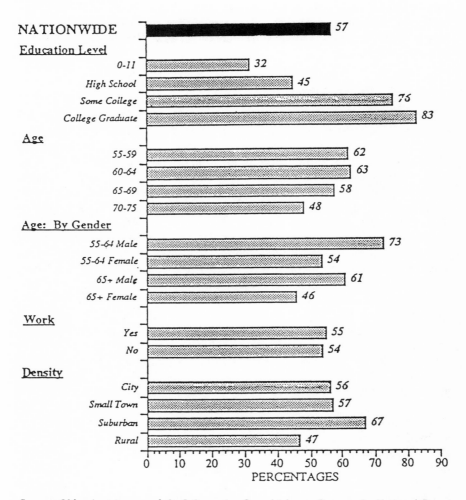

Source: Older Americans and the Information Superhighway: Report of a National Survey
(San Francisco: SeniorNet, 1994).

study does not assess if attitudes toward computers can transfer to other technologies. In another study, Jay and Willis (1988) examined personality, demographic, cognitive ability, and computer experience variables as predictors of the attitude of older women toward computers. They found that "the degree to which people believe they have control over their lives and intellectual functioning is associated with feelings of competence and gender equity of computer use and skill." They found that people with an internal locus of control are less anxious and more curious about using computers. They also noted that "indirect computer experience, particularly in the form of social influence, is an important factor influencing older women's computer attitudes." In other words, people who have social interaction with those who are computer users generally adopt their positive attitudes: interest in computers, acknowledging that people control computers, and believing women as well as men have technological skills.

Looking at the population as a whole, "between 25% and 50% of the American population are 'technophobic.' . . . Women are not more technophobic than men. Older people are not more technophobic that younger people" (Rosen and Weil 1994). According to Rosen and Weil, technophobia may include anxiety about interactions with computers and related technology or fears of the societal impact of computers and technology. It is not associated only with computers but influences avoidance of other technology, including VCRs, FAX machines, and even answering machines and digital watches. Technophobes of any age can be cured through careful and positive instruction in the use of technology (Rosen and Weil 1994). A recent national survey of older adults' views of the information superhighway reported by Adler and Furlong (1994) indicates that most older adults willingly use new technologies once they are well established in general use. The random sample survey of those aged fifty-five to seventy-five indicates that 89 percent have a microwave oven, 74 percent have a VCR, 62 percent have cable television, 42 percent have an answering machine, and 21 percent have a personal computer (see Figure 5.2). The older adults most likely to own personal computers are college graduate men under 65 years of age who live in urban areas of the western states. Two-thirds of those surveyed believe that older adults could benefit from help using computers, suggesting the importance of computer training and support services especially designed for the older learner (Adler and Furlong 1994).

Remembering that older adults are at least as diverse as any other age group is an important factor when assessing their attitudes toward technology. Some are eager to learn and experiment with electronic devices, and others are resistant.

COMPUTERS AND THE OLDER LEARNER

Mary Lou Kreidler was almost sixty when she decided that she wanted to learn about the computer because, as she puts it, "I hated it that my kids knew how to use it and I didn't."

In her youth, after a year at college and a year in the Air Force, Mary Lou had worked for thirteen years for a trucking company. She had taken typing in high school and bookkeeping in college, courses which helped her move from her first job of typing forms into responsibilities as a secretary. Later she

Figure 5.2
Penetration of High-Tech Products among Older Adults

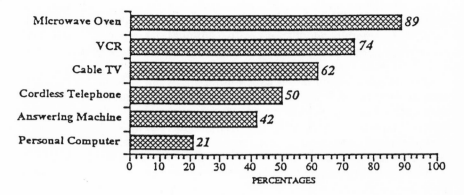

Source: Older Americans and the Information Superhighway: Report of a National Survey (San Francisco: SeniorNet, 1994).

was promoted to office manager and eventually became treasurer of the company. She has never shied from learning new skills and accepting new challenges, partly because she believes that work should be fun.

The next phase of her life found her at home raising six children. Always liking to stay busy, she found time to sew and read, especially business articles and historical novels. Mary Lou calls herself a "loner" because she is content to be by herself; in fact, she requires time by herself. She is also a good listener; "people have always told me their problems."

With one adult mentally challenged daughter still at home, Mary Lou enrolled in classes at an LRI institute located at the local university. At one of the first classes, the director of the program announced the need for a volunteer in the office. Mary Lou figured she could help out, and besides, she had seen the computer in the office. Soon Mary Lou was a regular volunteer, answering the phone and keeping records using the office's antiquated file card system.

She started to "play" with the computer when no one was using it. When the program director mentioned her wish to computerize the institute's financial records, Mary Lou volunteered to attend a workshop to learn Lotus 1-2-3. Before long she was manipulating spreadsheets and word processing programs with ease and had become the full-time volunteer secretary of the institute. As funds became available, she was put on the payroll, first part-time and then full-time. She is happy for the much-needed income, although the challenge, not the money, had been her initial motivation for learning about computers.

Now at sixty-five, Mary Lou is continuing to learn about computers; in her spare time, she is "playing with" WordPerfect 6.0.

Is Mary Lou unique, or are there other older adults who are challenged by new technologies? Mary Lou was sixty when she began retraining for a new job. At sixty-five she is valued for her computer expertise. Do computers hold potential for older learners and older workers?

Learning to Use Computers

One ubiquitous form of technology is the computer. Can older adults adapt to computer use? A study of attitudes toward older adults taking a computer course confirms the general attitude that older people are considered less likely to take and complete a computer course (Ryan, Szechtman, and Bodkin 1992). Those taking computer classes were considered atypical. Older adults themselves, however, believe benefits and services of the information superhighway, for instance, should be as available to all older adults as to all in other age groups (Adler and Furlong 1994).

In another study, healthy older and younger adults without prior computer use were given computer-assisted training in a word processing program (EDITOR). The results of the experiment show that "after twelve hours of instruction (six sessions) there were no differences between older and younger learners in recall of information about EDITOR or in correctness and efficiency with which computer operations were carried out. Older adults did, however, require more time to select and carry out the appropriate procedures" (Hartley, Hartley, and Johnson 1984).

Morris (1994) reports, however, that studies of older adults and computer use are contradictory: "Depending on which study is cited, older adults may be said to be either more negative than or equal to other age groups in their attitudes toward computer technology." The results of research on older adults enrolled in a basic computer course show that training them takes longer than training younger students. Also, older adults wanted to have an instructor available for answering questions (Morris 1994). Hales-Mabry (1993) reports more positive orientation toward computers by older adults in current surveys as compared to those conducted in the early 1980s.

Zandri and Charness (1989) found that training older adults takes almost twice as long as training younger people but that the two age groups are about equal in subsequent performance. Older adults respond to training that emphasizes "meaningfulness rather than rote approaches." Studies disagree on whether older adults should be trained individually in order to accommodate individual differences and questions or in small group sessions that encourage social reinforcement and the opportunity to learn from peers (Zandri and Charness 1989).

Computer classes were offered to older adults beginning in 1983 at the Syracuse All-University Gerontology Center. Some of the older adult learners expanded the program into the public schools and began to teach elementary school children how to use computers. One barrier to learning for some older adults who did not have computers at home was lack of practice time. In 1985 the Syracuse program established a computer education program in order to provide additional training and access to computers for older adults. The Syracuse program goals were to teach computer skills to older adults in an enjoyable way, giving them the skills to contribute their knowledge to society. They also researched the use of technology by older adults and provided an on-line network for older adults.

Learning Styles Related to Computer Use

Morris (1994) cites earlier studies that indicate some older people experience reduced spatial memory. This suggests that software designed for or meant to interest older people will be more readily accepted if it does not place demands on spatial skills; on-screen image or textual prompts are useful aids.

Some older adults may experience some sensory deficiency, such as reduced hearing, eyesight, and manual dexterity. Enhancements available in both computer hardware and software extend means of compensating for such losses. Large monitors and those with large type are readily available. Audio-enhanced and voice-activated modifications are also available. Software using combinations of text, visual images, and sound enhance the utility of computers for many people of all ages. "Hypermedia and multimedia systems offer great promise in meeting the information-processing needs of the senior user. Communication via multiple sensory modalities can compensate for a deficiency in one modality" (Morris 1994). One simple example is the word processor, an essential office tool, that has been adopted by numerous older adults who experience difficulty writing by hand for writing memoirs, family histories, and letters.

Benefits

Computers have remarkable potential to enhance the lives of the aging in ways as diverse as diagnosing and treating medical problems, enhancing safer living environments, and fulfilling information and educational needs. Hardware modifications such as text size and screen brightness can be adapted to particular needs. Communication networks can link older people with libraries, stores, government agencies, and each other. In other words, any application of computer technology that benefits other age groups can benefit older adults (Gorovitz 1985; Faris 1983; Engelhardt and Edwards 1986).

Eilers (1989) suggests that the most significant contribution of computerized technology to the lives of older people is its potential to "increase independence and control over one's environment." Eilers's study shows that older adults' use of computers helps them adapt behaviors to increase their options and to utilize multiple resources.

Eilers's study (1989) concerns older computer users at a senior center in California, where the computer education program is the "biggest ongoing educational activity." There, students learn BASIC programming and software review, including desktop publishing, word processing, database, and spread sheet. Similar projects have been undertaken by SeniorNet, with twenty educational projects for older adults at senior centers, universities, gerontological research centers, and a residential health care center. Based in San Francisco, SeniorNet is a nonprofit organization of 13,000 members over fifty-five who are interested in learning with and about computers. The twenty SeniorNet projects provide equipment and courses for teaching older adults how to use computers (Middleton 1990; Select Committee on Aging 1984; Owen 1991). One drawback of SeniorNet projects is the $15,000 to $20,000 start-up cost for equipment. Significant private-sector funding has aided in establishment of many of these centers.

The Eilers study finds that 85 percent of those in the senior center's computer club purchase personal computers after they begin participating (Eilers 1989). Although many utilize their computer knowledge for personal benefits, others apply their new knowledge and skill to serve others. For example, one man wrote an income tax program for small, in-home businesses, and another wrote a program to track membership lists and data for a local organization.

Physical limitations such as arthritis and hearing loss did not affect the older people's ability to learn to use the computers (Chin 1985). People originally enrolled in the computer courses because they were looking for a new challenge or hobby, wanted to communicate with children and grandchildren, or hoped to keep up with the times. Once they have learned basic computer skills, they continue to be involved for social reasons: sharing computer interests, maintaining friendships established in class, and making a contribution. While many people see the potential of computer technology to free older adults from restrictions of physical impairments, travel (especially at night), and to aid communication, others praise the possibilities of computers allowing older adults to remain independent (Adler and Furlong 1994).

COMPUTER-ASSISTED INSTRUCTION

In general, many older adults enjoy the benefits of computer technology for a variety of educational purposes. Do they benefit from CAI software? Are older adult educators utilizing CAI to supplement other teaching and learning techniques?

According to McNeely (1991), both educators and software developers are largely ignoring the potential impact of CAI for older learners. McNeely states that well-written CAI can accommodate learner needs through self-pacing, individualization, privacy, learner active participation, immediate feedback, and the opportunity for repetition or practice; these characteristics closely match the established instructional needs of older adults. This match suggests that CAI should be used successfully as a teaching and learning strategy with older learners. However, few studies have explored this connection; one involved teaching employment skills to disadvantaged elderly jobseekers, and two were related to health issues (McNeely 1991). One of the later studies found that learners' characteristics such as age, educational level, and previous experience with a keyboard were not related to learning using the CAI method. All three studies found the method led to effective older adult learning.

INFORMAL LEARNING AND COMMUNICATION

Two teams of just-retired and close-to-retired employees of the Los Angeles Department of Water and Power were given the task of making recommendations for the department's retirement planning program. One team was provided a personal computer network for its task while the other was not. Each of the forty-person teams of older adults completed the task, but the group using the personal computer network reaped some unexpected benefits.

By the end of the year-long study, 90 percent of the electronic group recognized each other (compared to 80 percent for the other group). The electronic group had more frequent contact with one another during the year and scheduled more face-to-face meetings, and more of them claimed to have made lasting friendships during the year.

This study suggests that computer networks for older people encourage and enable active social interactions and communications. "Like roads and highways, these networks help you get from place to place and stay in social and intellectual contact . . . [by providing] connectivity" (Bollier 1989).

Future research needs to determine whether older adults are taking advantage of opportunities to connect with the world through computers. Or are computers, in reality, devices that isolate the users, especially older adult users?

Older Adults Online

Older adults are connecting to the world through the Internet's global communications network. An estimated twenty-five million people world wide use the Internet to retrieve government documents, connect to discussion groups on various topics, and communicate through e-mail. Many older adults access the Internet from their home computer via a modem and the telephone lines.

Some seniors enjoy using computer technology for finding the information that they want or need. Using the Internet, they can access information from agencies and libraries in distant locations. In some cities, public libraries are establishing public access to the Internet for patrons. Some retired older adults access the Internet through connections with previous employers, especially universities. Many other older people subscribe to private online services for access. These services, including Prodigy and Delphi, do not currently have information on age of subscribers but, anecdotally, their members' services departments acknowledge growing use by older learners. For a yearly membership and monthly user fee, subscribers can access the Internet and a variety of services, from stock market reports to back issues of newspapers (Rushkoff 1994).

Another online service, America Online, recently made an arrangement to allow subscribers to access SeniorNet. In addition to the twenty SeniorNet project sites mentioned above, their services include on-line courses, information, and opportunities to communicate with one another on an electronic bulletin board. The organization's newsletter is also on-line.

DISTANT LEARNING

In many rural areas of the country, distance can be a barrier to education, particularly for older adults. At the same time, the needs of those isolated by distance are as great or even greater than of those in metropolitan areas which provide a plethora of opportunities for learning, enrichment, and involvement. Using distance learning, isolated older learners can take classes for a degree or diploma, gain skills for reemployment, and stay connected with learners elsewhere.

Initiatives at the federal and state level are developing the country's information highway network. For example, North Carolina initiated an information highway able to transmit voice, video, and data signals in an effort to improve government efficiency. There and in numerous other states, colleges and universities are ready partners with the state government even while they debate issues of control and maintenance of the electronic system. Many colleges and universities are already using telecommunications to control tuition costs while serving more students. In fact, Maine may soon be the first state to create an electronic institution rather than building a new campus (Blumenstyk 1994). Their initiative is not only to control rising costs, but also to serve many students who live in rural areas or on islands and to bring into the state degrees, such as library science, that are not currently offered.

Universities that encourage the electronic classroom must establish procedures for distant learners to access the library, receive counseling, and collaborate with other students. Although government and universities are involved with these satellite and fiber optic links, older adult educators and telecommunication organizations, such as telephone and cable television companies, need to collaborate to develop opportunities for older learners who also may be distant from college campuses or unable to attend traditional classes.

Presently, telecommunications technology is enabling older adult distant learning in such locations as rural areas of Michigan. According to Dekker (1994), interactive classes and workshops are held in multiple locations, including senior centers, high schools, and community centers. In western North Carolina communities separated by mountains, groups of older adults gather at local campuses of a community college for mutually interactive classes on community leadership issues that affect the represented communities.

PROGNOSIS FOR THE FUTURE

With ample benefits of computerized technology documented, why are older adults not flocking to community colleges and universities to become computer literate? Older adults offer some of the same reasons for why they choose not to enroll in any college or university courses: inconvenient location, inconvenient schedule (often evening), and expensive fees. They cite additional reasons that may prevent older adults from enrolling in computer classes: entrance requirements such as mathematics, fear of competition with younger students, and concern about the fast pace of class.

If such concerns can be addressed, we can expect a growing number of older adults to learn computer skills and thereby expand their own educational opportunities and their capacity to contribute to an increasingly electronic world community. "Policy planners in the fields of gerontology, adult education and microelectronics are encouraged to facilitate equitable computer learning opportunities for the curious and capable older American" (Eilers 1989). Senior centers and LRIs similar to the ones mentioned in this chapter may be leaders in providing viable opportunities for older adults who want to learn to use computers. By equipping computer laboratories open to retirees and providing educational and social support networks, they are attracting novice and expert older adult computer users.

Criticism of telecommunications and technology industries for being unresponsive to the interest of older learners is unwarranted, since older learners prefer using what other age groups are using. Older adult education professionals and older adults themselves need to vigorously explore the potential of computer technology. Using current and future technology, older adults can remain connected and productive without being affected by limitations of age or mobility. Given the dedication of many older learners, they may be instrumental in developing technology applications beneficial to other age groups.

REFERENCES

Adler, R., and M. Furlong. 1994. *Older Americans and the Information Superhighway: Report of a National Survey.* San Francisco: SeniorNet.

Ansley, J., and J. T. Erber. 1988. "Computer Interaction: Effect on Attitudes and Performance in Older Adults." *Educational Gerontology* 14: 107–119.

Blumenstyk, G. 1994. "Networks to the Rescue?" *Chronicle of Higher Education* 61(16): A21–A25.

Bollier, D. 1989. Review Conference on New Electronic Technologies for the Elderly: Issues and Projects. Report of an Aspen Institute Conference (5th, Queenstown, Md., March 8–10) ERIC Document Reproduction Service No. ED 315 678.

Bowe, F. 1988. "Why Seniors Don't Use Technology." *Technology Review* 91: 35–40.

Brickfield, C. F. 1984. "Attitudes and Perceptions of Older People toward Technology." In *Aging and Technological Advance*. Edited by P. K. Robinson, J. Livingston, and J. E. Birren. New York: Plenum Press.

Chin, K. 1985. "The Elderly Learn to Compute." *Aging* 348: 4–7.

Dekker, D. 1994. "Telecommunications Is the Wave of the Future." *The Older Learner* 2(2): 3

Eilers, M. L. 1989. "Older Adults and Computer Education: 'Not to Have the World a Closed Door.'" *International Journal of Technology and Aging* 2(1): 56–76.

Engelhardt, K. G., and R. Edwards. 1986. "Homebound Computing: Increasing Independence for the Aging." *Byte* 1(3): 191–196.

Faris, J. 1983. "Technology Promises Increased Convenience and Challenges to the Nation's Elderly." *Aging* 339: 12–17.

Gorovitz, S. 1985. "Bringing Senior Citizens On Line." *Technology Review* 88: 12–13.

Hales-Mabry, C. 1993. *The World of the Aging: Information Needs and Choices.* Chicago: American Library Association.

Hartley, A. A., J. T. Hartley, and S. A. Johnson. 1984. "The Older Adult as Computer User." In *Aging and Technological Advance*. Edited by P. K. Robinson, J. Livingston, and J. E. Birren. New York: Plenum Press.

Jay, G. M., and S. L. Willis. 1988. Predictors of Older Women's Computer Attitudes. Presented at Gerontological Society of America, San Francisco. Department of Individual & Family Studies. Penn State University, University Park, Pa.

———. 1992. "Influence of Direct Computer Experience on Older Adults' Attitudes toward Computers." *Journal of Gerontology: Psychological Series* 47(4): 250–257.

Kerschner, P. A., and K. Chelsvig Hart. 1984. "The Aged User and Technology." In *Communications Technology and the Elderly: Issues and Forecasts*. Edited by R. E. Dunkle, M. R. Haug, M. Rosenberg. New York: Springer.

McClintock, R. O., ed. 1988. *Computing and Education: The Second Frontier.* New York: Teachers College Press, Columbia University.

McNeely, E. 1991. "Computer-Assisted Instruction and the Older-Adult Learner." *Educational Gerontology* 17: 229–237.

Middleton, F. 1990. "Computers for Seniors." Resourceful Aging: Today and Tomorrow. Conference Proceedings (Arlington, Va., October 9–10). Vol. 5. Lifelong Education. Washington, D.C.: American Association of Retired Persons. ERIC Document Reproduction Service No. ED 344 041.

Morris, M. J. 1994. "Computer Training Needs of Older Adults." *Educational Gerontology* 20: 541–555.

Owen, O. 1991. The Computers and the Elderly Program at Syracuse University: A History. Kellogg Project Report. Syracuse, N.Y.: Syracuse Univeristy.

Pogrow, S. 1983. *Education in the Computer Age: Issues of Policy, Practice, and Reform.* Beverly Hills, Calif.: Sage Publications.

Rosen, L. D., and M. M. Weil. 1994. "What We Have Learned from a Decade of Research (1983–1993) on 'The Psychological Impact of Technology.'" *Computers and Society* 24(1): 3–5.

Rothstein, F. R., and D. J. Ratte. 1990. Training and Older Workers: Implications for U.S. Competitiveness. Contract Report. ERIC Document Reproduction Service No. ED 336 608.

Rushkoff, D. 1994. *Cyberia: Life in the Trenches of Hyperspace.* New York: HarperCollins.

Ryan, E. B., B. Szechtman, and J. Bodkin. 1992. "Attitudes toward Younger and Older Adults Learnng to Use Computers." *Journal of Gerontology: Psychological Sciences* 47(2): 96–101.

Select Committee on Aging. 1984. High Technology and Its Benefits to Aging Populations. Washington, D.C. ERIC Document Reproduction Service No. ED 259 703.

Zandri, E., and N. Charness. 1989. "Training Older and Younger Adults to Use Software." *Educational Gerontology* 15: 615–631.

6

Generations Learning Together

Where do older adults go to gain basic computer skills? For a group of seniors in Upper Arlington, a suburb of Columbus, Ohio, their first lessons came from a team of highly computer-literate children in the computer lab at Tremont Elementary School. According to local senior center program coordinator Susan Drenning, the three ninety-minute instructional sessions allowed seniors to experience "one-to-one, high tech, instructions by enthusiastic, well-trained, nonthreatening elementary students."

The special program, Computer Ease, had mutually beneficial results. The children were able to build self-esteem and a sense of competence, learn time- and lesson-planning skills, and begin to understand some of the excitement and responsibility of being a teacher. The older adults gained computer literacy skills, learned to design their own letterhead on stationery, and turned new word processing skills into letters to grandchildren. The children learned about the lives of the seniors and their continued capacity and desire to acquire new abilities, and the seniors found new ways to appreciate and relate to fifth and sixth graders (Drenning and Getz 1992).

Another beneficial outcome was political in nature. Passage of an Upper Arlington school district levy by a 168 vote margin was attributed, in part, to intergenerational programs like Computer Ease. In a town where 20 percent of the population is made up of people over sixty, it makes sense to foster positive relations between young and old.

Pittsburgh, Pennsylvania, also has a high proportion of older adult residents with a substantial number of low-income elderly residing in inner-city high-rises run by the city's housing authority. The University of Pittsburgh sought ways to improve the lives of some of these residents while looking for ways to assist first generation, mainly African-American, college students, typically from inner-city schools. The University's intergenerational studies program,

Generations Together, brought the two groups together. A one-credit service-learning course provided the context to team up a small group of high-rise residents with these inner-city undergraduates. As co-learners, they examined community services and the housing system while exploring, face to face, the needs of the elderly. The undergraduates and the elderly learned with and from one another as both groups gained new perspectives on how the lives of low-income elderly might be improved.

INTERGENERATIONAL LEARNING

The two examples above are drawn from hundreds of programs that link young and old together. Such programs have proliferated since the early 1980s and are on the increase nationally as judged by the number of conferences, newsletters, and articles, both professional and popular, on the subject. Private foundation support for many of these programs has been augmented by federal and state funds. For example, in the fall of 1993, the AOA at the U.S. Department of Health and Human Services funded seven intergenerational projects around the country (Generations United 1994). And earlier, in 1989, Linking Lifetimes, a multisite project designed to utilize older adults as mentors to at-risk middle school youth and young offenders was launched by Temple University's Center for Intergenerational Learning with major grants from a host of foundations (Center for Intergenerational Learning 1992). Even Elderhostel, which started as a travel, residential, college-level learning program for people over sixty, reported that a total of 140 intergenerational programs (mostly involving grandparents and their grandchildren) were offered during 1994.

Intergenerational programming has been defined as "activities or programs that increase cooperation, interaction or exchange between any two generations. It involves the sharing of skills, knowledge or experience between old and young" (Ventura-Merkel and Lidoff 1983). Such forms of learning may have serious impact on the future direction of older adult education. It is far from accidental that Congress, for the 1995 White House Conference on Aging, made increasing public awareness of the generational interdependence and the salient contributions of older adults a major focus for policy directions through the end of the century.

The subject of intergenerational relationships reflects the sensitivities and subtlties of aging in the United States. Age-based special interest groups have recognized the need for a coordinated agenda around issues of health, safety, poverty, education, housing, and work. They understand that young and old will both be losers if their advocacy organizations allow political polarization of their pursuit of goals to improve the condition of each group. The social and political forces that produced various intergenerational coalitions in the mid-1980s has also accelerated the number and type of intergenerational educational program.

This chapter cannot hope to cover the spectrum of intergenerational learning experiences and its accumulated literature—the research portion of which is in a fledgling stage. Our concern here is to limit the focus to those intergenerational programs and studies that emphasize education more than community service; programs that promote learning together through contact between generations.

Co-learning, as it is sometimes called, is related to but different in important ways from other types of intergenerational programs, such as (1) helping programs in which the young provide help to older persons or vice versa; (2) mentoring programs in which seniors counsel youth who are at risk of dropping out of school, unwed and pregnant teenagers, unemployed youth, or just average students including those in college; (3) intergenerational child care in which older adults are trained to look after young children or where preschoolers and frail elders interact in a cooperative day care facility; and (4) other types of programs with primarily a human service agenda.

What is the key distinction? Co-learning programs, such as Computer Ease and Generations Together cited above, involve people of different generations in learning from one another and in joint learning ventures. Education—the process of acquiring new skills and information, gaining insight and self-knowledge—is central rather than peripheral to the activity and contents of these programs. Co-learning ventures place less emphasis on unidirectional transfer of knowledge, that is, on helping, mentoring, or interactions whose primary goal is the provision of aid and support and where a major objective is attitudinal change on the part of young and old about one another.

Those seeking a broader, more encompassing perspective of intergenerational programs will find Sally Newman's "A History of Intergenerational Programs" useful, though current only to 1989 (Newman and Brummel 1989). For a summary of research on some fifty intergenerational programs that emphasize attitudinal change, see Susan Fox and Howard Giles's critical essay, "Accommodating Intergenerational Contact: A Critique and Theoretical Model" (1993). Our purpose here is to examine colearning types of intergenerational educational programs that are more consonant with the scope of programs described in earlier chapters of this book. Accordingly, our starting point is to examine the possible rationales for such programs.

RATIONALES FOR INTERGENERATIONAL EDUCATIONAL PROGRAMS

Numerous reasoned "goods", or rationales, have been advanced for intergenerational education. These include the following:

- To encourage young and old to overcome prejudice and stereotypes held by the other group
- To provide opportunities for nonpaid or stipend supported services by one group

for the other, an exchange-of-service model designed to foster better understanding and greater care between generations

- To build common bonds between generations as they discover shared life themes, challenges, and problems
- To open new conceptual frames of reference in shared study of subjects that benefit from narratives of lived history, multiple generational perspectives, and life course–related interpretations

These and related rationales fall into segments on a continuum with a human service model of program legitimation at one end and a communal/developmental learning legitimation orientation at the other. These objectives need not be mutually exclusive. However, project directors' approaches to intergenerational learning tend to operate from an orientation more towards one end of the spectrum than the other. The corollary to these orientations is the presuppositions about the nature of young or old. The human service model tends to assume that individuals are reducible to a collection of needs, attitudes, and personal desires; the communal/developmental model pictures people as social beings shaped by, benefiting from, and contributing to community ideals.

Moody and Disch (1989) argue that most intergenerational programs are too narrowly focused on providing a needed service (e.g., tutoring, chore services), overcoming age stereotypes, or providing companionship and personal contact between old and young. While valid, these instrumental objectives, they assert, lack appreciation for the juxtaposition of old and young in a society scrutinizing issues of equity between generations and facing overwhelming problems of violence, racism, poverty, homelessness, and limited opportunities for minorities and the elderly themselves. Too often, say Moody and Disch, intergenerational programs are conceived from either a "sentimental" (e.g., life satisfaction, attitude change, good feelings) or strictly utilitarian standpoint. In contrast to sentimental justifications, Moody and Disch urge planners and policy makers to consider how intergenerational programs can contribute to "civic education."

They cite four model programs designed to "contribute to vital social issues such as support of public education, urban planning, overcoming racial and ethnic conflict, or insuring opportunities for minorities." A brief description of the four programs follows. They're All My Kids takes place at a Brooklyn public elementary school with local, minority, and elderly volunteers conducting an after-school program with a group of twenty kindergarten children, providing structured extracurricular activities and serving as role models for "strengthening the children's school readiness skills and reinforcing values." In Brookline, Massachusetts, the school superintendent initiated a campaign to enlist older people to function as advocates for schools and as volunteers, while making public schools available to seniors as sites for hot lunches and other services such as health screening and recreation. A Life

Stories Project was conducted by Hunter College's Brookdale Center on Aging where black and Hispanic teenagers learned how to conduct life history interviews with the frail homebound elderly. The students gained knowledge of recent U.S. history and an appreciation for the lives of the elderly, who themselves benefitted from the opportunity to tell the stories and eventually receive a bound transcription. The fourth model is a long-running intergenerational urban planning project focused on development of the waterfront region of Long Island City (the Long Island City 2000 Project) involving older adults and high school and junior high school age students in collaborative learning activities focused on urban planning themes.

The actual contents of the programs highlighted by Moody and Disch are not that dissimilar to other intergenerational programs that emphasize sentimental justifications. But Moody and Disch focus on the ways these programs contribute to the common good, indeed to an awareness that there is such a thing as the common good, as opposed to special interest group rights and needs, private satisfactions, and strife between generations concerning access to services and resources. Perhaps it is not that these programs and related research on attitudinal change or life satisfaction are sentimental or philosophically impoverished, but that the organizers' and researchers' conceptual approaches and research/evaluation strategies are constrained by disciplinary protocol in drawing valid conclusions while avoiding overgeneralizations. We will return to this point shortly.

Besides civic education, a moral and political intergeneration program rationale is offered by Paul Nathanson (1989), who urges older adults to become allies and advocates for poor children. Nathanson, who sees this as an "imperative" from the point of view of poor children, wonders whether the elderly and their advocates will accept this perspective. His view is based on a kind of "realpolitik" which recognizes that the social view of competition between young and old could be dispelled if representatives of the elderly joined forces with advocates for poor children to present a united front. It would be "politically expedient for aging organizations to be in the forefront of intergenerational programming," argues Nathanson, and in doing so to "demonstrate to a world skeptical of the aging agenda a sense of caring for the issues important to children."

His second argument promotes an "elders of the tribe" concept: Their accumulated years and wisdom should create a sense of duty on the part of older people and their representative organizations "to lead and guide the society for the betterment of all its members."

Clearly, Nathanson would applaud establishment of Generations United in 1986, the national coalition of more than 100 organizations seeking to foster intergenerational harmony and advocacy through an agenda of programs and political reforms.

The changes in orientation advanced by Moody and Disch, Nathanson, and others include developmental, cross-cultural, social, and public policy advantages of intergeneration cooperation and collaboration. All are mindful of the advantages of forging an age-integrated form of consciousness. To do this, they need to alter conceptions of the life course based on the simile that stages of life can be equated with spaces on a life-stage pyramid or traditional staircase motif. The spatial analogy has to be transformed into a temporal–historical consciousness that can imagine the unity of the life course and the linking of generations in a common perception of contemporaneity (i.e., a shared sense of time, history, heritage, and destiny).

The theme of common plight or common destiny that would unite people of different ages has parallels with Marx's utopian vision of a classless society dwelling harmoniously at the end of history—that is, at the termination of strife between economic classes, out of which, according to Marx, history is made. Today's economic picture includes not only socioeconomic classes but generational classes based on market niches of children (e.g., cartoon shows and cereal ads), youth (the Pepsi Generation), yuppies ("You only go around once"), the middle-aged, and senior citizens ("Where's the Beef?" meets AARP discounts).

It would be naive to imagine the disappearance of age-cohort difference, whether natural or market driven. In addition, the liberation of old age from restrictive stereotypes has spawned a postmodernist ageless society, which, for some, means "you're only as old as you feel" and you can act youthful all your life. Politically, an ageless society has other implications: that social benefits and entitlements should no longer be distributed on the basis of chronological aging (e.g., Medicare and Social Security which are triggered by turning a certain age) but on the basis of need (means-tested).

Many older adults are caught in the paradox of ageless versus age-based categories. They resist age labels such as senior citizen, older adult, retiree, or senior. They prefer to mix with other age groups and may think of themselves as one of the gang and not one of the oldies. But when the opportunity arises to take advantage of senior citizens' discounts or special tax breaks, most would not hesitate to show their membership card.

Clearly, there is a difference between an ageless society and an age-integrated one. Not by rejecting the idea of age norms and responsibilities, but by discovering strengths and perspectives that it takes a lifetime to learn are mature adults fully capable of joining with other generations in pursuing a vision of the common good.

There are some contexts in which age-integration occurs commonly and naturally. Musical groups such as jazz bands, symphonies, choirs, choruses, and folk ensembles are often made up of players spanning a broad age spectrum—from those in their twenties to those in their seventies. Their love of music and dedication to collaborative mastery joins them in combining talents, experience, and enthusiasm. Frequently they learn from one another. It is not uncommon, especially among folk musicians, for younger players to revere those more senior and for the veteran players to encourage and mentor those coming up in talent and ability. Dedication to musical heritages forms the common bond—one that can well serve as an analogy to the common good that is otherwise so difficult to identify in a complex society more polarized by values and allegiances than conjoined by them.

Could intergenerational programs actually help bring about a more caring community? The small but growing body of research literature would suggest an answer in the affirmative.

TRANSFORMING EFFECTS OF INTERGENERATIONAL EDUCATION

Most of the research on intergenerational education focuses on certain narrow indicators and measures. This is typical of social science research, self-contained by criteria of quantitative verification and methodologies. Legitimately, researchers want to know whether such measures as pre- and posttest scores on attitude change, as reflected, for example, in semantic differential scales, actually show improvements in how one age cohort views another. A sampling of recent intergenerational studies shows they involve older adults and the following other groups: African-American teenagers (Aday, McDuffie, and Sims 1993); college students (Dellmans-Jenkins et al. 1994; McGowan and Blakenship 1994); children (McGuire 1986); premedical students (Reinsch and Tobis 1991); and middle-aged adults (Glass and Knott 1982).

Almost universally, the studies report that specific intergenerational programs lead to greater tolerance, increased comfort and intimacy, partial dissolving of rigid stereotypes, and less fear of the other group. Researchers are generally cautious in noting that these changes may be short-term, and they are probably correct, since a return to relative isolation between generations in everyday life may gradually erode the gains that have been achieved. If most of what you learn about another group is gained through newspaper reports, television news, and other media (or no information at all, for those who do not follow the media), then stereotyping is inevitable. No longitudinal studies have been reported in the literature to date.

One study (McGowan and Blankenship 1994) attempted to move beyond the limitations of attitude-based program assessment by using a phenomenological methodological strategy. The authors of the study sought to describe fundamental changes in the way college undergraduates interpreted the meaning of their experiences during a period of weekly visits with older homebound persons. The students conducted life history interviews, drawing upon social and historical frameworks, and produced a final paper documenting the older person's life. While carrying out this project, the students recorded their impressions in a journal in order to process, through self-mediation, the meaning of the experience. Subsequently, these journals were analyzed by the researchers using a content analysis technique.

McGowan and Blankenship reported that most students' journals revealed a four-stage process of conceptual change. The stages were (1) anticipation, consisting of apprehension (characterized by fear, uncertainty, and nervousness) and expectation (believing that a positive experience would result); (2) personal conflict (consisting of "personal challenges" brought on by unsettling real-life encounters with an older person) and "field challenges" (ethical uncertainties mixed with methodological ones); (3) reevaluation of self (personal insights and realizations), of "project role" (concerning how the life history narratives were evolving), of "intergenerational relationship" (with the older partner, but also of prior relationships such as with the students' own grandparents), and of "aging and the elderly" (the stereotypes begin to crumble); and (4) transposition (change in the student's perspective from identifying primarily as a researcher to becoming a friend).

The authors of the study consider these four steps part of an "ontological change" in students' perceptions, citing the philosophical work of Hans-Georg Gadamer (1991) and his theory of interpretation (hermaneutics). Gadamer, the authors point out, showed that personal experience is prestructured by culturally, socially, and linguistically inherited conceptual assumptions that are not themselves self-conscious. Their Life Histories Project engaged the students in a process that led to a collision or conflict between previously unreflective assumptions about old people and certain contrasting or contradictory perceptions and experiences that emerged through the deepening relationships with the real-life people they were getting to know. These unsettling experiences prompted the need for critical re-thinking of assumptions and a fundamental repositioning of role away from the disinterested observer to the involved friend or companion.

McGowan and Blankenship's project and evaluative research is unique because it addresses many perspectives. Students are taught how to conduct a life history interview and to learn about how social and historical changes may have shaped the lives of the individual subjects, and are invited to process their own ongoing experiences through journal writing. The outcomes are two sets of documents: the journals, available for analysis, and the life histories, on which the elderly have collaborated but which are not analyzed or reported in the available article.

McGowan and Blankenship's phenomenological approach is a microcosm of how intergenerational learning processes may work. Indeed, they are among the few who have attempted to study the actual process, formulate the stages, and highlight the somewhat painful but necessary disequilibrium (to use a term from Piaget, not the authors) that marks the transformation in meaning and perspective—albeit, a one-sided one insofar as the study provides a report only on the students and not on the homebound elderly subjects. The lack of symmetry in reporting on what, presumably, would be the mutually beneficial results of the study is an apparent contradiction of its goal (i.e., the transformation of intergenerational experiences). Leaving this issue aside, the study reveals the possibilities for intergenerational encounters that nurture self-change and the repositioning that makes the student not only a friend but a contemporary.

INTERGENERATIONAL VERSUS
AGE-SEGREGATED PROGRAMS

If building bonds of trust, mutual understanding, and contemporaneity are possible outcomes of intergenerational programs that help foster an age-integrated society, what then of the status of age-segregated programs, which form the bulk of older adult education endeavors?

Education is age-segregated into the college years. Those enrolled at urban colleges and universities will be more likely to experience classrooms with people ranging in age from eighteen to the mid-thirties or early forties. Corporate and other workplace education and training is even more likely to span decades of adult life. But beyond these institutional settings, education in the post-fifty age period is like the Senior Tour in golf or the AARP qualifying membership.

Reasons for grouping older adults in age-segregated programs are numerous: (1) commonality and greater likelihood of peer support through mutually perceived cohort and life-course development tasks; (2) practical matters such as convenient daytime scheduling, length and frequency of courses and semesters, affordable costs, and simpler registration procedures; (3) curriculum shaped to meet the intellectual, vocational, recreational, social, and, perhaps, spiritual interests of participants; and (4) opportunities for seniors to exercise a degree of control and leadership in influencing organizational and curricular aspects of programs they join on a voluntary basis.

But reasons for intergenerational education may complement these features of age-segregated programs. As Broomall (1992) points out, traditional college-age students may experience phases of adult development focused on appropriating a valid set of beliefs and values (knowing and valuing) that parallel developmental issues in the lives of older adults who may also be challenged by intellectual and emotional reevaluations. For Broomall, the socialization function of higher education provides a "ripe opportunity for adult development to be facilitated by interaction across developmental stages."

Based on this reasoning, should age-segregated programs linked to higher education—such as LRIs—be phased out in favor of mainstreaming older adults into regular course classrooms through tuition-waiver policies that reduce or eliminate costs to seniors? To an extent, mainstreaming of this type already goes on, though usually quite modestly, if at all. Rarely, however, is there an attempt to actually take explicit advantage of the presence of older adults in the classroom. In some instances there are reports that younger students resent older class members because they feel intimidated and overshadowed by them. In other instances, the arrangement is mutually stimulating and adds to the learning process. As Fox and Giles (1993) point out in their review of a multitude of intergenerational projects of many types and with different generational mixes, simply bringing different age groups into contact with one another does not guarantee positive results. Some projects have led to a preponderance of negative outcomes and stereotypes or biases were confirmed rather than overcome. However, where projects were thoughtfully conceived and where mutual educational benefits were involved, results were generally favorable as reflected by both age groups.

Age-segregated and age-integrated educational programs each have their own qualities, values, and applications. Hopefully we will not have to choose between them. More critical is the question concerning the infrastructure that makes both possible. It has taken several decades to establish the validity of campus-based LRIs or congregational-based Shepherd's Centers with their Adventures in Learning programs. National, state, and local coalitions to promote intergenerational education are an even more recent and tentative innovation. What institutions will claim lasting ownership of intergenerational educational ventures? What continuing funding sources will enable them to establish solid foundations?

THE INTERGENERATIONAL
IMPULSE AND IMPERATIVE

Geropsychologist David Gutmann (1987) has argued that across numerous and diverse cultures there is a phenomenon of instinctual grandparenting, not only of children related through kinship but beyond family ties. But, until recently, in the United States at least, we have viewed generations of young, old, and middle-aged as separated by gaps generated from cultural, economic, social, historical, technological, and even biological change. Many patriotic veterans of World War II were dismayed by Vietnam protesters but confused about the nature of a war with unclear goals and ambiguous allies. Postwar affluence, the rise of suburban lifestyles, and credit card household economics were a far cry from urban and rural life during the Great Depression. Some historians argue that one reason that the Social Security Act of 1935 was so popular was that it meant older parents could afford to live separately from their adult children. Family sitcoms of the 1950s and 1960s rarely included the presence of grandparents. The generation raised on radio was different from the one raised on television; the computer-entranced child of today may be quite different from his or her parents—at least in some respects.

Given this background of twentieth-century American life and the frozen conception of life stages as people are tagged and separated by cohort characteristics while they march unchanged through time, how does the intergenerational movement of mutual assistance and colearning make sense? Has the grandparenting instinct been released from social and cultural suppression?

Or is it simply that more people now have more time in retirement to think about and help out younger people?

There is no single answer or attributable cause to resolve these questions. Just as there are characteristics that determine which individuals are most likely to volunteer in earlier and later life, there are probably characteristics of older adults who are drawn to intergenerational service and colearning programs. Forms of motivation that one hears repeatedly are (1) "Our kids need help if the United States is to remain a strong and competitive nation"; (2) "I want to give something back to society and young people represent its future"; (3) "Working with young people helps me feel young and in touch"; (4) "I'm doing it for the sake of our African-American (Hispanic, Native American, etc.) children"; and (5) "I was a dropout (young offender, unwed and pregnant teen, etc.) and now want to help others in that situation."

While there is an emerging corps of motivated senior adults, any intergenerational program coordinator will tell you that recruiting volunteers for intergenerational programs is difficult and retaining them over time (six months, a year, two years) is even more difficult. Moreover, there is a constant struggle to establish close, well-organized partnerships with institutions that serve younger persons (e.g., schools, juvenile centers, youth clubs). To some degree, this administrative stretch may reflect adjustments to the increasing use of volunteers in general. But the presence of substantial numbers of the elderly, in many instances of highly skilled and knowledgeable seniors, in the halls of these institutions is still something of a shock to youth and to administrators. Will they truly be useful, or are they well-intentioned meddlers who do not really understand the nature of what is going on? There is little question but that running intergenerational programs is a labor-intensive activity that usually requires some paid professional staffing or, at least, the support of an institution willing to provide space and the necessary amenities to get the job done.

Intergenerational programs are unlikely to solve the nation's crime, poverty, dropout, drug, unwed mother, or low SAT score problems. They will make a difference in some children's lives and in some older adults'. They will make many more older adults aware of these issues as they involve real children and families, not newspaper headlines or politicians' quick fixes.

Is the growing movement of intergenerational programming—including colearning—a harbinger of change, reflecting closer identification of people in the later years with those in the earlier? Can we imagine a society in which separate age-group identification fades and is replaced by orientation to overarching communal values? Will older adults themselves seek to shed the nomenclature and identification of elderhood and instead perceive themselves as individuals who simply organize their days differently than when working?

The motivation to join in intergenerational service and educational programs must be related to the dawning awareness of the limits of one's own life and, therefore, of the shape of the life course. Seniors have the gift and burden of time, while, for youth, time is endless and measureless. The very personal sense of being part of the life course and of belonging to a generation probably does not occur until one's third decade, intensifying with succeeding decades. Consciousness of aging and of the brief span of our years (for what is human longevity when compared to evolutionary, geological, or cosmic time?) makes some people more sensititive to what they have in common with those in other generations and of whatever class and ethnic makeup. For others, the encounter with finitude and the inevitability of death leads to self-preoccupation and fear and avoidance of those perceived as being strangers in time.

Nevertheless, the growing visibility of intergenerational relationships, new emphasis on grandparenting, awareness of the need for whole communities to participate in the education of youth, and innovations in colearning ventures points to new frontiers of older adult education. As programs and organizations devoted to older learners continue to develop, they are ever more likely to encompass not only ideals of lifelong learning, but of communal belonging.

REFERENCES

Aday, R. H., W. McDuffie, and C. R. Sims. 1993. "Impact of an Intergenerational Program on Black Adolescent's Attitudes toward the Elderly." *Educational Gerontology* 19: 663–673.

Broomall, J. K. 1992. "Intergenerational Synergy." In *Students of the Third Age*. Edited by R. B. Fischer, M. L. Blazey, and H. T. Lipman. New York: Macmillan.

Center for Intergenerational Learning, Temple University. 1992. "Linking Lifetimes—Lessons Learned." *Interchange* (Fall).

Dellmann-Jenkins, M., L. Fowler, D. Lambert, D. Fruit, and R. Richardson. 1994. "Intergenerational Sharing Seminars: Their Impact on Young Adult College Students and Senior Guest Students." *Educational Gerontology* 20: 579–588.

Drenning, S., and L. Getz. 1992. "Computer Ease." *Phi Delta Kappan* 74: 471–472.

Fox, S. and H. Giles. 1993. "Accomodating Intergenerational Contact: A Critique and Theoretical Model." *Journal of Aging Studies* 7(4): 423–451.

Gadamer, H.-G. 1991. *Truth and Method*. Translated by J. Weinsheimeer and D. G. Marshall. New York: Crossroad.

Generations United. 1994. *Newsline* (Summer): 6–9.

Glass, J. C., Jr., and E. S. Knott. 1982. "Effectiveness of a Workshop in Aging in Changing Middle-Aged Adults' Attitudes toward the Aged." *Educational Gerontology* 8: 35 9–372.

Gutmann, D. 1987. *Reclaimed Powers*. New York: Basic Books.

McGowan, T. G., and S. Blankenship. 1994. "Intergenerational Experience and Ontological Change." *Educational Gerontology* 20: 589–604.

McGuire, S. L. 1986. "Promoting Positive Attitudes towards Aging among Children." *Journal of Social Health* 56: 322–324.

Moody, H. R., and R. Disch. 1989. "Intergenerational Programming in Public Policy." In *Intergenerational Programs: Imperatives, Strategies, Impacts, Trends*. Edited by S. Newman and S. W. Brummel. New York: Haworth Press.

Nathanson, P. S. 1989. "Political Imperative for Intergenerational Programs?" In *Intergenerational Programs: Imperatives, Strategies, Impacts, Trends*. Edited by S. Newman and S. W. Brummel. New York: Haworth Press.

Newman, S. 1989. "A History of Intergenerational Programs." In *Intergenerational Programs: Imperatives, Strategies, Impacts, Trends*. Edited by S. Newman and S. W. Brummel. New York: Haworth Press.

Reinsch, S., and J. S. Tobis. 1991. "Intergenerational Relations—Pre-Med Students at Senior Centers." *Archives of Gerontology and Geriatrics* 13: 211–224.

Ventura-Merkel, C., and L. Lidoff. 1983. *Program Innovation in Aging: Vol. 8, Community Planning for Intergenerational Programming*. Washington, D.C.: National Council on the Aging.

Appendixes

We have included information in the appendixes that we think may be useful to those interested in older adult education: policymakers, educators, gerontologists, as well as older adults themselves. The material here enhances the information, analysis, and discussion provided in this guide; it also provides some suggestions for finding additional information and resources, thereby opening the potential of new opportunities for cooperation and collaboration in developing innovative ideas and trends in older adult education.

Appendix A and Appendix B provide details on numerous national organizations that have interest and expertise in aging issues or older adult education. The description following each organization highlights the membership, goals, and mission of the organization. Readers may note that certain interests of other organizations may overlap with their own; therefore, sharing resources may be beneficial.

Appendix C suggests organizations that provide resources particularly designed for or useful to older adult education programs. The description of resources provided by each organization is a sampling rather than an extensive listing.

Appendix D provides a listing of the various titles and parts of the Older Americans Act. Those wishing details will need to refer to the complete Act; this summary is useful in understanding interconnections when reading this guide and other sources that mention titles and parts of the Act.

Appendix E, current to 1994, lists the tuition-waiver policies of each state and the District of Columbia in three categories: no policy, age-based, and needs-based. The chart is useful when comparing the declared policies in different states.

Appendix F lists guidelines established by the Library Services to an Aging Population Committee of the ALA. Because these guidelines represent optimum goals and services, they may be useful to other organizations considering their role in relation to the growing population of older adults. Although other organizations work extensively with the older adult population, this was the most comprehensive set of guidelines we uncovered.

Appendix G, the background paper on Life Enrichment Opportunities prepared for the North Carolina White House Conference on Aging (December 1994), provides a provocative discussion of the scope of life enrichment for older adults as well as an example of policies and programs in a particular state. Following the paper are the preliminary Life Enrichment recommendations of the North Carolina White House Conference on Aging.

Appendix H and Appendix I are schematics of the aging and education networks. These are particularly useful to those unfamiliar with those networks in order to understand their interrelationship and hierarchy.

A

Leadership Council of Aging Organizations

Professional groups serve older adults by furthering public understanding of their potential and their needs. The organization answers public and private initiatives by coordinating unified responses by members.

Alliance for Aging Research (AAR), 2021 K St., NW, Suite 305, Washington, DC 20006. Daniel Perry, Executive Director. Phone: 202–293–2856 Fax: 202–785–8574. *The AAR promotes and supports scientific research on human aging. It develops coalitions to create a national base of support for aging research, informs the public about current research in aging, conducts conferences on major aging issues, and serves as a voice in Washington for the health of older Americans. A list of publications is available.*

Alzheimer's Disease and Related Disorders Association, Inc. (ADRDA), 1319 F St., NW, Suite 710, Washington, DC 20004. Stephen McConnell, Senior Vice President, Public Policy. Phone: 202–393–7737 Fax: 202–393–2109. *The Alzheimer's Association is the only national voluntary health organization dedicated to research to find effective treatments, prevention, and eventually a cure for Alzheimer's disease and related disorders, and to support the more than four million Americans and their families who are living with these devastating illnesses. Through a fifty-state network of more than 200 local chapters, 2,000 family support groups, and 35,000 volunteers, the Association assists families with information and referral, support, respite services, and caregiver training.*

American Association for International Aging (AAIA), 1133 20th St., NW, Suite 330, Washington, DC 20036. Dr. Helen K. Kerschner, Executive Director. Phone: 202–833–8893 Fax: 202–833–8762. *The AAIA is an association of aging advocates, organizations, corporations, foundations, and individuals concerned with the needs of the aged worldwide, particularly in the Third World. The AAIA seeks to improve the socioeconomic condition of older people in developing countries through self-help and economic development. It provides small grants to projects for Third World aging.*

American Association of Homes and Services for the Aging (AAHSA), 901 E Street, NW, Suite 500, Washington, DC 20004–2037. Sheldon Goldberg, President. Phone: 202–783–2242 Fax: 202–783–2255. *The AAHSA is the national association of not-for-profit organizations dedicated to providing high-quality health care, housing, and community services primarily to the elderly. The AAHSA's mission is to represent the interests of its members and to promote its vision through ethical leadership, advocacy, education, information, and other services. Membership of close to 5,000 not-for-profit nursing homes, continuing care retirement communities, senior housing facilities, and assisted living and community services serve more than one million older persons.*

American Association of Retired Persons (AARP), 601 E St., NW, Washington, DC 20049. Horace B. Deets, Executive Director. Phone: 202–434–2300 Fax: 202–434–2320. *The AARP is the nation's leading organization for people age fifty and over with approximately thirty-three million members. It serves their needs and interests through legislative advocacy, research, informative programs, and community services provided by a network of local chapters and experienced volunteers throughout the country. For more information about older adult education, contact AARP, Consumer Affairs (202–434–6030). The Andrus Foundation supports education and aging research through grants to nonprofit organizations, universities, and colleges in areas such as literacy, technology, and lifelong learning.*

American Federation of State, County, and Municipal Employees (AFSCME) Retiree Program, AFL-CIO, 1625 L St., NW, Washington, DC 20036. Steve Regenstreif, Director. Phone: 202–429–1274 Fax: 202–429–1293. *The AFSCME Retiree Program organizes public employee retirees so that they can work together to improve their retirement benefits. The program currently includes twenty-nine chapters and over one-hundred fifty subchapters around the country with a dues-paying membership of 165,000. AFSCME retiree members are grassroots lobbyists, advocating at the local level for cost-of-living adjustments on pensions, employer contributions to retiree health-care coverage, and extension of health coverage to spouses and survivors. In addition, AFSCME retiree chapters work on such mainstream senior issues as preservation of Social Security and enactment of a national health plan.*

American Geriatrics Society (AGS), 770 Lexington Ave., Suite 300, New York, NY 10021. Linda Hiddemen Barondess, Executive Vice President. Phone: 212–308–1414 Fax: 212–832–8646. *The AGS is a medical specialty society of over 6,500 physicians and other health-care professionals dedicated to improving the health and well-being of all older adults. To achieve this goal, the AGS works to develop, support, and promote the clinical practice of geriatrics and to support practitioners providing such care; increase the number of health-care professionals knowledgeable about geriatrics and committed to the clinical care of the aged; promote effective, high quality research that addresses health-care problems of older people; and engage in a public policy effort that focuses on the improvement and study of health care for older people.*

American Society on Aging (ASA), 833 Market St., Room 516, San Francisco, CA 94103. Gloria Cavanaugh, Executive Director. Phone: 415–974–9600 Fax: 415–974–0300. *The ASA is an association of diverse individuals bound by a common mission. The mission of the organization is to promote the well-being of aging people and their families by enhancing the abilities and commitment of those who work with them. The ASA's 10,000 members include representatives of the public and private sectors, service providers and researchers, educators and advocates, health and social service professionals, students and the retired, and policymakers and planners. The Older Adult Education Network, a membership unit within the ASA, works to meet the needs of professionals who administer educational programs for older adults, who serve as instructors, or who plan activities with education components.*

Asociacion Nacional Pro Personas Mayores, 3325 Wilshire Blvd., Suite 800, Los Angeles, CA 90010–1784. Carmela G. Lacayo, President and CEO. Phone: 213–487–1922 Fax: 213–385–3014. *The Asociacion Nacional Pro Personas Mayores is a private, nonprofit corporation committed to promoting coalitions nationwide in order to improve the well-being of older Hispanics and other low-income elderly. The Asociacion administers a nationwide employment program for low-income older persons and provides training and technical assistance to community groups and professionals in the field of aging. The National Hispanic Research Center conducts national studies on the Hispanic community and their Media Center produces and disseminates bilingual information on older Hispanics.*

Association for Gerontology and Human Development in Historically Black Colleges and Universities (AGHD-HBCU), 1424 K St., NW, Suite 601, Washington, DC 20005. Dr. Delores D. Penn, President. Phone: 202–628–5322 Fax: 202–628–0939. *The AGHD-HBCU is a nonprofit organization fostering exchange of resources and sharing knowledge among individuals committed to improving the quality of life for the elderly, especially for racial/ethnic minorities and women. Its members are individuals and organizations com-*

mitted to education, research, training, and service programs in gerontology/ geriatrics. The membership includes educators, practitioners in health and human services, legal professionals, academic institutions, aging service organizations, students, and older adults.

Association for Gerontology in Higher Education (AGHE), 1001 Connecticut Ave., NW, Suite 410, Washington, DC 20036–5504. Elizabeth B. Douglass, Executive Director. Phone: 202–429–9277 Fax: 202–429–6097. *The AGHE is an organization of over 300 higher education institutions which represent gerontological education and research programs. It promotes education of people preparing for research or careers in gerontology and works to increase public awareness. The AGHE cooperates with public officials, voluntary organizations, associations, and others interested in aging and education.*

Catholic Golden Age (CGA), 430 Penn Ave., Scranton, PA 18503. Rev. Gerald N. Dino, President. Phone: 717–342–3294 Fax: 717–963–0149. *CGA is an organization of one million Catholics over age fifty emphasizing study of the meaning of longer life, religion, and spirituality and emphasizing means to self-fulfilling lives. It provides information designed to enrich the lives of older adults by confronting problems such as poor health, loneliness, loss of social status, inactivity, and insufficient financial resources.*

ELDERCARE AMERICA, Inc., 1141 Loxford Terrace, Silver Spring, MD 20901. Andrew Hofer. Phone: 301–593–1621 Fax: (same as phone). *Eldercare America, Inc. is a coalition of organizations, professionals, and concerned individuals interested in improving the well-being of the millions of family members who care for their older relatives. The only national organization that focuses exclusively on family eldercare, it promotes stimulating, supporting, and strengthening local self-help and community-based service initiatives.*

Families USA, 1334 G St., NW, Washington, DC 20005. Ronald Pollack, Executive Director. Phone: 202–737–6340 Fax: 202–347–2417. *The Families USA Foundation, with a membership of 150,000, is the nation's leading health-care reform advocacy organization working on behalf of consumers. It works nationally and locally to educate the public and mobilize consumers to fight for reform of the health-care system. Families USA provides information, policy analysis, and educational services.*

The Gerontological Society of America, 1275 K St., NW, Suite 350, Washington, DC 20005–4006. Carol A. Schutz, Executive Director. Phone: 202–842–1275 Fax: 202–842–1150. *The Gerontological Society of America is a 6,500-member multidisciplinary organization of professionals founded in 1945 to promote the scientific study of aging, to encourage exchanges among researchers and practitioners from the various disciplines related to gerontology, and to foster the use of gerontological research in forming public policy.*

Gray Panthers, 2025 Pennsylvania Ave., NW, Suite 821, Washington, DC 20006. Dixie Horning, Executive Director. Phone: 202–466–3132 Fax: 202–466–3133. *The Gray Panthers, with approximately 40,000 members, is a multigenerational nonpartisan membership organization with a global reach and a vision of peace and justice. Headquartered in Washington, D.C., the Gray Panthers hold consultative status to the Economic and Social Council of the United Nations. Major issues of concern include health, peace, housing, education, justice, the environment, and human potential.*

Green Thumb, Inc., 2000 North 14th St., Suite 800, Arlington, VA 22201. Andrea Wooten, President. Phone: 703–522–7272 Fax: 703–522–0141. *Green Thumb, Inc. is a national nonprofit organization that provides employment and training opportunities for older Americans in forty-four states and Puerto Rico. Green Thumb principally operates the Senior Community Service Employment Program authorized under Title V of the Older Americans Act and funded by a grant from the U.S. Department of Labor. Green Thumb's mission is to improve the quality of life of all Americans by using and developing the talents and skills of older individuals through training, employment, and community service. In 1994, Green Thumb provided employment, training, and service opportunities to over 26,000 older Americans.*

National Asian/Pacific Center on Aging (NAPCA), Melbourne Tower, Suite 914, 1511 Third Ave., Seattle, WA 98101. Don Watanabe, Executive Director. Phone: 206–624–1221 Fax: 206–624–1023. *The NAPCA is committed to advocating for the well-being of elderly Asian and Pacific Islander Americans and developing programs and service projects which enhance the quality of their lives.*

National Association for Home Care (NAHC), 519 C St., NE, Stanton Park, Washington, DC 20002. Val Halamandaris, President. Phone: 202–547–7424 Fax: 202–547–9559. *The NAHC, with approximately 6,000 members, is a professional association representing the interests of Americans who need home care (including acute, long-term, and terminal care) and the caregivers who provide them with in-home health and supportive services. Its primary mission is to promote and foster home care and hospice services. Top priorities remain the enactment of long-term care legislation based on home care, while protecting Medicare and other government programs from erosion based on growing costs and budget pressures and helping to increase the numbers and qualifications of people seeking employment in the home care field.*

National Association of Area Agencies on Aging (NAAAA), 1112 16th St., NW, Suite 100, Washington, DC 20036. Richard Browdie, Executive Director. Phone: 202–296–8130 Fax: 202–296–8134. *The NAAAA represents the interests of a network of local agencies dedicated to helping all older Americans remain healthy and independent and in their own homes and communities for* *as long as possible. Area Agencies on Aging, established under the federal Older Americans Act, address the needs of all older Americans aged sixty and over within every local community. Area Agencies on Aging coordinate almost $3 billion annually, including home delivered meals, senior centers, transportation, home care, respite and adult day care, and legal assistance. Area Agencies on Aging also provide information to older Americans and their caregivers about the availability of local agency services, handling over 15 million requests each year. Membership includes Area Agencies on Aging, Title VI Native American Aging Organizations, and corporations and other private organizations interested in providing services to older Americans.*

National Association of Foster Grandparent Program Directors (NAFGPD), Foster Grandparent Program (FGP), Laurelton Center, Laurelton, PA 17835. Mary Louise Schweikert, President. Phone: 717–922–1130 Fax: 717–922–4799. *The NAFGPD has approximately 300 members, including FGP program directors and other staff, public and private local FGP Sponsoring Agencies, and others who support the work of the FGP. It serves as the principal national advocate for the FGP in general, for the furtherance of the goals of the FGP, and for the well-being of Foster Grandparent volunteers. The purpose of the NAFGPD is to provide a national focus for issues which directly impact the quality of services provided to FGP volunteers and the children they serve, the visibility and viability of the broader senior and volunteer service communities, and the ability of FGP directors to manage their programs effectively and meet the changing needs of their communities.*

National Association of Meal Programs (NAMP), 101 North Alfred St., Suite 202, Alexandria, VA 22314. Margaret Ingraham, Legislative Director. Phone: 703–548–5558 Fax: 703–548–8024. *The mission of NAMP is to provide education, training, and development opportunities that will enable its members to provide quality nutrition, services, and programs to people in need. The 700 members of NAMP deliver Meals on Wheels and provide lunches at Senior Centers.*

National Association of Nutrition and Aging Services Programs (NANASP), 2675 44th St., SW, Suite 305, Grand Rapids, MI 49509. Connie Benton-Wolfe, Executive Director. Phone: 616–531–8700 Fax: 616–531–3103. *The NANASP is a professional membership organization of over 1,000 members from every region of the country representing the interests of nutrition and other direct service providers in the aging network. It provides training and information to service providers and lobbies for them and the older Americans they serve.*

National Association of Retired and Senior Volunteer Program Directors, Inc. (NARSVPD), Audubon Area RSVP, 1650 West Second St., Owensboro, KY 43201. Patricia S. Renner, President. Phone: 502–683–1589 Fax: 502–686–1614.

The NARSVPD is an association of 600 directors of programs sponsored by the Retired Senior Volunteer Program (RSVP). It provides national advocacy for the RSVP, facilitates communication among members, and acts as a representative for those served by the RSVP before national governmental bodies. The RSVP is made up of volunteers at least sixty years old who are willing to perform services on a regular basis through voluntary service to communities.

National Association of Retired Federal Employees (NARFE), 1533 New Hampshire Ave., NW, Washington, DC 20036. Judy Park, Legislative Director. Phone: 202–234–0832 Fax: 202–797–9697. *The NARFE strives to protect federal employee retirement benefits by uniting civilian employees, retirees, survivors, and spouses around the world. It serves those who have served the nation. Members of NARFE (nearly 500,000) are committed to and actively involved in volunteer community services. They are organized into more than 1,740 chapters and 53 state and territorial federations throughout the United States, Puerto Rico, Guam, the U.S. Virgin Islands, Panama, and the Philippines.*

National Association of Senior Companion Project Directors (NASCPD), Senior Companion Program, Lutheran Social Service of Minnesota, 2414 Park Ave., Minneapolis, MN 55404. John Pribyl, President. Phone: 612–872–1719 Fax: 612–753–3074. *The NASCPD is organized to provide an opportunity for expression and education for and by Directors of Senior Companion Projects. It provides a vehicle for communication between the Project Directors, organizations and agencies serving the Senior Companions Program, as well as the Corporation for National Service offices. The organization also encourages coordinated mutually supportive services within the aging network. A major goal of the organization is to avoid duplication of services and maximize both the quality and level of services provided for the elderly.*

National Association of State Units on Aging (NASUA), 1225 I St., NW, Suite 725, Washington, DC 20005. Daniel A. Quirk, Executive Director. Phone: 202–898–2578 Fax: 202–898–2583. *The NASUA is a national, non-profit, public interest organization dedicated to providing general and specialized information, technical assistance, and professional development support to State Units on Aging. The membership of the Association is comprised of the fifty-seven state and territorial government agencies charged with advancing the social and economic agendas of older persons in their respective states.*

National Caucus and Center on Black Aged, Inc. (NCBA), 1424 K St., NW, Suite 500, Washington, DC 20005. Samuel J. Simmons, President. Phone: 202–637–8400 Fax: 202–347–0895. *The NCBA is dedicated to improving the quality of life for African-American and other minority elderly, especially those of low income. The goals include eliminating poverty for all elderly Americans, improving the status of health and quality of health care for African-American seniors, and increasing minority participation in programs and services for the aged. It is a nonprofit organization which has nearly 3,000 members in thirty-two chapters across the United States. The NCBA provides services and programs in employment and training, housing, public policy and advocacy, and research.*

National Council of Senior Citizens (NCSC), 1331 F St., NW, Washington, DC 20004–1171. Lawrence T. Smedley, Executive Director. Phone: 202–347–8800 Fax: 202–624–9595. *The NCSC is an advocacy organization dedicated to the belief that America's elderly, like America's youth, is worthy of the best that this nation can give. The NCSC was founded in 1961 during initiatives for Medicare legislation. It now comprises over 5,000 senior citizens clubs with a total membership of five million and continues to speak out on behalf of the elderly, striving always to make this country a better place for older people . . . and for people of all ages.*

National Council on the Aging, Inc. (NCOA), 409 Third St., SW, Second Floor, Washington, DC 20024. James Firman, President. Phone: 202–479–1200 Fax: 202–479–0735. *The NCOA encompasses a varied membership united by a commitment to the principle that the nation's older people are entitled to lives of dignity, security, and physical, mental, and social well-being and to full participation in society. In all its efforts, the NCOA seeks to help meet the current and changing needs of all older persons—regardless of sex, race, color, creed, national origin, or special handicap—and to tap the vast resources that older people offer to the nation. It conducts research and demonstration projects, provides training and technical assistance, develops program standards, and disseminates information. The NCOA advocates for improvements in public and private policies that affect the aging. Membership includes both individuals and organizations.*

National Hispanic Council on Aging (NHCoA), 2713 Ontario Rd., NW, Suite 200, Washington, DC 20009. Marta Sotomayor, President. Phone: 202–745–2521 Fax: 202–745–2522. *The NHCoA is dedicated to improving the quality of life for Latino elderly families and communities through advocacy, training, projects, and education. Through newsletters in English and Spanish, it informs members about critical issues in health, income, education, employment, housing, and community that face Latino elderly and families. The NHCoA's network of chapters and affiliates consists primarily of dedicated volunteers who help educate families and communities about national, state, and local issues facing Latino elderly families and serve as catalysts for change on the local level.*

National Osteoporosis Foundation (NOF), 1150 17th St., NW, Suite 500, Washington, DC 20036. Sandra Raymond, Executive Director. Phone: 202–223–2226 Fax: 202–223–2237. *The NOF is the nation's leading resource for patients, health-care professionals, and organizations seeking up-to-date, medically sound information and program materials on the causes, prevention, and treatment of osteoporosis. The NOF includes a network of individuals, healthcare professionals, and organizations who support its goals. It advocates for increased research support, provides direct support for research, increases public awareness and knowledge about osteoporosis, educates physicians and other health professionals, and informs patients and their families.*

National Senior Citizens Law Center (NSCLC), 1815 H St., NW, Suite 700, Washington, DC 20006. Burton Fretz, Executive Director. Phone: 202–887–5280 Fax: 202–785–6792. *The NSCLC was established to help older Americans live their lives in dignity and free from poverty. It pursues this goal by practicing law in support of legal services programs and on behalf of elderly poor clients and client groups.*

National Senior Service Corps Directors Associations (NSSCDA), 4958 Butterworth Place, NW, Washington, DC 20016. Alan Lopatan, Washington Represenative. Phone: 202–244–2244 Fax: 202–244–2322. *The NSSCDA is an umbrella association for the directors of the three national senior service corps: Foster Grandparent Program, Senior Companion Program, and Retired and Senior Volunteer Program.*

Older Women's League (OWL), 666 11th St., NW, Suite 700, Washington, DC 20001. Dianna Porter, Public Policy Director. Phone: 202–783–6686 Fax: 202–638–2356. *The OWL is a national grassroots membership organization whose sole mission is to address the special concerns and needs of women as they age. The OWL works to provide mutual support for its members to achieve economic and social equity and to improve the image and status of midlife and older women. The OWL's programs and activities seek to achieve their mission of mature women in control of their lives, managing their health, their problems, and their needs with dignity, strength, and independence. Membership now totals approximately 20,000.*

United Auto Workers (UAW) Retired and Older Workers Department, 8731 East Jefferson Ave., Detroit, MI 48214. Tim Foley, Director. Phone: 313–926–5231 Fax: 313–824–5750. *The UAW Retired and Older Workers Department provides programs and services to UAW retirees. In addition to supporting a national health-care program and protection of Social Security and Medicare, the UAW Retired Workers Department includes a section on subjects of interest to retirees in UAW's monthly and quarterly magazines.*

B

Additional Organizations Interested in Older Adult Education

American Association for Adult and Continuing Education (AAACE), 112 16th St., NW, Suite 420, Washington, DC 20036. Judith A. Koloski, Executive Director. Phone: 202–463–6333. *The AAACE is a 4,000-member organization providing leadership in advancing education as a lifelong learning process. It works to stimulate local, state, and regional adult and continuing education efforts. The AAACE encourages cooperation, monitors legislation, conducts special studies, and bestows awards.*

Association for Continuing Higher Education (ACHE), 1800 Lincoln Ave., University of Evansville, Evansville, IN 47722. Lynn R. Penland, Executive Vice President. Phone: 812–479–2472. *Institutional members are accredited colleges or universities that award undergraduate or higher academic degrees; individual members are faculty or staff of a university continuing education division. The ACHE promotes professional excellence, stimulates faculty leadership, and cooperates with other organization and groups.*

Elderhostel, Inc., 80 Boylston St. Suite 400, Boston, MA 02116. William D. Berkeley, President. Phone: 617–426–7788. *Elderhostel is an international network of colleges, universities, and other educational institutions interested in lifelong learning and the elderly. Elderhostel offers low-cost, short-term, residential academic programs for adults fifty-five and over, their spouses of any age, and companions at least fifty years old. Elderhostel offers noncredit liberal arts and science courses taught by college faculty.*

National Education Association (NEA), 1201 16th St., NW, Washington, DC 20036. Don Cameron, Executive Director. Phone: 202–833–4000. *The NEA is a 1,600,000-member professional organization of elementary and secondary school teachers, college and university professors, administrators, principals, counselors, and others concerned with education.*

National University Continuing Education Association (NUCEA), One Dupont Circle, Suite 615, Washington, DC 20036. Kay J. Kohl, Executive Director. Phone: 202–659–3130. *The members of NUCEA include 400 public and private institutions of higher education with continuing education programs and 2,000 professional staff at member institutions. The NUCEA has a division of continuing education for older adults.*

C

Older Adult Education Resources

American Association of Retired Persons (AARP), 601 E St., NW, Washington, DC 20049. Phone: 202–434–2277 Fax: 202–434–2320. *The AARP publishes a wide variety of materials on consumer, economic, health, international, work, and legal issues. Examples of publications include* AARP's Catalog of Publication and Audiovisuals, Education Projects Idea Book: A Guide for Volunteers, *and* All About AARP.

American Library Association (ALA), 50 Huron St., Chicago, IL 60611. Phone: 800–545–2433, ext. 7 Fax: 312–440–9374. *The ALA offers a variety of resources especially for libraries.* Book Discussions for Adults: A Leader's Guide *is helpful for library-sponsored discussion groups. The Reference and Adult Services Division provides additional resources for working with older people. See also* The Whole Person Catalog *and* Let's Talk About It.

Association of Learning in Retirement Organizations (ALIROW), 1607 Angelus Ave., Los Angeles, CA 90026. Phone: 213–664–1322. *ALIROW offers publications such as* Compendium for Curriculum Ideas for Learning in Retirement Organizations and Institutes *and* The Handbook for Learning in Retirement Organizations and Institutes.

Audio Store, 821 University Ave., Madison, WI 53706. Phone: 800–972–8346. *Audio Store sells a variety of educational audio tapes made for Public Radio. Topics include American history, music, literature, ethics, and nutrition. Some programs have discussion leader guides. A catalog is available.*

Bi-Folkal Productions, Inc., 809 Williamson St., Madison, WI 53703. Phone: 608–251–2818 Fax: 608–251–2874. *Bi-Folkal Productions is a non-*

profit organization which provides theme kits to spark discussion among older adults. Kits may include slides, videos, booklets, activities, and resources. Themes include the Depression, worklife, fashion, pets, music, automobiles, train rides, and African-American artists.

Choices Education Project, Brown University, Box 1948, Providence, RI 02912. Phone: 401–863–3465. *A project called Choices for the 21st Century provides resources, including "Changes in the Former Soviet Union: Debating U.S. Aid," and suggestions for supplemental reading.*

Documentary Educational Resources, 101 Morse St., Watertown, MA 02172. Phone: 617–926–0491. *This company produces, distributes, and promotes anthropological and sociological films for educational purposes.*

Great Books, Adult Program Coordinator, 34 East Wacker Drive, Suite 2300, Chicago, IL 60601. Phone: 800–222–5870. *Great Books curricula are designed to encourage reading and discussion of outstanding works of literature.*

Great Decisions, Foreign Policy Association, Programming and Community Affairs Department, 729 Seventh Ave., New York, NY 10019. Phone: 800–628–5754 or 212–764–4050. *Offered by the nonprofit, nonpartisan Foreign Policy Association, Great Decisions is a lecture and discussion series on world affairs and international issues vital to the longterm interests of the United States. Great Decisions seeks to promote better understanding of world issues that affect foreign policy. Topics include nuclear proliferation, the United Nations, international financial markets, immigration, and relations with China and the Middle East. The curriculum and materials are available for a fee.*

Let's Talk About It, American Library Association (ALA) Public Programs, 50 E. Huron St., Chicago, IL 60611. Phone: 800–545–2433, ext. 5053 or 5055, or 312–280–5053. *A national humanities program for adult book discussions about contemporary life and culture. Usually participants read several books related to a single theme and discuss them under the guidance of a humanities scholar following the scholar's overview of the books and key ideas. Examples of themes include work and its rewards, nationalism and the Civil War, and individual rights and community.*

National Council on the Aging (NCOA), 409 Third St., SW, Washington, DC 20024. Phone: 800–424–9046. *The NCOA provides information and publications on services, programs, and policies in the field of aging. Publications on health, eldercare, work, housing, arts, humanities, and retirement issues are available for a fee.*

National Council on the Aging (NCOA), Discovery Through the Humanities, 409 Third St., SW, Washington, DC 20024. Phone: 800–424–9046 or 202–479–6990. *Discovery through the Humanities provides program materials for reading and discussion groups. Anthologized selections in the books are adapted for series of five to twelve sessions. Materials include a book for each participant, a guide for discussion leader, audio tapes, and posters. Materials may be borrowed for a fee. Examples of titles include* Remembering World War II; Roll on, River; The Search for Meaning; Work and Life; The Remembered Past: 1914–1945; *and* A Family Album: The American Family in Literature and History.

National Issues Forums (NIF), 100 Commons Rd., Dayton, OH 45450–2777. Phone: 800–433–7834 or 513–434–5567 Fax: 513–439–9084. *The NIF prepare nonpartisan study materials for participants and guides for leaders. Three challenging domestic issues are selected each year on topics such as health care, violence, and free speech. Materials are available for a fee.*

National Recreation and Park Association (NRPA) Publications Center, 2775 S. Quincy St., Suite 300, Arlington, VA 22206. Phone: 703–820–4940 Fax: 703–671–6772. *The Final Report from the NRPA's Comprehensive Leisure and Aging Study is available for thirty-five dollars to nonmembers. The 1994 study assessed programs and services for older adults by municipal recreation departments nationwide. It provides information for local governments in organizing and evaluating recreation and leisure programs and provides suggested resources.*

SeniorNet National Office, 399 Arguello Boulevard, San Francisco, CA 94118. Phone: 415–750–5030 Fax: 415–750–5045 or Internet address: seniornet@aol.com. *Fifty-four learning centers in twenty-six states and SeniorNet Online are some services of this membership organization for beginning and intermediate level computer uses.*

State Arts Councils. *Many state arts councils provide resources and visiting artists. For information, inquire from National Assembly of State Arts Agencies, 1010 Vermont Ave., NW, Washington, DC 20005. Phone: 202–347–6352 Fax: 202–737–0526.*

State Humanities Councils. *Many state humanities councils provide resources, including a Speaker's Bureau of humanities scholars willing to lecture on a variety of subjects. Ask for* National Endowment for Humanities Overview of Endowment Programs *from Public Information Office, 1100 Pennsylvania Ave., NW, Washington, DC 20506. Phone: 202–606–8438.*

Study Circles Resource Center (SCRC), Route 169, PO Box 203, Pomfret, CT 06258. Phone: 203–928–2616. *The SCRC is a nonprofit organization that promotes the study circle concept from Sweden which involves members in democratic, highly participatory, small-group discussions on critical social and political issues. It provides resources on organizing and conducting study circles, training materials, and course materials. Program topics include government, society, health, cultures, environment, ethics, and religion.*

Teaching Company, The, PO Box 17524, Arlington, VA 22216. Phone: 800–832–2412. *In cooperation with the Resident Associate Program of the Smithsonian Institution, the Teaching Company has produced fifteen different eight-part videotaped lecture series available for rental or purchase. One example is "Detective Fiction: The Killer, The Detective & Their World." A catalog is available.*

Whole Person Catalog, The, American Library Association (ALA) Graphics, ALA, 50 Huron St., Chicago, IL 60611. Phone: 800–545–2433, ext. 5048, 5049, or 5050 Fax: 312–440–9374. The Whole Person Catalog *is a resource particularly for libraries. It describes humanities-oriented reading and discussion programs, exhibitions offered by libraries and nonprofit organizations, and how to receive further information.*

D

The Older Americans Act of 1965 (as Amended in 1992)

Title I   Declaration of Objectives: Definitions

Title II   Administration on Aging

Title III   Grants for State and Community Programs on Aging
  Part A   General Provisions
  Part B   Supportive Services and Senior Centers
  Part C   Nutrition Services
    Subpart 1   Congregate Nutrition Services
    Subpart 2   Home-Delivered Nutrition Services
    Subpart 3   School-Based Meals for Volunteer Older Individuals
       and Multigenerational Programs
    Subpart 4   General Provisions
  Part D   In-Home Services for Frail Older Individuals
  Part E   Additional Assistance for Special Needs of Older Individuals
  Part F   Preventive Health Services
  Part G   Supportive Activities for Caregivers who Provide In-Home
       Services to Frail Older Individuals

Title IV   Training, Research, and Discretionary Projects and Programs
  Part A   Education and Training
  Part B   Research, Demonstrations, and Other Activities
  Part C   General Provisions

Title V   Older Americans Community Service Employment Program

Title VI   Grants for Native Americans
  Part A   Indian Program
  Part B   Native Hawaiian Program
  Part C   General Provisions

Title VII   Vulnerable Elder Rights Protection Activities
       Part A   State Provisions
             Subpart 1   General State Provisions
             Subpart 2   Ombudsman Programs
             Subpart 3   Programs for Prevention of Elder Abuse, Neglect,
                       and Exploitation
             Subpart 4   State Elder Rights and Legal Assistance Development
                       Program
             Subpart 5   Outreach, Counseling, and Assistance Program
       Part B   Native American Organization Provisions
       Part C   General Provisions
Title VIII   Amendments to Other Laws: Related Matters
       Part A   Long-Term Care Workers
       Part B   National School Lunch Act
       Part C   Native American Programs
       Part D   White House Conference on Aging
Title IX   General Provisions

E

Survey of Age-Based Tuition-
Waiver Policies

STATES WITH NO LEGISLATION OR STATE POLICY TO
WAIVE OR REDUCE TUITION FOR SENIOR CITIZENS

STATE	POLICY
Alabama	None
Arizona	None
California	None
Colorado	None
Iowa	None
Mississippi	Individual institutions have policies based on age
Missouri	Individual institutions have policies based on age
Nebraska	None
Oregon	Individual institutions have policies based on age
Vermont	Individual institutions have policies based on age
West Virginia	Individual institutions have policies based on age
Wyoming	Up to 20 percent of tuition may be waived and most individual colleges provide this waiver for senior citizens on space-available basis

STATES WITH AGE-BASED TUITION WAIVER

STATE	POLICY, MINIMUM AGE REQUIREMENT
Alaska	Sixty, enrollment on a space-available basis
Arkansas	Sixty, general student fees, space available
Connecticut	Sixty-two, space available
Delaware	Sixty, formal degree candidates only, space available
District of Columbia	Sixty, credit or audit
Florida	Sixty, credit courses but no credit awarded, space available
Georgia	Sixty-two, space available
Hawaii	Sixty, credit courses, space available
Idaho	Sixty, reduced fees and tuition, space available
Illinois	Sixty-five, credit courses, space available
Indiana	Sixty, high school graduate, retired, and not employed full-time, 50 percent in-state tuition up to nine semester hours
Kansas	Sixty, audit but not credit, space available
Kentucky	Sixty-five, for those admitted, space available. Donovan Scholars—audit or credit without limit
Louisiana	Sixty; for those fifty, reduction in cost of textbooks and instructional aids
Maine	Sixty-five with financial need, credit or noncredit, space available
Maryland	Sixty, retired with chief income from retirement benefits, not employed full-time, space available, credit or noncredit, up to three courses per term
Massachusetts	Sixty, space available, credit or noncredit
Michigan	Sixty, community colleges
Minnesota	Sixty-two, credit, audit or noncredit excluding noncredit adult vocational education courses, space available
Montana	Sixty-two
Nevada	Sixty-two, credit or audit
New Hampshire	Sixty-five, fees vary among institutions
New Jersey	Sixty-five, credit or noncredit, space available
New Mexico	Sixty, credit and noncredit if enrolled for less than six hours and meet all course requisites
New York	Sixty, audit or credit, space available
North Carolina	Sixty-five, credit on noncredit, must meet admission standards, space available

STATE	POLICY, MINIMUM AGE REQUIREMENT
North Dakota	Sixty-five, audit, space available
Ohio	Sixty, noncredit, space available
Oklahoma	Sixty-five, space available
Pennsylvania	Retired persons, space available
Rhode Island	Sixty, permanent resident, household income less than twice the federal poverty level as established by the U.S. Department of Health and Human Services, space available
South Carolina	Sixty, credit or noncredit, must meet admission standards, space available
South Dakota	Sixty-five, 75 percent of normal tuition, credit
Tennessee	Sixty-five, audit or credit, space available
Texas	Sixty-five, audit, space available
Utah	Sixty-two, space available, audit senior must pay full tuition to receive credit
Virginia	Sixty, up to three noncredit per quarter or semester; sixty, audit only if income exceeds $10,000, for credit if income below $10,000; space available unless has completed 75 percent of degree requirements
Washington	Sixty, credit or audit up to two courses per quarter or semester if course credits not for increasing credentials or salary increases, subject to prerequisites
Wisconsin	Sixty-two, vocational adult courses

STATES WITH NEEDS-BASED TUITION WAIVER

STATE	POLICY
Illinois	Annual household income below threshold in Section 4 of Senior Citizens and Disabled Persons Property Tax Relief and Pharmaceutical Assistance Act, credit courses, space available
Maine	Sixty-five, with financial need credit or noncredit, space available
Rhode Island	Sixty, permanent resident, household income less than twice the federal poverty level as established by the U.S. Department of Health and Human Services, space available

Table E.1
State Tuition-Waiver Policies (additional regulations or requirements may apply)

State	Age	Needs	By institution	No policy	Credit	Noncredit	Audit	Space Available
Alabama				•				
Alaska	•							•
Arizona				•				
Arkansas	•				•			
California				•				
Colorado				•				
Connecticut	•							•
Delaware	•				•			•
District of Columbia	•				•		•	
Florida	•				•			•
Georgia	•							•
Hawaii	•				•			•
Idaho	•							•
Illinois	•	•			•			•
Indiana	•							•
Iowa			•	•				
Kansas	•						•	•
Kentucky	•				•		•	•
Louisiana	•							
Maine	•	•			•	•		•
Maryland	•							•
Massachusetts	•				•	•		•
Michigan			• Age					
Minnesota	•				•	•	•	•
Mississippi			• Age	•				
Missouri			• Age	•				
Montana	•							
Nebraska				•				

210

Table E.1 (continued)

State	Age	Needs	By institution	No policy	Credit	Noncredit	Audit	Space Available
Nevada	•				•		•	
New Hampshire	•							
New Jersey	•				•	•		•
New Mexico	•				•	•		
New York					•	•		•
North Carolina	•				•	•		•
North Dakota	•						•	•
Ohio	•					•		•
Oklahoma	•							•
Oregon			•	•				
Pennsylvania	•							•
Rhode Island	•	•						•
South Carolina	•				•	•		•
South Dakota	•				•			
Tennessee	•				•		•	•
Texas	•						•	•
Utah	•						•	•
Vermont			• Age	•				
Virginia	•	•			•	•	•	•
Washington	•				•		•	
West Virginia			•	•				
Wisconsin	•							
Wyoming			• Age					•

F

Guidelines for Library Service to Older Adults

The importance of library services to meet the particular needs of older adults increases along with this group's numbers. These guidelines suggest means whereby librarians can meet those needs.

1.0 Exhibit and promote a positive attitude toward the aging process and older adults.

1.1 Actively seek to improve communication skills with people of all ages.

1.2 Educate its administrators, librarians, and library staff regarding physiological, psychological, social, and cultural development of people throughout the lifespan.

1.3 Participate in continuing education which will enhance skills in working with older adults.

1.4 Avoid labeling and look beyond the stereotypes and mythologies of aging.

1.5 Exhibit the same level of interest, comfort, and respect with older adults as with any other patrons.

2.0 Promote information and resources on aging and its implications not only to older adults themselves but also to family members, professionals in the field of aging, and other persons interested in the aging process.

2.1 Assess the information needs of the older population in order to build a collection which meets the real needs of
   a. people interested in understanding the aging process;
   b. people planning for a change in lifestyle or employment;
   c. individuals who act as advocates for the aging;
   d. service providers; and
   e. younger people learning about the potential for growth over the lifespan.

2.2 Assure that library selection and weeding policies lead to the acquisition of current and useful materials which reflect diverse formats and information needs. Collection development should include information on
    a. lifelong learning;
    b. older adults as consumers of aging services;
    c. behavioral implications;
    d. cultural, ethnic, economic, and regional differences;
    e. leisure time activities; and
    f. issues raised by the rapid aging of our society.

2.3 Locate sources of appropriate materials including large print books, pamphlets, and audiovisual materials (e.g., talking books, tapes, films, videotapes, etc.) which are available for purchase, for loan, or at no cost.

2.4 Survey the existing gerontological resources within the community and make available the materials or information about them.

2.5 Organize information on community agencies, activities, and resources for use by older adults and those who work with them.

2.6 Provide ready access to an information and referral service which includes current information on
    a. human services agencies serving older adults;
    b. speakers, reviewers, and other resource people available for programming; and
    c. publications, reports, community population profiles, funding agencies, and other research sources.

2.7 Publicize the availability of resources by
    a. providing reading lists, advertisements, and exhibits of interest to the publics identified above;
    b. introducing the materials, demonstrating their use, or cosponsoring with other agencies and organizations, discussion series and programs at the library or in the community;
    c. mailing informative brochures to club presidents, committee chairpersons, interested individuals, and concerned agencies and organizations; and
    d. attending meetings, giving presentations, and working actively towards community involvement.

3.0 Assure services for older adults which reflect cultural, ethnic, and economic differences.

3.1 Become knowledgeable about the cultural, ethnic, and economic composition of the community.

3.2 Use this information to purchase materials and arrange service, to train staff, to conduct programs, and to develop and maintain interagency cooperation.

3.3 Actively participate with existing agencies to serve the literacy needs of the older population.

4.0 Provide library service appropriate to the special needs of all older adults, including the minority who are geographically isolated, homebound, institutionalized, or disabled.

4.1 Provide trained staff to serve older adults.

4.2 Provide special materials such as talking books or large print books and periodicals.

4.3 Provide special equipment such as tape recorders, magnifying devices, page turners, reading machines, etc., to help in the reading process.

4.4 Identify the homebound or institutionalized who are in need of library service.

4.5 Provide personalized library service to meet the special needs of the individual within the institution (i.e., bed-to-bed, etc.) or the home.

4.6 Cooperate with the institutional administration in the planning and implementation of library services for the institutionalized.

4.7 Provide on-site service to the homebound and institutionalized, with training and transportation provided by the library.

5.0 Utilize the potential of older adults (paid or volunteer) as liaisons to reach their peers and as a resource in intergenerational programming.

5.1 Develop and implement well-organized training sessions for the individuals carrying out the library program.

5.2 Invite staff (including volunteers) to participate in library staff meetings so that they can be kept current about resources and policies.

5.3 Work closely with staff to solicit ideas, ensure a meaningful work experience, and provide as much autonomy as is desirable.

6.0 Employ older adults at both professional and support levels for either general library work or for programs specifically targeted to older adults.

6.1 Make certain that older adults are given serious consideration as candidates for either professional or support staff positions as available.

6.2 Request volunteer help only when funding is not available for paid positions.

7.0 Involve older adults in the planning and design of library services and programs for the entire community and for older adults in particular.

7.1 Identify representative older adults in the community to participate in library planning.

7.2 Assure that adequate needs assessment is conducted to represent the needs and interests of the older adults of the community.

7.3 Actively plan and implement programming to meet the needs identified.

8.0 Promote and develop working relationships with other agencies and groups connected with the needs of older adults.

8.1 Identify agencies, organizations, and groups in the community which are interested in older adults. Confer with agency leadership about ways in which the library can contribute to the achievement of their goals and objectives through
a. providing resources, materials, and services for older adults and for professional and lay workers in the field;
b. cooperating in programming, service delivery, and in-service training; and
c. involving key persons in cooperative library and interagency planning.

8.2 Identify organizations of older adults in the community and involve them in the planning and delivery of services.

8.3 Enlist participation of area librarians in developing cooperative collection development, and in developing services, programs, continuing education, and staff training to improve library service to older adults.

8.4 Work toward comprehensive cooperative planning for older adults by
   a. working with educational institutions to promote lifelong learning opportunities for older adults;
   b. locating and working with preretirement groups sponsored by business, industry, and other agencies;
   c. coordinating with other agencies to eliminate unnecessary duplication of services;
   d making available a list of community resources for information and referral which would then be available to older adults and the agencies which serve them; and
   e. asking that professional staff and administration keep abreast of current developments in gerontology and geriatrics regionally and nationally so that informed interagency communication can be facilitated.

9.0 Provide programs, services, and information for those preparing for retirement or later-life career alternatives.

9.1 Develop a collection of materials and information on preretirement planning, retirement, and career alternatives, and provide bibliographies on these topics.

9.2 Cooperate with other community agencies to provide workshops, programs, and seminars on such topics as preretirement planning, retirement, and career alternatives.

9.3 Serve as a clearinghouse for information on retirement, alternate employment, and other career opportunities.

10.0 Facilitate library use by older persons through improved library design and access to transportation.

10.1 Make sure that both the collection and meeting rooms are physically accessible to older adults, with special regard for the impaired elderly, by providing as necessary ramps, hand bars, and other design features.

10.2 Provide or be knowledgeable about the availability of assistive devices such as audio loops, infrared listening systems, etc.

10.3 Provide furniture for use with wheelchairs.

10.4 Strategically locate large-print signage, including informational and safety guides.

10.5 Inform or assist older adults in securing transportation by utilizing public or volunteer transportation, new or existing van services, or dial-a-ride systems.

10.6 Seek and secure funding for any of the above.

11.0 Incorporate as part of the library's planning and evaluation process the changing needs of an aging population.

11.1 Conduct periodic needs assessments to determine whether library resources and programs are satisfying the changing needs of older adults.

11.2 Use the results of the needs assessments and continuing evaluation of current programs and services to assist with planning.

12.0 Aggressively seek sources of funding and commit a portion of the library budget to programs and services for older adults.

12.1   Use these funds to acquire resources, assign or recruit staff, promote services, conduct staff development, and forge interagency cooperation.

12.2   Pursue sources of additional funds in order to provide for special or one-time-only projects.

NOTE

Prepared by the Library Services to an Aging Population Committee, Reference and Adult Services Division, American Library Association. Adopted by the reference and Adult Services Division Board of Directors, January 1987. (Supersedes Guidelines for Library Services to an Aging Population, July 1975.)

ANNOTATED BIBLIOGRAPHY

Balkema, J. B., ed. 1983. *Aging: A Guide to Resources.* Syracuse, N.Y.: Gaylord Professional Publications, in association with Neal-Schuman. *Reference tools for librarians, such as directories, bibliographies, statistical tables, and handbooks, and working tools for social gerontologists and students, such as manuals, outlines, and guides, are included in this annotated bibliography of books, pamphlets, and journal articles. The classified arrangement follows that of the National Council on Aging Library's verticle file, and indexing is by name and subject.*

Casey, G. M. 1984. *Library Services for the Aging.* Hamden, Conn.: Library Professional Publications. *Discussions of U.S. demographics, the intellectual abilities of the elderly, and educational opportunities for senior citizens lead into chapters on current trends in library services for the elderly, information resources for both the aging and researchers in the field of aging, and the professional education of librarians. A chapter on program planning for public librarians and an annotated bibliography of library service to the aging round out this work.*

Monroe, M. E., and R. J. Rubin. 1983. *The Challenge of Aging: A Bibliography.* Littleton, Colo.: Libraries Unlimited. *Nontechnical works, including creative literature, comprise this fully annotated list on aging. Organized according to an outline of life-tasks and indexed by author-title and subject, it is intended for individual readers, librarians serving them, social gerontologists working with groups, and senior-center activities directors. Materials available in nonprint format are noted.*

Turock, B. J. 1982. *Serving the Older Adult: A Guide to Library Programs and Information Sources.* New York: R. R. Bowker. *Various types of service programs and delivery systems are explored in this practical work. Also covered are a history of relevant legislation; demographics; theories of aging, program planning, and management; and the all-important funding issues. A valuable reference/collection development section offers an annotated core collection on aging; lists of fiction and nonfiction works, periodicals, and films about aging; and a selective directory of organizations and associations involved in the aging network.*

G

Life-Enrichment Opportunities

Background Paper Commissioned by the North Carolina Division of Aging

**THE NORTH CAROLINA WHITE HOUSE CONFERENCE ON AGING
DECEMBER 7–9, 1994
RESEARCH TRIANGLE PARK, N.C.**

Ronald J. Manheimer, Ph.D.
*Executive Director, North Carolina Center
for Creative Retirement, University of North Carolina at Asheville*

What Is Life Enrichment?

During this century, the average life expectancy at birth in the United States has risen from age forty-seven to seventy-five and the period of retirement from a handful to approximately sixteen years. The quantitative lengthening of the life course—adding years to life—has provoked the question: How do we add life to our added years? In other words, what makes a longer lifetime also an enjoyable, meaningful, and productive one?

Life-enrichment opportunities offer a powerful answer to this question. Through education, recreation, participation in civic affairs, cultural life, and spiritual searching, people of retirement age may find the benefits of renewed vitality, intellectual stimulation, fellowship, a shared sense of legacy with other generations, and, generally, a reason to get up each morning with a sense of purpose and dignity.

Life enrichment can have a wide variety of meanings. It can be the one-to-one conversation between a frail, bed-ridden older person in a nursing home sharing her life story with a volunteer trained in helping people turn reminiscing into a permanent record that can be shared with family and friends. It can be a class on nutrition, yoga, or crime prevention at a senior center. And it can be the jubilant shout of accomplishment as one crosses the finish line of a one-mile or long-distance race at the Senior Olympics.

Life-enrichment opportunities are not just ways of keeping busy or maintaining the status quo. They are avenues to new roles, relationships, and responsibilities as the waves of senior adults redefine and expand the possibilities of the latter part of life. What researchers at the AARP's think-tank, New Roles in Society, have said about education could be extended to life enrichment in general. "The future well-being and quality of life in an aging society will depend in large part on new thinking and initiatives that promote education in its broadest forms" (Harootyan and Feldman 1990).

What then of life-enrichment opportunities in North Carolina? How are these determined; who pays for them; how are they accessed; when and how are they influenced by state legislation or federal regulations; and what role does the private sector play? Before answering these questions and exploring future possibilities, it may be useful to place life enrichment in North Carolina in the bigger and changing picture of life enrichment in the United States.

Life Enrichment: The National Picture

Until recently, the topic of life enrichment has not been central in public policy discussion of larger concerns about the well-being of older people. Lawmakers, social activists, and researchers were busy trying to move a third of the aging population in the United States (in 1959) from below the poverty level; to create income supports (Supplemental Security Income) and health care benefits (Medicare and Medicaid); to eliminate age discrimination in employment (the Age Discrimination in Employment Act); to help low-income people find new employment through job retraining (the Senior Community Services Employment Program); and a myriad number of other improvements to the dismal existence of a vast number of America's elderly. The primary focus was on ameliorating the impoverished state of older persons; life enrichment remained on the periphery.

Of course, regardless of wealth or the lack of it, many elderly Americans practiced their own form of life enrichment through folk music and folk arts, traditional crafts, storytelling, dancing, culinary traditions, and so on. These traditions were and are an important part of North Carolina's heritage. They were transmitted in families and small communities but began to die out as the young moved away for better economic opportunities and as traditional lifestyles were overwhelmed by the modernized life course. Fortunately, government and church organizations help to rediscover and support these traditional cultural forms. This side history illustrates the positive role that can be played by the public sector in sustaining life-enrichment opportunities.

A landmark event that brought life enrichment more centrally into the national aging picture was the inclusion of a background paper on the positive outcomes of educational opportunities for seniors as part of the 1971 White House Conference on Aging. Educational gerontologist Howard McClusky (1970) urged policymakers to recognize the following: "Education is a basic right for all persons of all age groups. It is continuous and henceforth one of the ways of enabling older people to have a full and meaningful life and a means of helping them develop their potential as a resource for the betterment of society."

Subsequent recommendations of the White House Council on Aging led, in part, to expanded language in amendments of the 1973 Older Americans Act that encouraged the nation's multipurpose senior centers to promote educational opportunities as part of their missions.

Among national aging organizations, it was the NCOA, a Washington-based trade and advocacy organization of professionals in the field of aging, that since the mid-1970s advanced the importance of life enrichment as part of its annual policy recommendations. In 1975, the NCOA launched the Senior Center Humanities Program (now the Discovery through the Humanities Program), with major funding from the NEH, which has provided educational programming materials (large-print anthologies accompanied by audio tapes, leaders, guides, etc.) to thousands of groups across the United States for reading and discussion groups meeting in senior centers, libraries, nursing homes, congregational settings, and other community sites. The NCOA program demonstrated that high quality, intellectually stimulating programming could be attractive to and actively involve seniors, a third of whom had no more than eight years of formal education.

With federal guidelines and priorities often determining state-level aging policy, it is not surprising that few state-level aging plans addressed life enrichment. Growing awareness of older people's lives tended to concentrate on the problems that needed to be solved. Moreover, since aging was regarded by biomedical researchers as a period of cumulative decline, a decrement model of aging tended to predominate, one that emphasized the failure dimensions of old age, not the strengths or potential for successes.

The absence of policy positions on enrichment opportunities does not mean that funding streams and program development were dormant. Federally, significant dollars flowed from such sources as the AOA, NEH, NEA, programs of the Department of Education, and other agencies to help support everything from resident artists in seniors center to drama groups in nursing homes. At the state level, humanities and arts commissions frequently funded related projects. Many senior centers found inexpensive ways (usually through volunteers) to offer arts, crafts, and recreational programs, as did parks and recreation departments.

State level legislation did emerge, especially during the 1970s, to offer tuition-free courses on a space-available basis at colleges and universities for those over sixty or sixty-five (currently, these policies exist in twenty-eight states including North Carolina) and almost or completely free course opportunities through community colleges (U.S. Senate Special Committee on Aging 1991).

It is not that a range of opportunities was completely lacking, but that funding and the programs themselves were often episodic and lacked clear commitment from sponsoring institutions, so that, with the exception of institutions such as senior centers, community colleges, and agricultural extension programs, organizations like four-year colleges, public libraries, school districts, museums, and foundations rarely made life enrichment for seniors part of their institutional mission. Moreover, when life-enrichment opportunities were offered (and funds from foundations or government sought), they were justified by a human services model or mental health approach to aging.

Hence, programs were deemed valuable because they could help seniors overcome isolation and depression, prevent premature institutionalization, enable seniors to come to terms with death, and fill other needs. While there is considerable truth in claims for these benefits, they still reveal uncertainty and discomfort with the intrinsic value of seniors' participation in educational or cultural activities, such as studying current events, learning a foreign language, participating in a reminiscence group, acting in a play, or running in a race.

The idea that older persons might simply like to learn new things, make their own talents and skills available, assume planning and leadership roles, or better handle their own or a spouse's household management or self-care was just beginning to emerge. The empowerment theme which came to prominence in the field of aging in the 1980s helped to change this orientation from one of *doing for* to *doing with*, or enabling seniors to do for themselves. Active participation in life enrichment was advanced as well as the realization that seniors may have wants and interests as well as needs; that later life may be a time of new perspective with its own unique developmental qualities (Moody 1988).

Life-enrichment opportunities can now be seen to benefit older persons and, through them, society in general, by fostering some of the following:

- Intellectual stimulation that promotes continued growth and enables individuals to function in society as well-informed citizens
- A sense of personal meaning and life purpose through activities that engage the mind and body while in fellowship with others
- Life goals that generate self-fulfillment and that may lead to contributions to society whether through artistic expression, volunteerism, or social activism
- The realization that one is never too old to learn

The conflicting needs versus wants models of aging also reflect the changing demographic picture of later life in the United States. As indicated earlier, as recently as the 1960s, more than one-third of U.S. citizens sixty-five and over were in poverty, the majority lived in rural areas, the median level of educational attainment was eight years of schooling, and decent health care for many was unaffordable or unobtainable (U.S. Bureau of the Census 1992). Early efforts to ameliorate the suffering and deprivation of older persons concentrated on these problems and, inadvertently, succeeded in projecting images of aging that gained popular acceptance. Unintentionally, these efforts tended to foster a negative view of aging as an inevitable process of cumulative decline and social isolation.

Today, some things have changed. The 1990 census tells us that just over 12 percent of seniors are at or below the poverty level (in large part because of Social Security benefits) and that the average elderly couple have a household income of just over $25,000 (compared to the median income of households of individuals 18 to 64 of $34,000). Today's elderly are more likely to live in metropolitan areas (74 percent), the majority of them in suburbs. As of 1993, the majority of seniors (over 60 percent) had completed high school and 12 percent had completed four years or more of college. Healthwise, over 70 percent of older Americans report they are in excellent or good health.

In other words, older adults span an incredibly broad spectrum of income and educational levels. Given the diversity of older adults, generalizations about them are difficult to frame. It is now as appropriate to ask how seniors can contribute to their communities, run their own programs, and continue their development (a strengths of aging model) as.to ask how the problems of decline, poverty, and debilitation can be solved or ameliorated.

Paradoxically, the gains in the lives of older Americans and the rise of the concept of successful aging have created a new set of issues which bear on life-enrichment opportunities. Have seniors been too successful while other generations, most notably children, are showing high levels of social and economic deprivation? Since 1974, the poverty level for persons under age seventeen has exceeded that of persons over sixty-five. In 1990, the poverty rate for those under seventeen was 20.6 percent (Tauber 1992). Aggregate data of this sort unfairly generalize, since high levels of poverty are found among elderly women, seniors living alone, African-American and other minority groups, and rural elderly, particularly those in southern states. Most children are poor because their families are poor. The older generation should not be blamed for the very necessary gains it has achieved. Rather, these gains should be a model for improving the lives of children and Americans in general. Every effort must be taken to avoid intergenerational conflict over allocation of limited resources. A major national trend is toward intergenerational solidarity as reflected in such advocacy organizations as Generations United and the Families USA Foundation.

The issue still remains: How are opportunities that add to the quality of life of older Americans to be justified in relation to the needs of other groups? What obligations and responsibilities should obtain between generations? How can enrichment opportunities not only benefit senior adults but serve to link them with other generations in mutually beneficial endeavors? These issues of social justice must form the broader context of any discussion of enrichment opportunities for seniors. We will return to this matter after surveying the situation in North Carolina.

Life-Enrichment Opportunities in North Carolina

The elderly population in North Carolina is close to the national average (12.4 percent over sixty-five in North Carolina as compared to 12.7 percent for the nation). Fifty-one percent of state residents over sixty live in rural parts of the state. The majority of North Carolina's 100 counties have 65-plus populations that exceed the national average, and counties in the northeastern and southwestern parts of the state are much higher (the top ten counties range from 17 percent to 24 percent over sixty-five). Indeed, North Carolina's is one of the fastest growing aging populations among states, in part because of low birth rates, extended life expectancy, and the influx of migrating retirees who, in some counties, account for over 50 percent of senior population growth during the past ten years.

At the same time that North Carolina is attracting relatively affluent and well educated retirees (the state is now the fifth most popular retiree destination), it has one of the highest levels of poverty among the U.S. elderly (19.5 percent). With its large pockets of poor and disadvantaged elderly, North Carolina fits the profile of national conditions from the 1950s.

North Carolina's elderly are more likely to live in rural versus urban or suburban areas, creating transportation, service delivery, and access problems. On the positive side, somewhat higher than reported in national studies, 84 percent of North Carolinians aged sixty-five to seventy-four say they are in good health with no impairment to mobility or the ability to care for themselves, though this percentage drops to 64 percent for those over seventy-five and declines sharply for those over eighty-five. The African-American elderly population makes up 22 percent of the total elderly population as compared to a national average of 8 percent.

Turning now to review the current status of life-enrichment opportunities in North Carolina, we divide our discussion as follows: (1) education (including literacy), (2) recreation, (3) volunteerism and social activism, (4) culture, and (5) spirituality and the role of churches and synagogues.

Education. Among the most popular and accessible sources of education (continuing, vocational, and credit-bearing toward a degree) is the multitude of community colleges in North Carolina. Thousands of seniors take advantage of free or low-cost community college courses. Usually these are not specifically or exclusively offered to seniors but are scheduled during daytime hours and, hence, attract many retirement-aged persons. Courses range from health-promotion activities like water aerobics, yoga, and walking (including postsurgical, rehabilitative programs such as "heart path" classes) to practical skill-building classes in home maintenance, household financial management, caregiving, and legal matters (topics of elder law). Many community colleges also offer self-help seminars such as widowhood support groups.

Community colleges have often offered these classes on campuses and in senior and other community centers, thus reducing barriers to access. But since 1987, reduction in state appropriations to community colleges has resulted in limited numbers of free classes for persons over sixty-five. For example, while 33,693 persons aged sixty-five and older participated in extension courses at community colleges in 1993–1994, that number represents a 50 percent decrease of those enrolled in 1987.

Clearly, reduced funding to community colleges has taken its toll of senior participants. Nursing homes, park and recreation departments, and senior centers are among the hardest hit by this reduction. One leader of a statewide organization of activity professionals estimated that, because of community college cutbacks, educational opportunities to nursing home residents has declined by at least 20 percent (Zimmerman 1994). The difficulty for nursing homes is that activity directors are burdened with broad duties and considerable paper work while they are mandated to develop diverse and individualized programming for residents. With activity staff to resident ratios of from 50:1 to 300:1, high-quality programming becomes almost impossible and outside help is needed.

Although North Carolina is one of the twenty-nine states with a tuition-free/space-available policy for state resident seniors over sixty-five, the program at four-year colleges and universities is underutilized, as in most states, because it is not well publicized, often involves large school-generated fees (tacked on to tuition) that cannot be waived, is intimidating to those with no college-level experience, and fails to accommodate adult learning styles and schedules.

The shrinking of low-cost courses delivered through community colleges is inversely related to a new trend of fee-based college and university LRIs. LRIs are often semiautonomous programs in which retirement-age persons help to administer, govern, and teach one another through an affiliated unit usually placed under continuing education departments. Currently, North Carolina has nine LRIs at both state-funded schools like the University of North Carolina (UNC) at Asheville, Chapel Hill, North Carolina State, and Wilmington and at community colleges such as Blue Ridge (Henderson area) and Mayland (Spruce Pine). Private schools such as Duke and Gardiner-Webb (Boiling Springs) also have programs. Several of these programs are nationally well known. For example, UNC Asheville's NCCCR has been featured in the *New York Times* and on the cover of *Parade* magazine.

While not especially expensive (yearly fees range from $35 to $250), these programs generally attract the more affluent, well-educated senior. Noteworthy, many of these program invite seniors to teach one another (usually on a volunteer basis), and several have established outreach community service programs such as tutoring youth in reading and math. For example, the NCCCR has a Seniors in the Schools volunteer program and, yearly, also places several hundred volunteers in community nonprofit organizations.

While LRIs still reach only a small portion of the state's retirement-age population (an estimated 4,000 to 5,000), they are part of a growing trend. Currently, there are over 200 LRIs nationally, the majority of which have been established in the last seven years. Equally important, LRIs represent a growing trend of lifelong learning connected to community service, thus fostering new roles for older adults (Manheimer and Snodgrass 1993).

Related to community service roles for seniors, since 1989 the NCCCR, with help from private foundations, assisted ten other North Carolina communities in establishing community leadership programs specifically for older persons. Six of these are now ongoing organizations.

Educational programs are fine, but what about older persons who cannot read? While literacy programs generally target young adults, some focus on the senior population, which has the highest level of illiteracy of any age group. A third of those classified as functionally illiterate are over sixty years of age nationally but only 6 percent are served annually by literacy tutoring programs. North Carolina literacy groups include efforts to reach older persons. For example, in 1993–1994, North Carolina's community colleges provided Adult Basic Eduction (ABE) courses to 2,481 people aged sixty-five and over who had less than 8.9 years of schooling. This figure represents 2 percent of the total community college population served. Other literacy groups utilizing volunteer tutors reached 376 people over sixty in a comparable period, which is about 6 percent of total persons served. Additionally, many groups draw upon older persons themselves to serve as tutors. While statewide figures are not available, the Buncombe County Literacy Council reports that of 133 tutors, one-third (44) are sixty-five and over. Literacy is a good example of those programs and services that not only enrich and improve older persons' lives but in which seniors play volunteer roles to serve fellow seniors and those of other generations.

Senior centers are another major purveyor of educational opportunities for seniors. With over 120 senior centers in North Carolina, enrichment opportunities that span recreation to education to community service fill the monthly calendars for the estimated 15 percent of state residents who attend these programs. But senior centers exhibit great variation in size, facilities, budgets and staffing, and program scope. Many are limited to providing hot lunches, subcontracting with regional area agencies to deliver in-home services, and filling out their activities with hobby-level arts and crafts activities, bus trips, and dances. A small percentage of senior centers offer more intellectually stimulating programming, skills development, or get involved in volunteer projects outside center services.

While senior centers are loosely affiliated through state-level organizations, few mechanisms exist to support ongoing training and resource sharing, especially in the area of life enrichment. Staff turnover and inadequate training of activity directors often limits the quality and continuity of senior center programming. Moreover, senior centers are finding themselves in competition for new waves of retirees as other organizations, such as colleges, religious congregations, public libraries, and others have targeted seniors with programs geared for the well, mobile older population.

Discussion of programs for older learners should not omit Elderhostel, the travel/learning program first started in 1975 and designed to attract persons sixty and over to college campuses, conference centers, national parks, and other sites where they are offered college-level courses and residency at low cost. There were thirty-three locations in North Carolina in 1994 providing Elderhostel classes that attracted seniors from throughout the country, while almost 11,000 North Carolinians participated in Elderhostel programs somewhere in the United States or abroad.

Recreation. Enrichment is not limited to mental work, study, or volunteering; it can also be physical and competitive. The nationally conducted Senior Games has found enthusiastic reception at the community and state levels in North Carolina. More than 20,000 adults fifty-five and over participated at forty-seven local programs governed by North Carolina Senior Games (a nonprofit organization with both public- and private-sector financial support) in 1994. In addition, North Carolina Senior Games helps promote year-round health and wellness education opportunities at the local level through affiliated groups. Also sponsored by Senior Games is SilverStriders, a statewide walking club for those over fifty, and SilverArts that offers participants the opportunity to demonstrate their talents through visual, literary, performing, and heritage art forms.

Parks and Recreation departments also offer some type of special recreation programs for older adults. Most assist in developing walking clubs, aerobics classes, and swimming programs. Many parks and recreation departments added staff members designated as aging specialists who were responsible to handle all senior programming. While there has been some attrition in these positions, they have held relatively stable (Austin 1994).

Volunteerism and Social Activism. Should volunteerism be considered a part of enrichment? While some may consider enrichment a matter of getting or receiving some good, and volunteer as giving, volunteering is another way in which people give and receive as they continue to learn (through training, exposure to community issues and groups, etc.), find fellowship, and experience a sense of usefulness.

Volunteer programs include the long-running Retired Senior Volunteer Program (under the federal Action program), Foster Grandparents, and the more recent Senior Companion program. These programs involve thousands of the state's elderly in vitally important roles in which seniors not only help other seniors but assist children and those of other generations.

Senior activism and involvement in the political life of the state is yet another aspect of life enrichment. Through groups such as AARP chapters, the North Carolina Coalition on Aging, and the Senior Tar Heel Legislature, older residents may draw on their life experiences and expertise in advancing the cause of their age peers and that of other generations. Political activism is truly a learning and caring process.

Culture. Culture in North Carolina can mean anything from banjo players gathered informally at the rural general store to gospel choirs to the North Carolina Symphony. The state's Humanities and Arts councils have made numerous grants to organizations attracting seniors to cultural programming. African-American churches, cultural organizations, and fraternal and sorietal groups have also played a major role in promoting African-American heritage. Other groups such as Jewish Community Centers and Greek Cultural Centers have special older member groups engaged in cultural programming.

Spirituality and the Role of Churches and Synagogues. Among congregational-based organizations is the Shepherd's Center movement which started in 1975 in a Kansas City, Missouri, Methodist church. Shepherd's Centers are volunteer-led senior centers based singly or collaboratively in churches and synagogues. Shepherd's Centers include an Adventure in Learning component of courses that range from current events to art history and foreign languages. These programs are financed through modest membership fees and church/synagogue funds, with some sites securing public and private foundation money for special programs and services. Currently, there are five Shepherd's Centers in North Carolina.

Shepherd's Centers are only one strand of congregational-based life-enrichment programs. While relatively late on the scene of offering programs and services to seniors, church and synagogue leaders have come to realize that, especially for mainstream Catholic, Protestant, and Jewish congregations, more than half of their congregants are over fifty-five. Indeed, besides health and social needs, spiritual practice and concern tends to intensify as people age, especially for those who already have some religious orientation.

Churches in the African-American community are especially important as a focal point of life-enrichment opportunities. Many of the black churches now have senior citizens clubs. Many of these clubs are made up of low-income seniors for whom life enrichment means having the leisure time to do a little traveling as part of tours (for which they raise money to make the trips affordable to all members) and to get involved in the political process of improving conditions for themselves and their aged peers (Myles 1994). For example, there are some 400 seniors clubs in black churches that belong to the North Carolina Senior Citizens Federation, an organization connected to the North Carolina State Baptist Association which itself has developed an aging plan and aging committee to look after the large percentage of seniors among its 400,000 members.

Critical Issues

Given the vast expansion in the nation's and our state's senior population in years to come (a projected 32-percent increase in the senior population in North Carolina by the year 2010), planners and policymakers need to look ahead as they consider current institutional readiness and adequacy. The value, variety, and benefits of life-enrichment opportunities must be factored in as economic, health, housing, and other quality-of-life issues for seniors are examined. Given the rich diversity of life-enrichment programs and range of sponsoring organizations that have emerged during the past thirty years, one might conclude that life enrichment seems to be taking care of itself without special policies or public funding. However, episodic and sporadic life-enrichment programs have not led to well-organized, financially viable and substantial institutionally based activities. And low or no-cost programming continues to fluctuate or disappear. The following critical issues need to be addressed before acceptance of the status quo:

1. The quality-of-life enrichment opportunities vary dramatically depending on the awareness and financial capability of the host organization or the participants' ability to pay.
2. Life-enrichment opportunities are still regarded as marginally important in most settings. Staff members generally are poorly prepared to offer guidance or leadership and are often unaware of available resources.
3. Little or no rationale has been articulated among organizations serving seniors as to the intrinsic value and benefits of life-enrichment opportunities. The strength model of aging is slow to be acknowledged, while serving the well elderly is still low on the aging agenda of most senior service organizations.
4. Infrastructure for life-enrichment programs is slow to be formed except in fee-based programs hosted by organizations outside the aging network such as colleges, universities, and congregations. Hence, a growing inequity exists between those who can pay for and gain access to life-enrichment activities and those who cannot.
5. The potential of life-enrichment opportunities to help keep seniors in the mainstream of society and to link them to other generations is underdeveloped. Even in university-level gerontology programs, life enrichment, education for seniors, the contributive abilities of seniors, and the like are rarely mentioned.
6. A clear sense for how life enrichment for seniors may be linked to the needs, interests, and wants of young people and those of other generations requires further elaboration and implementation.

These and related critical issues lead to reflection on a number of public policy options.

Choices and Options

The North Carolina state government has demonstrated a progressive attitude toward life-enrichment opportunities. The state's first comprehensive Aging Services Plan (1991) included discussion of and recommendations for cultural, recreational, and educational opportunities for at-risk seniors (and, by implication, for older state residents generally), as well as a chapter on "Improving Services to and Investment in Well Older Adults." This latter chapter viewed the well older person as both self-sufficient and a community resource. The document argued that "planning and program development that recognizes only the problems and dependencies associated with aging are themselves deficient and shortsighted."

The Aging Services Plan sought to embrace a "successful" or "productive aging" viewpoint regarding the older generation. Nevertheless, that chapter of the State Plan limited the scope of discussion to primarily instrumental goals such as employment of older adults, volunteerism and self-help, preretirement planning, and health promotion/disease prevention among the well elderly. While these are vitally important areas of concern, the plan does not adequately examine educational, cultural, recreational, and spiritual enrichment opportunities for the well elderly and how these may be linked to intergenerational activities.

The State Plan does, however, reflect the national trend of recognizing the contributive potential of older adults (and, hence, the state's interest in seniors as an "investment in the future") while recognizing that individuals in the later part of life continue to exhibit strong signs of growth and development.

Leaders in state-level policy making will be challenged by the following facts: (1) North Carolina's senior population is projected to double during the period 1980–2010 and the population of the old-old 85-plus) will triple; (2) the state will likely continue to attract a significant number of migrating retirees; (3) North Carolina will continue to have a substantial percentage (20 percent) of African-American elderly and a rising number of Hispanic, Native American, and Asian American elderly; and (4) more than half of the state's 100 counties will have large populations of rural-dwelling seniors.

Therefore, the following policy matters require careful consideration:

1. How should life-enrichment opportunities be viewed? Are they essential to the quality of life of older adults of the state? Can they promote personal development, community participation, wellness (both physical and mental), personal autonomy, intergenerational relationships, and spiritual growth?

2. Should the state play a role and assume some level of responsibility for helping provide enrichment opportunities through development and circulation of resources, training in utilization of these resources, and coordination among organizations? Is this best handled at the county level? Or should life-enrichment opportunities be determined by marketplace economics.

3. Who should pay for access to and use of enrichment opportunities? Should this be based on ability and willingness to pay or should some opportunities be made more accessible through state funding?

Strategies and Recommendations

While it is beyond the purpose of this background paper to arrive at solutions or answers to the questions and problems discussed here (these will be addressed at statewide forums and at the state-level White House Conference on Aging), the author offers the following suggestions as a catalyst for reflection:

1. That the Division of Aging (under the Department of Human Resources) help to initiate a Coalition for Life-Enrichment Opportunities for Older Adults that would include senior centers, community colleges, four-year colleges and universities, public library systems, retirement and health-care facilities, senior housing groups, and other organizations interested in promoting productive aging. The coalition would forge mutual agreements for a statewide plan to promote life-enrichment opportunities through sharing resources, training, and expertise. The coalition would also focus on intergenerational learning opportunities and community service, and would seek both private- and public-sector funding for well-coordinated, efficient, statewide programs.

2. That a cadre of life enrichment for seniors facilitators be formed through volunteers from such organizations as AARP chapters, AAUW chapters, retired teacher associations, and from Volunteers in Service to America (VISTA). These people would receive training on how to help community organizations plan, initiate, and run life-enrichment programs. They would learn to use a standard assessment tool for determining life-enrichment needs in their communities, would be familiar with a wide range of inexpensive and easily accessed programming resources, and would have a protocol to follow for organizing, planning, and implementing high-quality programming for and with older persons.

3. That exploration be undertaken to determine the feasibility of using cable television networks to broadcast life-enrichment programs that have an interactive component. Courses already being taught by retirees to retirees at several North Carolina universities could be broadcast through a variety of networks. Some of the IRLs are already looking into using campus telecommunications linkages.

4. That a showcase of vintage artists of North Carolina be established, perhaps through SilverArts. This would be a juried show open to persons sixty and over. The show would travel for exhibition around the state.

5. That a guide for developing life-enrichment opportunities for seniors be developed to be used at the county level to inspire local leaders and make them aware of the resources that are available and how to plan and initiate good programming for their local senior population that also involves many of these seniors in the planning process.

REFERENCES

Austin, M. 1994. Telephone conversation with the Chair, Senior Program Division, North Carolina Parks and Recreation Society.

Harootyan, R. A., and N. S. Feldman. 1990. "Lifelong Education, Lifelong Needs: Future Roles in an Aging Society." *Educational Gerontology* 16(4): 347–358.

Manheimer, R. J., and D. Snodgrass. 1993. "New Roles and Norms for Older Adults through Higher Education." *Educational Gerontology* 19: 585–595.

McClusky, H. Y. 1971. "Education: Background and Issues." Paper Presented at the 1971 White House Conference on Aging. Washington, D.C.: U.S. Government Printing Office. ERIC Document Reproduction Service No. ED 057 335.

Moody, H. R. 1988. *Abundance of Life*. New York: Columbia University Press.
Myles, I. 1994. Telephone conversation with Executive Director of the North Carolina Senior Citizens Federation.
Tauber, C. M. 1992. Income and Poverty Trends for the Elderly. Testimony March 26, 1992, to Subcommittee on Retirement Income and Employment. Washington, D.C.: U.S. House of Representatives, Select Committee on Aging.
U.S. Bureau of the Census. 1992. "Sixty-Five Plus in America." In *Current Population Reports; Special Series*. Washington, D.C.: U.S. Government Printing Office.
U.S. Senate Special Committee on Aging. 1991. *Aging in America: Trends and Projections*. Washington, D.C.: U.S. Department of Health and Human Services.
Zimmerman, B. M. 1994. Telephone conversation with the North Carolina Activity Professionals Association President.

NORTH CAROLINA WHITE HOUSE CONFERENCE ON AGING

Preliminary Recommendations on Life Enrichment, December 1994

Issue 1: Strategies to Support Life-Enrichment Programs

- Establish a statewide Life-Enrichment Center for Older Adults to coordinate, promote, and extend the capacities of life-enrichment programs. Funding could be through the university or community college system.
- Develop a statewide funding plan for life-enrichment programs based on need. Rationale: population-based funding may penalize rural areas where there are fewer resources for life enrichment. No additional funding required—redirect and reallocate existing resources.

Issue 2: Expansion and Enhancement of Life-Enrichment Opportunities

- Create a state-level Life-Enrichment Coalition: a network for sharing resources, training, and information among professionals from different settings who are involved in life enrichment. Would require state funding for staff position and overhead expenses possibly supplemented by membership fees.
- Designate a person in every county to be a life-enrichment specialist. This person would be a county representative to the network mentioned above. Use existing resources.

Issue 3: Reduce Barriers to Delivery of and Access to Life-Enrichment Programs

- Pursue public/private partnerships for innovative funding for life enrichment such as state arts and humanities councils, corporations, and chambers of commerce.

• Allow greater county-level flexibility in allocating transportation and other resources to enable more people to benefit from life-enrichment opportunities. Existing funding could be redirected.

Issue 4: Organizing Volunteer Opportunities

• Establish a volunteer information center and computer skills bank in each county. Fund with participating organization user fees and state funds.
• Expand existing professional volunteer programs such as RSVP, Foster Grandparent Program, and Senior Companion program. Would require federal or state funding such as current proposed legislative allocation.

Issue 5: Intergenerational Programs such as Mentoring, Counseling, Co-Learning, and Grandparenting

• Conduct an assessment of community needs, expertise, and resources concerning intergenerational programs. To be carried out in relation to county aging plans by designated lead agency with help of student interns or volunteers. Could be funded with existing resources.
• Provide for planning and training of senior adults who want to work in child care programs. Incorporate as a part of Smart Start or other early childhood initiatives.
• Initiate a memorandum of understanding between the Division of Aging and the Department of Public Instruction to promote the use of older people as volunteers in schools.

H

The Aging Network

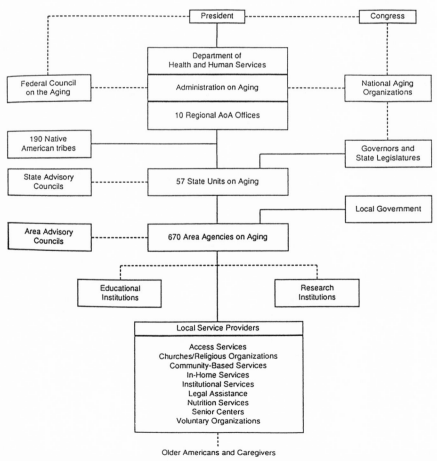

Source: *Directory of Aging Resources*, Nancy Aldrich, ed. (Silver Spring, Md.: Business Publishers, 1992).

I

U.S. Department of Education Organizational Chart

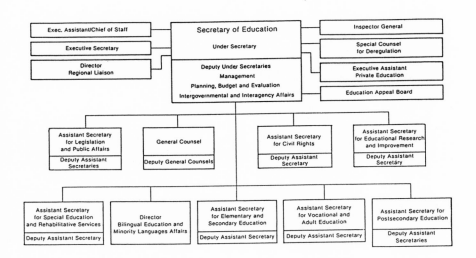

Source: U.S. Department of Education, *Annual Report*, fiscal year, 1984.

Index

Academy of Lifelong Learning, University of Delaware, 26
Academy of Senior Professionals at Eckerd College (ASPEC), 94
Adler, Richard, 161, 163, 167
Administration on Aging (AOA), 128, 133
Adult Basic Education Program, 137
Adult education: in colleges and universities, 148–150; colonial period, 130; defined, 126, 128; twentieth-century, 131; in University of Wisconsin system, 149–150; U.S. history of, 40–42; versus older adult education, 45–46
Adult Learning Institute, Columbia Greene College, 96
Adult literacy, 123, 136, 137
African-Americans: educational attainment of, 18
Age cohort: generation gaps, 182; theme of common destiny, 178
Age Discrimination in Employment Act (ADEA), 72
Ageless society: political implications, 178
Aging: attitudes toward, 10, 12; decrement model of, 42; impact of

Aging *(continued)*
and technology, 161; women's movement, 10
Aging Network. *See* Appendix H
Aging organizations. *See* Appendix A; Appendix B
Aging society: baby boomers, 115, 119; as defined in United States, 5; demographic trends of, 114–16; needs of, 115–116, 129; role of education in, 137–138; sociopolitical reality of, 32
Agricultural Extension, 148; mission defined, 148; programs for older adults, 148
American Association of Retired Persons (AARP), 122–123, 134, 140, 150; policies on older adult education, 150–151
American Library Association (ALA), 146; Adult Services Division, 146; Library Services to an Aging Population, 146–147. *See also* Appendix F
American Society on Aging (ASA), 151; Older Adult Education Network, 151
Arbeiter, Solomon, 19

Areawide Agencies on Aging (AAA), 133–134, 140

Baltes, Paul B., 44–45
Barriers to education of older adults: distance, 169; fear of competition, 170; fees, 170; location, 169; in older learner programs, 122, 127; schedule, 170
Bartunek, Carol, 52
Binstock, Robert H., 135–136
Birren, James E., 46
Blankenship, Sara, 179–181
Bollier, David, 168
Butler, Robert N., 32, 42

Center for Lifelong Learning, University of Texas at El Paso, 96
Charles, Richard R., 52
Charner, Ivan, 21
Charness, Neil, 165
Chautauqua: Institution, 70; movement, 40, 130–131
Chelsvig, Kathleen A., 142
Clark Foundation, Edna McConnell, 47
Clayton, Vivian P., 46
Coalition for Older Adult Learning (COAL), 145
Cognitive development: trade-off view, 44; and wisdom, 45
Cole, Elbert C., 70, 109
Cole, Thomas R., 10
Co-learning: distinguishing characteristics, 175
College at Sixty, Fordham University, 53
Committee on Aging and Geriatrics, 133
Communications networks, 166; online, 168–169; and social interactions, 168–169
Community College Educators of Older Adults (CCEOA), 32
Community colleges, 25, 32, 40, 49–53, 85
Community service, 85, 110
Computer-assisted instruction (CAI), 160, 165, 167; and instructional need of older adults, 167–168; and learning styles, 168

Computer Ease, 173
Computer technology: and communication networks, 166; and increased independence in older adults, 166; impact on education, 160; potential of, 170
Computers: benefits of, for older adults, 166–167; and effect of social influence, 163; and independence in older adults, 167; and influence of age, 165; and learning styles, 160; older adults' attitudes toward, 161–163; and older learners, 159–160, 163–165; older women's attitudes toward, 162–163; and social interactions, 168–170; training older adults using, 165–168
Continuing education. *See* Adult education
Cost sharing, 140
Curricula, 103–104

de Beauvoir, Simone, 10
Department of Health, Education, and Welfare (DHEW), 133
Dickerson, Ben E., 15
Dienstbach, Genevieve, 37–38
Directory of Older Adult Education Programs (AARP), 84
Disch, Robert, 176–177
Donovan Scholars Program (DSP), University of Kentucky, 28
Doucette, Don, 52
Duke University's Institute for Learning in Retirement (DILR), 59

Education: in computer age, 160; financial support of, 137; impact of computer technology on, 160; and reconstructed life course, 10–11
Education for Later Maturity: A Handbook, 41
Educators: as stakeholders in older adult education, 125. *See also* Appendix I
Eilers, Merry Lee, 166–167, 170
Eklund, Lowell, 128
Elderhostel, 12, 54–55, 127; intergenerational programs, 174

Elderhostel Institute Network (EIN), 56, 109, 151
Elderly: median level of education among, 92
Elders Share the Arts (ESTA), 66
Empowerment, 85
Erikson, Erik H., 42

Facilitating Education for Older Learners, 1, 24
Federal Council on Aging (FCA), 133, 136
Fischer, Richard B., 49
Florida Atlantic University, 58
Fox, Susan, 175, 182
Franklin, Benjamin, 40
Friedan, Betty, 10
Furlong, Mary, 161, 163, 167

Generational equity, 117–118, 131, 136
Generational investment paradigm, 118
Generations Together, University of Pittsburgh, 174
Generations United, 177
Gerontologists: as stakeholders in older adult education, 129
Gerontology Program, University of Massachusetts (Boston), 60
Giles, Howard, 175, 182
Gutmann, David: instinctual grandparenting, 182

Hartley, Alan A., 165
Hartley, Joellen T., 165
Hitchcock, Earl and Marabeth, 2–4, 29–30
Hospital Audiences, Inc. (HAI), 65–66
Houston, Elizabeth, 4–5, 29–30
Humanities Programming for Older Adults, 65

"Identifying Critical Pathways in Organizing Educational Programs for Older Adults" (research project of N.C. Center for Creative Retirement), 87; critical pathways taxonomy (fifteen stages), 88–89, 90–91; need for study, 86–87; research method of, 87–88; survey response rate, 89

"Identifying Critical Pathways in Organizing Educational Programs for Older Adults," research findings of: by-products, 108; continuity and growth, 107–108; delivery, 106; determinants of success, 108–109; determining the need for older adult education, 93; evaluation, 106–107; funding and resources, 98–100; how programs are governed, 101–102, organizational positioning, 96, participants, 100–101; planning process, 93–94; prospects for future, 109–110; rationale, 97; scale, 105–106; staffing, curriculum, and pedagogy, 102–104; strategy, 104–105; when and how program started, 89–93
Information highway, 131, 159, 161, 163, 165, 169; and electronic classroom, 169
Institute for Retired Professionals, New School for Social Research, 56, 149
Institute of Study for Older Adults, 68
Institutional rationales, 24–28; in higher education, 24; participant motives, 26–28; social responsibility, 28
Intellectual functioning: cognitive stimulation, 44; crystallized and fluid intelligence, 44; of older adults, 42–45
Intelligent computer-assisted instruction (ICAI), 160
Intergenerational education: rationales for, 175–178; transforming effects of, 179–181; versus age-segregated education, 181–182. *See also* Co-learning
Intergenerational experiences, 129, 138, 144, 149
Intergenerational programs, 173–174; defined, 174; four models, 176–177; funding sources, 174; relationships, 174
Intergenerational service: motivation for, 183–184
Internet, 159, 168–169
Iowa City/Johnson County Senior Center, 68

Janowitz, Bob, 159–1160
Jay, Gina M., 161–163
Johnson, Shirley A., 165
Johnson City Senior Center, 94

Knowles, Malcolm S., 14, 45, 126
Kreidler, Mary Lou 163–165

Labouvie-Vief, Gisele, 43–44
Laslett, Peter, 39–40, 45, 46
Later life: as extension of middle age, 46;
    as unique developmental stage, 46
Leadership Council of Aging Organiza-
    tions, 140. *See also* Appendix A
Learning, self-directed, 130
Learning in Retirement Institutes
    (LRIs), 14, 56–59, 127, 148;
    acronyms of, 56; curricula of, 23, 57;
    defined, 56,84; relationship with host
    institution, 148–149; types of, 56–59
Learning styles: effect of computers on
    160; related to CAI, 167–168; related
    to computer use, 166
Libraries, public, 146–148; Brooklyn
    Public Library Service to the Aging
    (SAGE), 63; history of service to
    older adults, 61; Information and
    Referral Services, 63; Monroe
    County Library System (MCLS) of
    Rochester, N.Y., 63; older adults as
    patrons of, 61
Library Service to an Aging Population
    Committee (of American Library
    Association), 61
Library Services and Construction Act
    (LSCA), 61
Life course: age norms, 8; changes in,
    115; distribution of education, 7;
    extension of, 7; linear, defined, 126;
    reconstructed, 10; stages, 127–128;
    work and leisure, 7
Life enrichment. *See* Appendix G
Lifelong learning: applied to older
    learners, 42; compared to older adult
    education, 127, 140; emerging trends
    in, 5; national plan of, 139; presuppo-
    sitions in later life, 12–13

Lifelong Learning Act, 121, 124,
    139–140, 142
Lifelong Learning Society, Florida
    Atlantic University, 107
Linking Lifetimes, Center for
    Intergenerational Learning, Temple
    University, 174
Long, Huey B., 143–144
Longino, Charles F., 4
Louis Harris and Associates, 49
Lowy, Louis, 23, 124–125, 128
Lyceum movement, 130–131

Mackintosh, Esther, 65
Manheimer, Ronald J., 24
Marketing to the over-fifty population,
    119
McClusky, Howard Y., 137–139
McGowan, Thomas G., 179–181
McMahon, Alexander T., 129
McNeely, Elizabeth, 167–168
Means test, 135, 140
Medicare, 116, 123; legislation, 133
Minorities: recruiting as participants, 100
Mission statement, 97
Moody, Harry R., 10, 13, 32, 41, 46,
    176–177; on public policy, 141; view
    on older adult education, 123–124, 129
Morris, Morgan J., 165
Motivation: expressive and instrumental
    motives, 20–24; fear of cognitive
    decline, 21; institutional rationales,
    26–28; intellectual stimulation, 28; of
    older learners, 20–24; volunteerism, 29
Museum One, 66
My Turn, Kingsborough Community
    College, 60

Nathanson, Paul, 177
National Center for Education Statistics
    (NCES), 49
National Conference on the Aging, 133
National Council of Senior Citizens
    (NCSC), 140, 150
National Council on the Aging
    (NCOA), 140, 147; Discovery
    Through the Humanities Program,

National Council on the Aging *(continued)* 22, 63, 64–65, 152; National Institute of Senior Centers (NISC), 67; policies on older adult education 151–152; Silver Editions Projects, 147

National Endowment for the Humanities (NEH), 147–148

National Recreation and Park Association, 152

National University Continuing Education Association (NUCEA), 153

North Carolina Center for Creative Retirement (NCCCR), 120; College for Seniors, 3, 57, 159; Humanities Outreach Programs, 58; Leadership Asheville Seniors (LAS), 3, 58; Retirement Planning Program, 58; Senior Academy for Intergenerational Learning (SAIL), 58; Senior Wellness Program, 58; Seniors in the Schools, 4, 29; volunteer programs, 149

O'Connor, Darlene, 23, 124–125, 128, 143

Older adult education: benefits of, 38; and changing demographics, 5–8; compared to lifelong learning, 127–128, 140; defined, 127; emergence of (in United States), 40–42; empowerment, 14; five models of, 84–85; funding for, 13, 84, 113; new organizational structures of, 14; new paradigm of, 29–32, 168; philosophical presuppositions of, 12–13; politics of, 32–33; and self-actualization, 13, 14, 46, 123. *See also* Appendix B; Appendix C

Older Adult Education Network (OAEN), 109

Older adult education policies: agricultural extension, 148; colleges and universities, 148–150; compared to lifelong learning policies, 140; and educational leadership, 114; equity issues in, 123, 124–125; federal, 137; and goals, 139; libraries, 146–148; national organizations, 150–153;

Older adult education policies *(continued)* shaped by economics, 113–114, 123, 124–125, 153–154; shaped by values, 113–114; stakeholders in, 122–130

Older adult education policies, state, 141–143; Michigan, 145–146; New Jersey, 145; New York, 145; in state education or aging plans, 144. *See also* Appendix G

Older Adult Service and Information System (OASIS), 37, 68–70, 85, 106; intergenerational tutoring program of, 106

Older adults: dependency in, 116; diversity of, 121, 122–123, 127, 152, 153; "greedy geezers," 131, 136; income of, 119; industry, 119; needs of, 136–137, 142; new roles of, 14–15; new stereotypes of, 15; participation in educational programs, 125; policies for well and at-risk, 121; quality of life for, 116; as resource, 128–129; as stakeholders, 122–123; stereotypes of, 135, 141

Older Americans Act, 122, 133–136, 140–141; amendments of 1973, 12, 47; authorization of education and training, 76; Title III, 62. *See also* Appendix D

Older learner programs: certificate programs, 60–61; at Chautauqua Institution, 70; community colleges, 49–53; Elderhostel, 54–55; four-year colleges and universities, 48–49; growth of, 83; humanities and arts, 64–66; Learning in Retirement Institutes (LRIs), 56–59; Older Adult Service and Information Systems (OASIS), 68–70; role of public libraries, 61–64; senior centers, 65–68; Shepherd's Centers, Adventures in Learning, 70–72; support of, 75–77; workplace education, 72–75

Parker, A. Kern, 159–160

Participation rates: barriers to increase at colleges and universities, 53;

Participation rates *(continued)*
  future growth of, 15–20; of older
  adults in educational programs, 125;
  of people over fifty-five, 11; National
  Center for Education Statistics
  (1984), 16, 49
Perkins, Hugh V., 143
Peterson, David A., 1, 24, 41, 129
Physical limitations, computers and: in
  older adults 167, 170
Productive aging, 32
Public and private partnerships, 125, 154
Public policy: changing context,
  116–119; influence of market
  demand on, 120; on older adult
  education, 46–48, 113–114; role in
  educational programs, 120; targeting
  services, 116, 153–154; trends
  related to older adults, 117–119;
  values reflected in, 122, 154;
  workplace education for older adults,
  172–175

Recollections (publication of Seniors'
  Studies, Ryerson Polytechnical
  Institute), 108
Recruitment: of minorities, 100; of
  participants, 100; of younger age
  groups, 100
Reminiscing: discouraged among older
  people, 42; life review process, 40
Renaissance Society, California State
  University at Sacramento, 59
Retirement Institute, Westchester
  Community College, 93
Retraining older workers, 123–124, 136
Riley, John W., 43
Riley, Matilda White, 43
Robertson-Tchabo, Elizabeth A., 143
Romaniuk, Jean G., 142
Rosa Keller Campus, University of New
  Orleans, 101
Rosen, Larry D., 163

Scanlon, John, 53
Schaie, K. Warner, 43
Schlachter, Stephany S., 113, 123

Second middle age, 8
Senior centers, 65–68, 85; changing name
  of, 97; serving frail and elderly, 97
Senior Citizen Program, Portland
  Community College, 106
Senior Enrichment Program, Delta
  College, 104
Senior Neighbors of Chattanooga, 5,
  29, 105
Senior Theater, 66
SeniorNet, 106, 167, 169
Sensory deficiency, computers and: in
  older adults, 166
Shepherd's Centers, 14, 85, 93;
  Adventures in Learning program,
  70–72, 104
Shuldiner, David, 64
Sioux Land Senior Center, 68
Sixty-Plus Club, California State
  University at Bakersfield, 105;
  Instructional Television Committee
  of, 108
Social Security, 116–117, 123, 140;
  Act, 132–133, 135
Spatial memory, computers and: in
  older adults, 166
Squaring of the population pyramid, 115
Star Trek, 30–31
Stuhr, Elsie J.: Leisure Center, 93
Swindell, Richard F., 44

Teaching methods, 104
Technology: diversity of attitudes by
  older adults on, 163; impact of aging
  and, 160–161; impact of changes in
  on older adults, 160–163; impact on
  quality of life, 161; uses of by age,
  161; uses of by educational level,
  161; uses of by gender, 161; uses of by
  income, 161; uses of by location, 161
Technophobia: defined, 163; influence
  of education on, 163
Third age: ideas of, 38–40; individual
  and societal meanings of, 38; as
  perspective, 27, and subjective time, 46
Timmermann, Sandra B., 142
Townsend Movement, 132

Tuition-free programs, 25, 76, 84
Tuition-waiver policies, 47, 120, 121, 122, 141–144; barriers to participation, 142; and formula funding, 142, in Maryland, 143; in Massachusetts, 143; of University of Kentucky, 142. *See also* Appendix E

University for Seniors, University of Minnesota, 96
University of the Third Age (U3A), 39

Vellas, Pierre, 39
Ventura-Merkel, Catherine, 52
Volunteerism, 29, 123, 124, 129, 136

Weil, Michelle M., 163

Weinstock, Ruth, 53
White House Conference on Aging (1961), 135, 138–139
White House Conference on Aging (1971), 12, 41, 47, 124, 136–137
White House Conference on Aging (1981), 62; final report of, 121, 140
White House Conference on Aging (1995): intergenerational policy focus, 174
White House Conference on Aging Act, 133
Willis, Sherry L., 161–163
Wilmington Senior Center, 97
Wirtz, Philip, 21

Zandri, Elaine, 165

ABOUT THE AUTHORS

RONALD J. MANHEIMER is the executive director of the North Carolina Center for Creative Retirement at the University of North Carolina at Asheville, where he is also Research Associate Professor of Philosophy.

DENISE D. SNODGRASS is assistant director of the North Carolina Center for Creative Retirement.

DIANE MOSKOW-McKENZIE has over fifteen years of work experience in the field of adult education.

ISBN 0-313-28878-X

90000>

EAN

9 780313 288784

HARDCOVER BAR CODE

DATE DUE

DEMCO 38-297